Anglo-Saxon Studies in Archaeology and History

21

Edited by
Helena Hamerow

Oxford University School of Archaeology

Published by the Oxford University School of Archaeology
Institute of Archaeology
Beaumont Street
Oxford

Distributed by
Oxbow Books
The Old Music Hall, 106–108 Cowley Road, Oxford, OX4 1JE, UK
Tel: 01865 241249   Fax: 01865 794449

Distributed in North America by
Casemate Academic
1950 Lawrence Rd, Havertown PA 19083, USA

www.oxbowbooks.com

ISBN 978 1 905905 44 7
ISSN 0264 5254

A CIP record for this book is available from the British Library

Cover image: Anglo-Saxon bronze mount from Tessem, Steinkjer.
© Bergen University, drawing by Per Rasmussen.

Designed and typeset by Oxford Book Projects
Printed in Great Britain by
Short Run Press, Exeter

Foreword

Anglo-Saxon Studies in Archaeology and History is a series concerned with the archaeology and history of England and its neighbours during the Anglo-Saxon period.

ASSAH offers researchers an opportunity to publish new work in an inter- and multi-disciplinary forum that allows for a diversity of approaches and subject matter. Contributions placing Anglo-Saxon England in its international context are as warmly welcomed as those that focus on England itself.

Papers submitted to ASSAH must be comprehensible to non-specialist readers. They must, furthermore, conform to the journal's house style. A copy of the style-sheet is available on-line, at: **http://www.arch.ox.ac.uk/assah**. A hard copy can be obtained from the Editorial Assistant, Dr. Laura Morley (Laura.morley@arch.ox.ac.uk). All papers are peer-reviewed.

The Editor is grateful to the contributors to this volume for their prompt and efficient responses, and to those peer reviewers who have taken the time to read and comment upon submissions. She would also like to thank the Archaeological Solutions for a generous subvention towards the publication of this volume.

All papers for consideration for future volumes should be sent to the Editor.

Professor Helena Hamerow
(helena.hamerow@arch.ox.ac.uk)
Institute of Archaeology
34–6 Beaumont Street
Oxford OX1 2PG

Contents

Contributors

Aina Margrethe Heen Pettersen
Department of Historical Studies, The Norwegian University of Science and Technology, NO-7491 Trondheim, Norway

John Hines
Department of Archaeology, Cardiff University, Adeilad John Percival Building, Rhodfa Colum Drive, Cardiff, Wales CF10 3EU

Antony Mustchin
Archaeological Solutions Ltd., Unit 6, Brunel Business Court, Eastern Way, Bury St Edmunds IP32 7AJ

Letty ten Harkel
School of Archaeology, University of Oxford. 1 South Parks Road, Oxford OX1 3QY

Richard Shaw
Our Lady Seat of Wisdom, 18 Karol Wojtyla Square, PO Box 249, Barry's Bay, Ontario, K0J 1B0, Canada

Anglo-Saxon Studies in Archaeology and History 21, 2018

Ethnic identity or something else? The production and use of non-ferrous dress-accessories and related items from early medieval Lincoln

Letty ten Harkel

Abstract

This paper asks, what can decorative metalwork tell us about the way in which identities were expressed in Viking-Age Lincoln? It presents the non-ferrous metalwork material from early medieval Lincoln, England (c. AD 800–1100), for the first time as a coherent assemblage. The artefact types – mainly dress-accessories and related decorative objects – are described in terms of their art-historical and stylistic characteristics, and placed within the context of manufacturing evidence from Lincoln. The question is asked, did the production of decorative metalwork play a key role in the deliberate creation or manipulation of 'ethnic' identities? Many of the objects found in Lincoln reveal Anglo-Saxon, Scandinavian, Hiberno-Norse and Frankish influences, and provide insights into the complex identities of Lincoln's ninth- to eleventh-century inhabitants on multiple levels. However, the manufacturing evidence, providing an insight into the deliberate choices that were made by Lincoln's metalworkers with respect to the manipulation of such identities, suggests that ethnic considerations may perhaps have been less important than is sometimes assumed.

Introduction: metalwork and ethnicity

What was the role of decorative metalwork in ninth- to eleventh-century England? Writing a decade and a half ago, Hadley and Richards stated that 'many archaeologists of the early medieval period … still work within a broad culture history framework … individual artefacts are commonly classified, on stylistic and art-historical grounds, as Anglo-Saxon or Scandinavian, and by implication the racial identity of their makers and wearers is identified'.[1] More than fifteen years on, we acknowledge that the relationship between material culture and ethnicity is problematic on theoretical grounds, and that identities are multi-faceted and exist on different scales, but often Viking-Age metalwork studies in England are still concerned with 'Anglo-Saxon', 'Scandinavian' or hybrid 'Anglo-Scandinavian' identities.[2] Sometimes allowance is made for other ethnic influences: for example, based on the increasing number of 'Frankish' dress-accessories from metal-detected contexts in England, Gabor Thomas has argued that 'the adoption, adaptation, and strategic manipulation of Carolingian/northern Frankish identity formed an embedded component of cultural dynamics in Viking-Age England'.[3] This is a step forwards from depictions of Viking settlement that imagined the situation as rigidly dichotomous, involving two static cultures, one Anglian, the other Scandinavian.[4] But it does not ask the question, how important *was* ethnicity? To quote Hadley and Richards once more, we need 'to address the question of what people thought of themselves and their 'ethnic' allegiances, if, indeed, they ever or normally thought in those terms'.[5]

The roots of culture historical analyses lie in a period when 'national' identities were at the forefront of European socio-political consciousness, and it is thus unsurprising that a scholarly focus on ethnicity has been the result. But did the ninth- and tenth-century inhabitants and settlers of the Anglo-Saxon kingdoms share this concern with ethnicity? Walter Pohl has pointed out that 'we should not be surprised to find more evidence on the ethnic perceptions of others than on ethnic self-identification', and although his comment was made in the context of contemporary groups describing 'others', it can also be applied to modern scholarship describing 'others' in the past.[6] This is a pertinent point in the current context: in a recent synthesis of the archaeology of Lincoln's Lower City, the authors remarked that few of the finds from Flaxengate, probably the most important site for our understanding of Lincoln's Anglo-Scandinavian phase, were distinctly 'Viking'.[7]

This paper addresses the question of whether ethnicity was expressed through decorative metalwork in Lincoln between the ninth and eleventh centuries AD. In a previous paper analyzing descriptions of Vikings in contemporary historical and literary sources, I have argued that religious and regional identities were more important than ethnic ones.[8] The texts were predominantly written from a (West) Saxon perspective at this date, however, providing an insight into how the native population viewed the incoming 'others'. Through a focus on metalwork, it may be possible to gain insight into the process of self-identification of the settlers.

This paper is not the first to attempt such an approach, but differs from other studies in terms of selection of evidence. The success of the Portable Antiquities Scheme, which catalogues stray finds made by members of the public (mostly metal-detectorists), has led to a number of recent high-quality studies of dress-accessories of the period, but the selection of material tends to be typological, rather than regional or context-specific.[9] Other studies that have emphasized the central role of decorative metalwork for the expression of ethnic identities have also tended to focus on selected artefact types, such as a recent paper by Ingunn Marie Røstad, who considers a group of eleventh-century brooches from central places in eastern Norway that display 'Danish' influences as referring to a 'Danish' identity.[10] Yet by focusing on a single artefact type or decorative style, we automatically introduce bias into our analyses. The same issue affects the recently-published Lower City volume, which singles out the handful of 'Viking' artefacts in the discussion of occupation evidence from Flaxengate, providing a one-sided impression of the nature of the material.[11] This paper argues that, to understand the role of decorative metalwork *in the past*, a holistic, site-specific or regional study of all available evidence is required, not just of those objects that share certain decorative or typological traits. For that reason, reference will also be made to other, previously published objects from Lincoln that were made from different materials.[12] Only then is it possible to appreciate the relative importance, context and significance of the material in its contemporary society.

The assemblage that stands central to this paper is the material from excavations in the city of Lincoln, held by 'The Collection: Art and Archaeology in Lincolnshire', which has never before been comprehensively published.[13] The Lincoln material is suited particularly well to the current study, as Lincoln is considered one of the main towns of Anglo-Scandinavian England, one of 'five boroughs' that were reportedly under Scandinavian control for some time. As such, it provides a good comparison for the material from York, which is better known and published, and whose experts have commented on a lack of a discernible 'Scandinavian' identity.[14] Urban assemblages have an advantage over studies of metal-detected finds because – although not without depositional issues either, as discussed below – they provide more contextual information, including manufacturing evidence, which usually remains unidentified in rural unstratified contexts. Evidence for manufacturing – which forms the first part of this paper – is important: it provides insight into the interplay between supply and demand, in particular the selection of certain artefactual styles for production, or the deliberate manipulation of identities.

It is not the aim of this paper to present an exhaustive catalogue, as new discoveries will continue to come to light; however, a comprehensive and representative selection has been included. With the exception of a small number of hooked tags made of iron, ferrous metalwork has largely been excluded, although a significant assemblage deserving of conservation and further analysis does exist. One object worth mentioning in passing is a Viking spearhead from Flaxengate, dated to the later ninth or tenth centuries.[15] Coinage has also been excluded from this study, as this has formed the basis of another, separate publication by the author.[16] A catalogue of decorative metal artefacts from Lincoln is included at the end of this paper. Relevant catalogue numbers are referred to in the text in brackets. Illustrations are included in many cases; obvious exceptions are objects that have already been published elsewhere (unless inclusion here was deemed to add meaningful information, for example for comparative reasons) and objects that have not been cleaned and conserved.

There are some interpretative challenges. Because of its well-preserved historic town centre, excavations in Lincoln have been piecemeal.[17] The most extensive ones took place in the mid 1970s at Flaxengate in the Lower City, revealing evidence for manufacturing activities including pottery production and metalworking, both ferrous and non-ferrous (Fig. 1).[18] Much of the following discussion will therefore concern the Flaxengate material, but it is important to emphasize that this reflects an excavation bias.[19] Moreover, as a result of the deep stratigraphy on most sites in the city, with evidence for frequent levelling and intercutting of features, the majority of objects are residual, which means their dating often depends on the combination of a *terminus ante quem* in combination with art-historical criteria, and contextual information can only be addressed at site level. This was exacerbated on some sites by the excavation methodologies that were adopted, which sometimes left early medieval deposits *in situ* because of their great depth, and in other cases favoured machine or spit excavation of post-Roman layers.[20] Although this inhibits very detailed interpretations of depositional circumstances, the situation is nevertheless more favourable than for ploughsoil finds, not least because undiagnostic or difficult-to-date objects – such as manufacturing waste – are more likely to be retained from excavated sites. This paper is therefore best read in conjunction with the excellent publications on the urban stratigraphy in the Lincoln Archaeological Studies series.[21]

Ethnicity, identity and metalwork: theoretical considerations

In order to address the question of whether ethnicity was actively expressed through decorative metalwork, it is

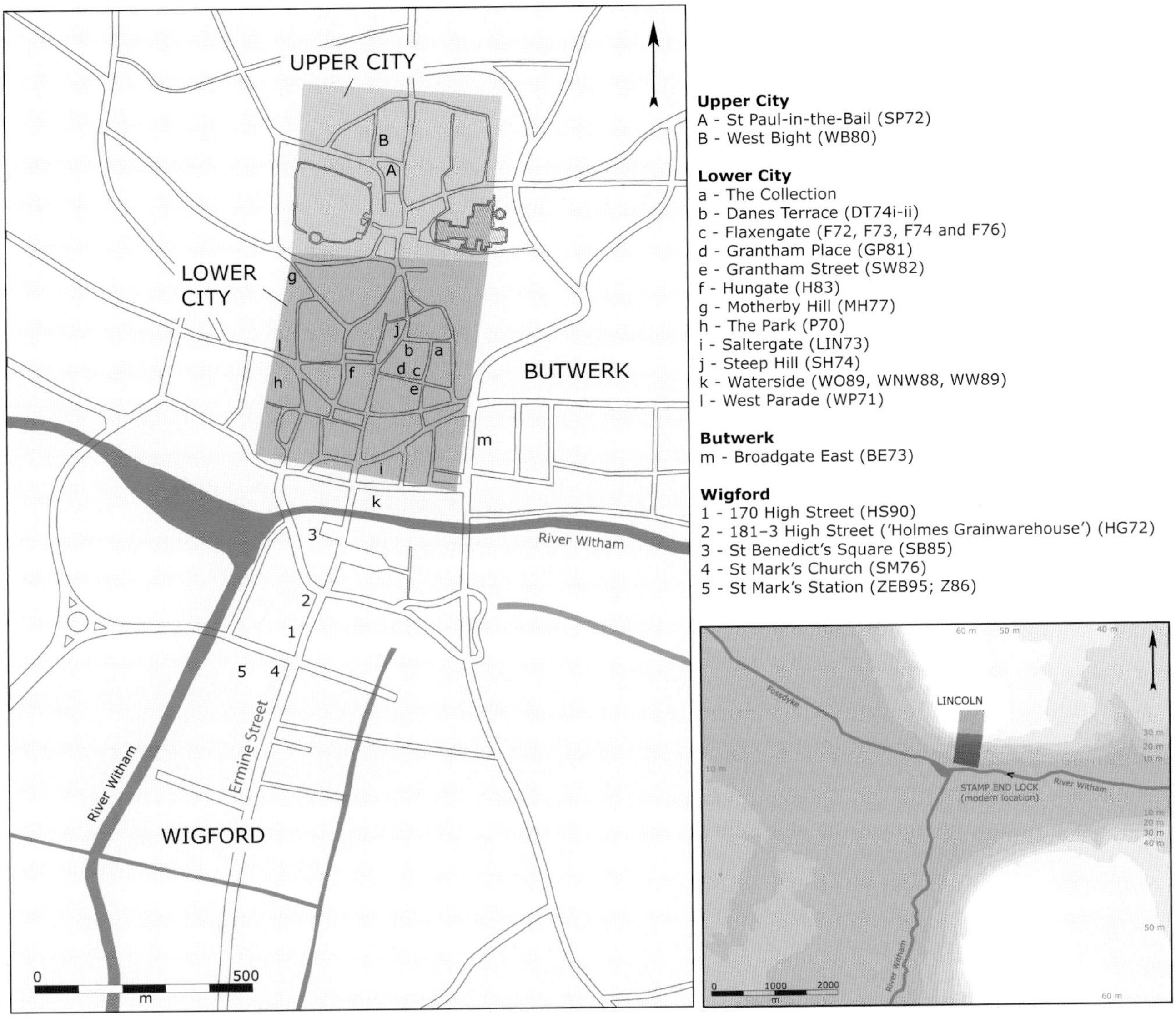

Fig. 1 Sites in Lincoln, mentioned in the text (drawing by Letty ten Harkel, after Stocker (ed.) 2003, fig. 1).

necessary to define what we mean by the term. Ethnicity is only one aspect of more complex identities, also including (and sometimes difficult to distinguish from) affiliation with kinship groups, territorial or regional groupings, urban identities, military groups, and religious or political identities.[22] Given the modern emphasis on 'identity' as an *active* choice, it is important to remember that expressing one's identity is an act of performance, a deliberate association with a specific social group.[23] In trying to understand early medieval identities, it is therefore not a question of whether we can identify the provenance of an object or even the geographical childhood origin of its producer, but whether (and how) the wearer's contemporaries would have understood the significance of this object in any given context. This is not an easy task, as objects can change in their significance: for example, a brooch type commonly produced in Denmark (but not in England) would almost certainly be more 'exotic' when worn in Wessex, simply because there would be fewer in circulation. It would possibly be perceived as explicitly signifying a 'Danish' identity if the person who wore it spoke with a Danish accent, even though the wearer her/himself might not readily associate it with anything of the sort. Its exotic decoration might be copied by local producers, but the perceived significance of its decorative elements might become lost in translation as the new 'fashions' became firmly engrained in West Saxon society. How, then, can we begin to unravel such complexity?

The only way to understand the complexity of associated meanings of decorative metalwork is by placing the whole process of metalwork production and use in Lincoln – from the personal possessions of Scandinavian settlers to the organized mass-production of low-cost dress-accessories in the blossoming Anglo-Scandinavian town – in its socio-political context. For that reason, the next section first involves a brief summary of Lincoln's early medieval archaeology. If – as I have explored in a previous article – metalwork production in Lincoln was subject to changes in 'fashion' that can be tied to broader developments in society, we might expect to be able to explain changes in metalwork styles by reference to broad changes in the city's archaeological record.[24] If this can be done, we should be able to identify whether the immigration of a substantial Scandinavian population was enough in itself to explain changes in contemporary metalwork styles, or whether other dynamics – such as the increased production scale characteristic of the emerging towns – were equally important. These issues will be returned to in the final section of this paper.

The bulk of the paper is divided into two parts, focusing first on the evidence for metalworking, to determine which types of objects were actively produced in the town, and then on the additional artefactual evidence from Lincoln. Dagfinn Skre has highlighted the difficulty in distinguishing between these – sometimes overlapping – categories, and the distinction here should not be seen as dichotomous.[25] The objects included in the section on metalworking include moulds, unfinished products and objects with close parallels that could have indicated the use of a single mould for their production, rendering it likely that they would have been produced nearby. The objects in the second part include the rest.

A brief consideration of the identities of metalworkers will conclude the analysis. As stated already, evidence for manufacturing provides insight into the deliberate manipulation of identities. Yet the relationship between supply and demand can be hard to unravel, which is why this section also includes a brief consideration of the identity of metalworkers and the socio-economic context in which they worked. An important consideration is the degree to which changes in production mode – the emergence of mass-production in specialized workshops – affected the styles of the objects being produced. Decorative metalwork of the period *c.* 870–1100 (after the Scandinavian settlement) is typically made of base metals, in particular copper and lead alloys, whilst silver – used in much larger quantities during the earlier ninth century and before – was largely restricted to the production of coinage. The choice of cheaper materials may well relate to increased scale of production and a different type of market.[26] Mass-production can also affect decorative style, resulting in a preference for simpler designs and methods of decoration.[27] Indeed, many of the objects discussed in this paper that were (probably) produced in Lincoln were executed in simple decorative styles requiring relatively little effort and expertise. Yet equally important in the context of changing market demands is the creation of a recognizable product, which may result in the development of regional styles. This possibility will also be explored below.

In writing about the question of whether ethnicity played a role or not, I am continuing an established tradition with its own, ethnically-laden, jargon. I will make no attempt to change this, as I believe that the terminology does reflect regional characteristics of the origin and spread of specific styles adequately; it is merely the implication of this classification for our understanding of the wearers' identities that I question. Therefore I will label objects with an explicitly 'Scandinavian' style that were unlikely to have been produced in Anglo-Saxon England or on the Continent – such as the *Borre*- or *Jellinge*-styles in their pure, unaltered forms – as 'Scandinavian'. Hybrid styles combining, for example, Scandinavian decoration with Anglo-Saxon object types, will be labelled 'Anglo-Scandinavian' or 'Hiberno-Norse'. Finally, I will refer to objects with no discernible Scandinavian elements as 'Anglo-Saxon', 'Frankish' or 'Irish'.

Setting the scene: Lincoln *c.* 800–1100

Excellent summaries of early medieval Lincoln exist elsewhere, but a few aspects are worth repeating to set the scene.[28] (Near-) contemporary written sources commenting on the socio-political circumstances in the town have resulted in a lasting perception of Lincoln as a 'Viking' – or at least 'Anglo-Scandinavian' – town, similar in many ways to the 'Viking' city of York.[29] One of the first documentary references to Lincoln comes from an entry in the *Anglo-Saxon Chronicle*, which mentions Lincoln, Nottingham, Derby, Leicester and Stamford as five boroughs (*burga fife*) which King Edmund 'freed' from Norsemen in AD 942, and alludes to the fact that Lincoln's inhabitants were, at some point, 'Danes' (*Dane*).[30] The chronicler's emphasis on the Scandinavian identity of its inhabitants is beyond doubt, and it is not surprising that subsequent scholars have therefore regarded these boroughs as the urbanized outcomes of the military camps of the Viking 'great army'.[31] It should not, however, be overlooked that Lincoln's development was more complex.

A former Roman *colonia,* Lincoln was situated in a dominant position in the relatively flat landscape of Lincolnshire, at the crossroads of a number of riverine and land-based communication routes (Fig. 1).[32] Unsurprisingly, therefore, despite evidence for widespread abandonment of the town after the Roman period, Lincoln continued to function as a place of some importance.[33] It is possible that a post-Roman ecclesiastical centre continued to exist at the site of St Paul-in-the-Bail in the Upper City, consisting of a sequence of small buildings interpreted as chapels/churches with associated burials, although the evidence could also be middle Anglo-Saxon in date (Fig. 1).[34] By that stage, Lincoln was undoubtedly important: it was at Lincoln that the seventh-century missionary Paulinus 'built a stone church of remarkable workmanship' following conversion of its *praefectus*, a man called Blæcca, and a few years later it was also at Lincoln that the new archbishop of Canterbury was consecrated.[35] A number of ecclesiastical foundations existed in the Lower City before the period of Scandinavian settlement in the middle of the ninth century.[36] In this context, a heavily-corroded copper-alloy fragment with a splayed terminal from the Lower City deserves mention as it is possibly a *stylus*-fragment, usually found in ecclesiastical contexts, although it has no clear parallels amongst the *styli* found at nearby Flixborough (no. 138; Fig. 2).[37]

Fig. 2 Photograph of H83 ⟨269⟩, Catalogue **no. 138** (photograph by Letty ten Harkel).

Lincoln was not exclusively an ecclesiastical enclave, however. More recently, excavations to the south of the Lower City have revealed tentative evidence for a middle-Anglo-Saxon settlement core, providing a possible parallel to the extra-mural sites of *Eoforwic* in York or *Lundenwic* in London.[38] Economic activity within the walled town did not start until approximately the third quarter of the ninth century, however, more or less contemporary with documented Scandinavian settlement in the Anglo-Saxon kingdoms of Northumbria, Mercia and East Anglia.

The evidence for non-ferrous metalworking emphasizes the importance and status of Lincoln during this period, as this has only been recognized to date in a limited number of ninth- to tenth-century towns in England, also including York, Thetford, Northampton, London and Winchester.[39] Unlike in York, however, where evidence for non-ferrous metalworking has been found that can be dated to both the middle Anglo-Saxon and the Anglo-Scandinavian periods, currently all production evidence from Lincoln belongs to the later part, after the Scandinavian settlement.[40] The majority of the evidence comes from the Flaxengate site, which was excavated in the 1970s and also yielded evidence for other crafts, such as pottery production, bone- and antler-working and glass-working. The excavations provided a unique insight into the development of what seems to have been a single urban property, as all the buildings across the whole site were periodically levelled and rebuilt. This resulted in high levels of residuality, with the majority of artefacts coming from levelling and demolition layers between building phases.[41]

The importance of Lincoln prior to the Scandinavian settlement is often overlooked and it is commonly assumed that the Scandinavian conquest and settlement was a direct cause of intense urban growth – even if 'little of the Scandinavian contribution to urbanization can be described as being characteristically Scandinavian'.[42] Indeed, early coinage produced in these 'Scandinavian' urban centres was typically based on Anglo-Saxon prototypes (or revealed Frankish and Byzantine influences), and named moneyers often bore Frankish names, Lincoln being no exception in this respect.[43] What is more, many of the emerging towns in the Scandinavian-occupied regions of England, including Lincoln, reveal evidence for pottery industries from the mid- to late ninth century onwards, producing, for the first time since Roman times, wheel-turned wares that were similar to contemporary Frankish wares. The evidence for these industries has caused a debate over the ethnic origins of the people responsible for their inception. Scholars such as Kathy Kilmurry and Alan Vince have argued that these innovative changes in pottery production happened at the instigation of itinerant Frankish potters arriving in England in the wake of the Scandinavian settlement, whilst more recently, Paul Blinkhorn has challenged the argument that there was a Scandinavian impetus behind these developments on the same 'ethnic' grounds.[44]

The interpretation of Viking-Age urbanization betrays the same preoccupation with ethnicity as the study of Viking-Age dress-accessories, and is indicative of a broader predilection for ethnic explanations in early medieval studies. But what if this says more about the development of our discipline than about the realities of the early medieval past? Do we really need to refer to the Scandinavian settlement to explain the changes in metalwork production in Lincoln, or was this the logical outcome of socio-economic processes that were already in motion? Put simply, can we identify the deliberate copying of new incoming object types or decorative styles that some may have associated with a 'Scandinavian' identity, and is there any evidence that they were selected *because* of their 'Scandinavian-ness'?

Metalworking in Lincoln

Introduction

Non-ferrous metalwork production evidence from Lincoln is plentiful, and has been discussed in more detail elsewhere.[45] The discussion here will focus mainly on the evidence that is relevant to a discussion of decorative styles. The first type of evidence to be considered is metalworking moulds, of which only a handful of relevant examples survive, spanning the ninth to eleventh centuries. In addition to moulds, there are a small number of artefacts that may shed more light on the issue. These are artefacts that may have been produced in Lincoln, based on the presence of unfinished specimens or the possible identification of mould duplicates. They include a large assemblage of hooked tags, some finger rings, wire rings and pins, two identical brooches, and two probably identical openwork discs. Like the moulds, none displays undeniably Scandinavian characteristics.

Moulds

An ingot mould made of soapstone from Saltergate in the Lower City might date to the later ninth century. As there seems to be a positive correlation between areas of Scandinavian settlement and finds of soapstone (mostly of Norwegian provenance), Justine Bayley has interpreted this mould as possibly indicating the presence of an itinerant Scandinavian metalworker in Lincoln in the early period of settlement.[46] Identifying the identity of the 'owner' of a single object is, however, tentative at best, and requires corroborating evidence, such as was, for example, found in the so-called 'Frisian merchant's house' in contemporary Kaupang, Norway, but which is to date absent from Lincoln.[47]

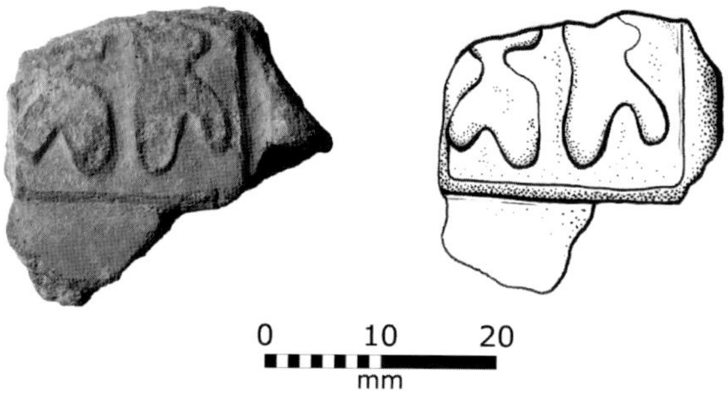

Fig. 3 Photograph of F75 ⟨p241⟩ and reconstruction drawing of object it would have created (photograph and drawing by Letty ten Harkel; note the object was photographed upside down).

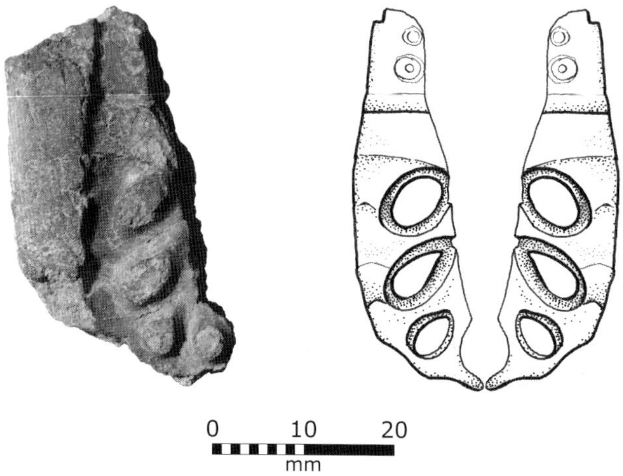

Fig. 4 Photograph of F75 ⟨p116⟩ and reconstruction drawing of object it would have created (photograph and drawing by Letty ten Harkel).

Soapstone ingot moulds are also known from Coppergate, York, including a re-used sherd of a soapstone vessel, like the Lincoln example.[48]As soapstone vessels are rare in English urban contexts, with only a few other vessel sherds known from Lincoln and a handful from York, which also had Scandinavian connections, the argument for a Scandinavian presence (or at least close contacts with Scandinavia) is compelling.[49] However, this does not mean that the products that emanated from the Lower City conveyed a 'Scandinavian' identity.

The production of ingots – if used for bullion purposes – would fit a Scandinavian context. However, although ingot moulds made from other materials were also found elsewhere in Lincoln, there is at present no evidence that a bullion economy functioned within the town of Lincoln.[50] In contrast to York and Torksey, no decorated weights are known from the city to date, and no hack silver has been found. What is more, the evidence for silver-working from the Lower City (presumably for coinage, as the later-tenth-century reverse die for a Crux penny of Æthelred (991–7) from nearby Flaxengate would suggest) means that this ingot mould could also have been used to rationalize raw materials for silver smithing.[51] In that case, the evidence may support the Scandinavian

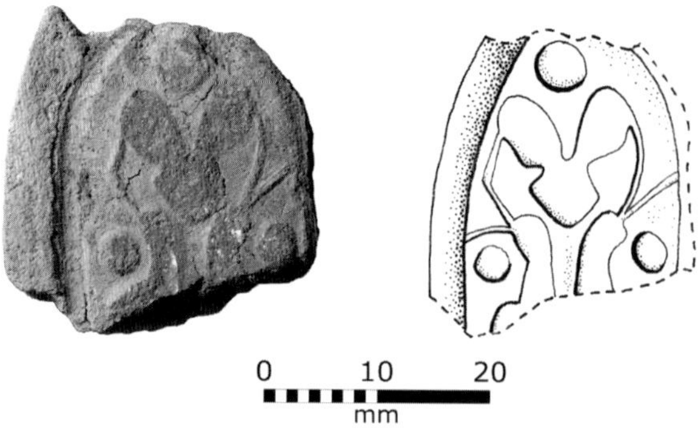

Fig. 5 Photograph of F75 ⟨p206⟩ and reconstruction drawing of object it would have created (photograph and drawing by Letty ten Harkel; note the object was photographed upside down).

background (or contacts) of the metalworker, but not the deliberate expression or manipulation of a Scandinavian identity. Instead, the soapstone may have been valued for its materiality rather than its Scandinavian connections, an argument that can also be applied to the ubiquitous hone stones of Norwegian Ragstone that occur on many sites of this period in the southern North Sea basin, even if their importation into England may have started as a result of the Scandinavian settlement.[52]

Most other moulds from Lincoln are made of clay, and – as a result of the aforementioned high levels of residuality on the Flaxengate site – few have been well enough preserved to identify the objects they would have created.[53] There are a handful of exceptions, none of which can be argued to have any Scandinavian affinities. By contrast, the Flaxengate excavations have produced two clay mould fragments used for the production of tongue-shaped strap-ends, ultimately derived from Continental styles, but with a wide distribution in tenth- to eleventh-century England. These include F75 ⟨p241⟩, a strap-end with debased Winchester-style foliate ornament, and F75 ⟨p116⟩, a Winchester-style openwork strap-end of Thomas Type E1 (Figs. 3–4). Similar strap-ends are known from Coppergate, York.[54] F75 ⟨p206⟩ (Fig. 5) would have created a strap-end with convex sides, a split attachment end and a zoomorphic terminal, which Gabor Thomas has identified as morphologically earlier, belonging to Thomas Class A, with a broad distribution across England in the ninth century.[55]

Excavations at Flaxengate also brought to light a fragment of a decorated stone mould, possibly used for casting lead.[56] A different design is visible on either side, one possibly for a flat disc brooch and the other for a cross-shaped ornament with lobed protrusions (Fig. 6). If this identification is correct, the flat disc brooch shows certain similarities to a copper-alloy specimen from Domburg in the Netherlands and to lead-alloy brooches of Weetch Types 5 and 24 (with a distribution in eastern England) from the eleventh-century Cheapside hoard in London, although the detail is different.[57] The lobed ornament shows similarities to Weetch Type 25, typically made of lead alloy and

Fig. 6 Photograph of stone mould from Flaxengate, possibly used for lead brooch casting (copyright Historic England).

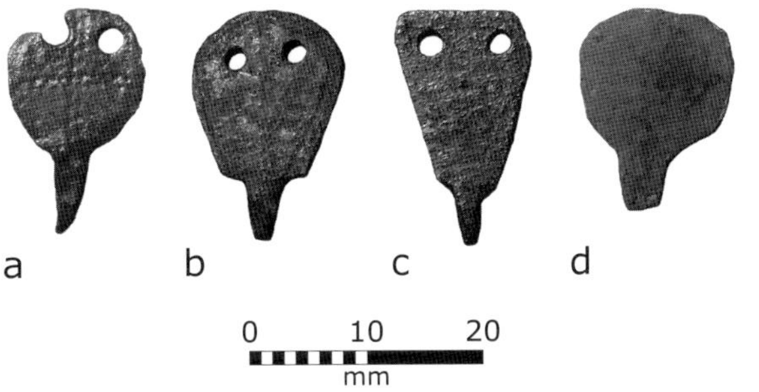

Fig. 7 Examples of finished hooked tags from Lincoln with different plate forms (a: F72 ⟨ae15⟩, Catalogue **no. 6**; b: F72 ⟨ae294⟩, Catalogue **no. 10**; c: BE73 ⟨ae37⟩, Catalogue **no. 76**; d: WP71 ⟨ae24⟩, Catalogue **no. 73**) (photographs by Letty ten Harkel).

with a distribution in London, Lincolnshire and Yorkshire, although the protrusions are spaced further apart in the shape of a simple cross.[58] Although it is abstract, it is possible that this cross-shape would have signalled a Christian identity.

Hooked tags

Hooked tags represent the most common type of manufacturing evidence from Lincoln and, rather than lending themselves for ethnic interpretations, their main characteristics seem to have been ease and (relatively) low cost of manufacture. They are fasteners of some sort, consisting of a plate with two attachment holes at the top and a protruding hook at the other end. The Lincoln hooked tags were largely made of copper-alloy or iron; the only recorded exception, made from silver, is no. 74 from West Parade in the Lower City. Iron examples were common in and near the Lower City and Wigford, where the waterlogged nature of deposits near the river (as opposed to the drier soils of the Upper City) may have aided their preservation (nos. 48–62, 64, 66–9 and 77). In a previous paper, drawing on a smaller selection of artefacts than those included here, I have linked such choices of 'cheaper' materials to increased scale of production.[59] Of course, the use of iron was not always a 'cheaper' alternative, and it may indicate a functional difference instead, as suggested by a hooked tag from Gloucester that was made of iron but also gilded and decorated.[60] However, none of the Lincoln tags made of iron seems to have been gilded.

The majority of the *c.* 80 hooked tags were found in association with Flaxengate Structure 20, interpreted as a possible workshop for the (relatively large-scale) production of these objects, and dated to the eleventh century (although the stratigraphic complexity of the site means that earlier, residual artefacts may also be included).[61] The shape of the plate varied between triangular and (sub-)circular (Figs. 7–8). Both finished and unfinished examples – as well as other forms of metalworking debris and crucible sherds – have also been found on other sites across Lincoln, however, suggesting that metalworking took place in several locations in the city (Figs. 7d, 8m and 8o–p).[62] This is suggestive of a specialist household mode of production, whereby craft activity, albeit increasingly specialized, still took place on a household level, a suggestion that is confirmed by the evidence for combined working and living space in single dwellings at Flaxengate.[63] These issues will be returned to further below.

In terms of their decoration, one of the hooked tags from Flaxengate, dated to the eleventh or earlier twelfth centuries, was decorated with an abstract design (no. 7; Fig. 9). Although it is much cruder and different in execution, the abstract nature of the decoration and its possible reference to zoomorphic or anthropomorphic mask-like features are vaguely reminiscent of a silver specimen found at Coppergate, York.[64] Dominic Tweddle has suggested that the York specimen possibly contained elements of the originally Scandinavian *Ringerike*-style, which became popular in England after the accession of Cnut, although he acknowledges that the decoration could have other stylistic origins as well.[65] The decorative pattern of the Lincoln hooked tag is even more abstract and is unlikely to have carried overtly ethnic associations of any kind.

Many of the Lincoln tags were decorated even more simply, with rocked-tracer decoration around the outline of the plate and the attachment holes, and sometimes forming lines or cross-shapes across the plate. The latter may again refer to a 'Christian' identity, although such abstract cross-shapes can also be interpreted as simple geometric patterns with no additional significance (nos. 6, 8, 10, 47 and 76; Fig. 10). Rocked-tracer decoration of hooked tags is not restricted to Lincoln: roughly contemporary examples have been found in York, Winchester, Gloucester and Hereford.[66] Other common types of decoration, such as the ring-and-dot motifs found on one of the York hooked tags, are not known from the large assemblage of Lincoln tags.[67]

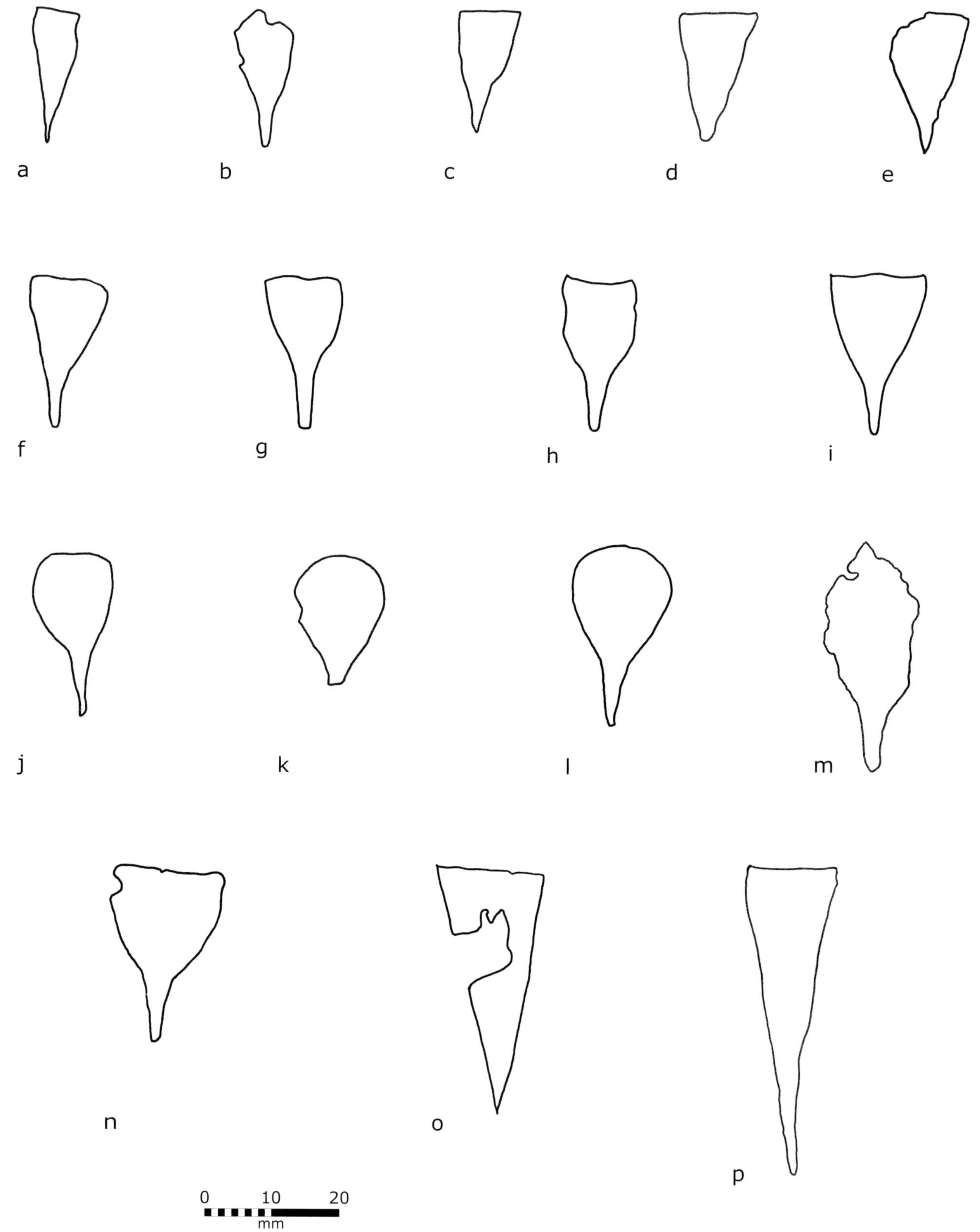

Fig. 8 Outline drawings of unfinished hooked tags from different excavations in Lincoln, showing a variety of plate forms (a: F74 ⟨ae165⟩, Catalogue **no. 16**; b: F74 ⟨ae240⟩, Catalogue **no. 25**; c: F74 ⟨ae335⟩, Catalogue **no. 38**; d: F74 ⟨ae166⟩, Catalogue **no. 17**; e: F74 ⟨ae335⟩, Catalogue **no. 38**; f: F74 ⟨ae485⟩, Catalogue **no. 43**; g: F74 ⟨ae259⟩, Catalogue **no. 29**; h: F74 ⟨ae281⟩, Catalogue **no. 30**; i: F74 ⟨ae242⟩, Catalogue **no. 27**; j: F74 ⟨ae289⟩, Catalogue **no. 32**; k: F74 ⟨ae169⟩, Catalogue **no. 19**; l: F74 ⟨ae169⟩, Catalogue **no. 19**; m: WW89 ⟨193⟩, Catalogue **no. 72**; n: F74 ⟨ae254⟩, Catalogue n**o. 28**; o: GP81 ⟨147⟩, Catalogue **no. 65**; p: WB80 ⟨ae13⟩, Catalogue no. 3) (drawings by Julia Warszewski).

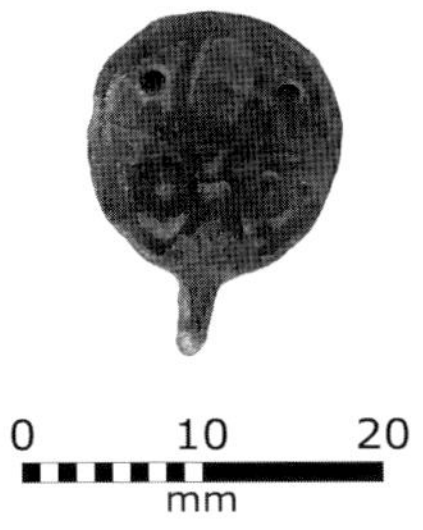

Fig. 9 Photograph of F72 ⟨ae45⟩, Catalogue **no. 7** (photograph by Letty ten Harkel).

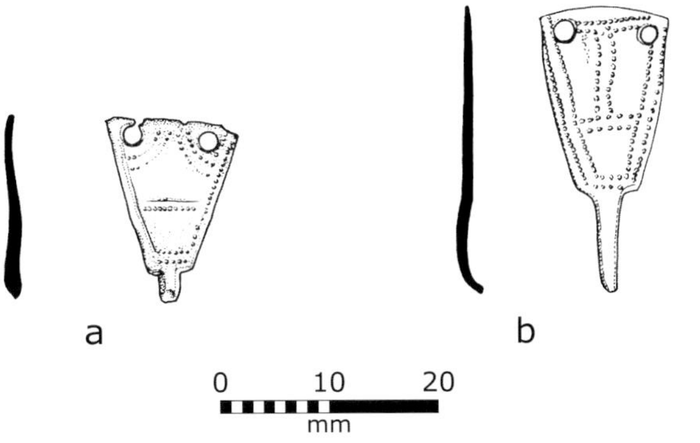

Fig. 10 Drawings of hooked tags from Flaxengate, showing the typical rocked-tracer decoration (a: F72 ⟨ae213⟩, Catalogue **no. 8**; b: F74 ⟨ae546⟩, Catalogue **no. 47**) (drawings by Dave Watt, copyright City of Lincoln Council).

I have argued elsewhere that copper-alloy hooked tags with rocked-tracer decoration from rural Lincolnshire – a growing number of examples brought to light through metal-detecting – were Lincoln products.[68] Given the evidence for contacts between York and Lincoln, it is possible that the York specimen – which fits well with the Lincoln style – should be included in this. By contrast, the rocked-tracer decoration on the example from Gloucester differs from the Lincoln examples, with diagonal rather than vertical and horizontal lines, suggesting that distinct 'workshops' – possibly linked to regional 'identities' focused on different production centres – can be identified also in the case of more simple decorative styles.

Rings

The evidence from the hooked tags presents the largest production assemblage of a single artefact type from Lincoln, and the only evidence that can rightly be seen as indicative of incipient mass-production for a regional market. In other cases, the evidence is less conclusive. There are three finger-rings made from tapering strips of copper alloy (nos. 113, 115–16). Two, both from Wigford, were unfinished. Like the hooked tags and the smaller pins discussed below, these rings were characterized by simple decoration consisting of punched dots. They are similar in form to some finger rings from York, although the latter are decorated with punched ring-and-dot motifs, which also occurred on the aforementioned hooked tag from York.[69] Ring-and-dot motifs do not occur often on the Lincoln metalwork known to date, except on a group of small hexagonal bells (discussed below). They also occur on finds made from different materials, such as a bone and antler comb from Flaxengate with an in-turned animal-head terminal.[70] This might suggest that, in addition to being regionally varied, simple decorative styles also varied in terms of the materials to which they were applied.

Excavations have also yielded a relatively large number of undecorated wire rings, possible finger- or earrings, some with their ends twisted together (nos. 103–12, 114). As copper-alloy wire was produced at Flaxengate, it is likely that these were local products.[71] Similar rings are known from both Fishergate and Coppergate in York, spanning the middle and late Anglo-Saxon periods, although some could also be Roman in date.[72] They may also have had a rural distribution, although the objects are too fragile to render their survival (and recognition by metal-detectorists) likely. In addition to copper-alloy rings, excavations at Flaxengate have yielded some plain jet finger-rings and a fragment of an amber finger-ring as well, similar to types manufactured at the Hiberno-Norse site of Wood Quay (Dublin) and Coppergate.[73] Amber probably originated in the Baltic (although it also occurs on the east coast of England, as it floats on sea water), but jet was probably sourced closer to home, for example from Whitby in Yorkshire.[74] This suggests that Lincoln was tied into (supra-)regional economic networks, connected not only to the cities of York and Dublin, but – either directly or via York – also to more rural areas that provided raw materials for craft production.

Pins

Given the evidence for the production of copper-alloy wire, as well as glass, production at Flaxengate, it is possible that two copper-alloy wire pins with glass heads were also produced in Lincoln (nos. 95 and 98).[75] They are similar to finds from Winchester from eleventh- to twelfth-century contexts.[76] Although the objects are undiagnostic and – like the wire rings – may have been produced more generally in a number of different production centres, it is not unthinkable that the pins indicate further economic contacts between Lincoln and Winchester, situated outside the area of Scandinavian settlement. Coin finds from Lincolnshire demonstrate that Lincoln was increasingly tied in to 'national' economic networks from the later tenth century onwards, with increasing numbers of coins with 'southern' mint signatures (including Winchester).[77]

Brooches

Moving on to more diagnostic decorative metalwork, there are two lead-alloy brooches of tenth- to eleventh-century date from the Lower City, which represent possible mould duplicates (nos. 84–5; Fig. 11).[78] With the possible exception of the stone mould discussed previously, which was used for ornaments in a different style, no definite lead alloy production evidence (moulds or lead-melting crucibles) has been found. However, because lead has a much lower melting point than copper alloy, moulds could have

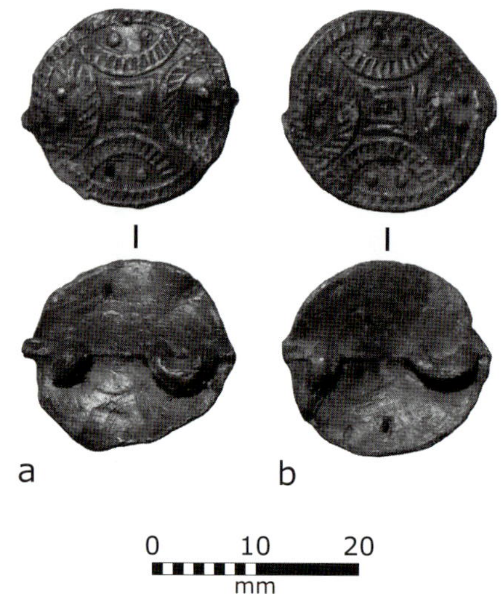

Fig. 11 Photograph of a) P70 ⟨pb13⟩, Catalogue **no. 85** and b) SW82 ⟨386⟩, Catalogue **no. 84** (photograph by Letty ten Harkel).

been made of wood or antler, and domestic cooking pots were suitable for use as lead-melting crucibles, leaving no identifiable vitreous residues.[79] This means that production evidence for lead alloys may be severely under-represented in Lincoln's archaeological record.

The flat disc shape and the form of the attachment fittings of the two Lincoln brooches indicate Anglo-Saxon and Frankish rather than Scandinavian fashions.[80] Decoration consists of a stylized curved-armed cross-design common across England and the nearby Continent; examples from England include one found at Barrow-upon-Humber in North Lincolnshire.[81] A variety of disc brooches with designs including crosses, foliate patterns, animals and coin-designs, and reflecting fashions current in southern England as well as the Ottonian realm, are known from York also, although the variety there is larger; for example, no animal or coin brooches are currently known from Lincoln.[82]

Pendants

The final objects to be considered in the section on metalworking are two openwork copper-alloy discs, again possible mould-duplicates, both from the Lower City (nos. 89 and 91; Fig. 12c).[83] A very small fragment of a metalworking mould found at Flaxengate (F72 ⟨p79⟩) tentatively strengthens the suggestion that objects *of this type* were produced in Lincoln. Fig. 12a shows this mould fragment with a reconstruction of the partial object it would have created, alongside a broadly similar disc from Wimborne St Giles (Dorset) (Fig. 12b) with a similar double border and some features that may depict a claw gripping or adjoining the border, although the fragment is admittedly too small to be definitive.

In a previous article I noted that the central animal motif shares elements with eleventh- to twelfth-century finds from Denmark in the Scandinavian-derived *Ringerike-* and *Urnes*-styles and early Romanesque Agnus Dei brooches, and suggested that their pendant form – a type of dress-accessory that had gone out of fashion in Anglo-Saxon England – points to a Scandinavian context.[84] However, as other metal pendants from Lincoln (discussed later in this paper) also belong to the eleventh century or later, it seems that the revival of this fashion was not a direct result of the initial Scandinavian settlement in the ninth century, but occurred at a later date, possibly after the reign of Cnut. Having said that, pendants made from different materials such as amber and jet occur more broadly in both York and Lincoln, some belonging to a slightly earlier time period.[85] The York assemblage in particular includes a significant number of pendants made from amber, a material that in itself could be argued to have Scandinavian, or at least Baltic, connotations.[86]

If the fashion of wearing pendants was reintroduced into England from Scandinavia, the decoration of the two Lincoln objects seems to imply a religious, rather than an ethnic, statement. Additional examples that share certain decorative elements are now known from England,

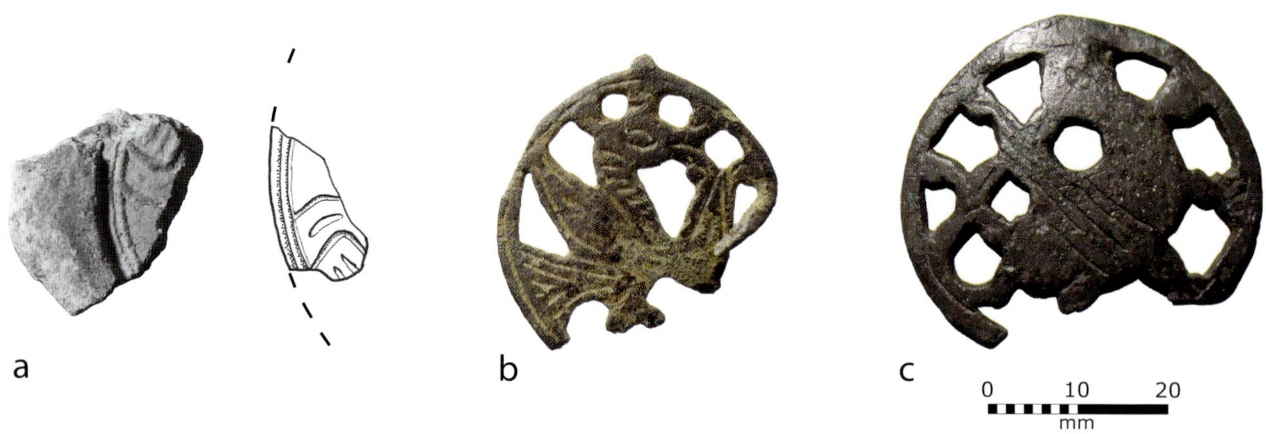

Fig. 12 Photograph of a) F72 ⟨p79⟩ alongside reconstruction of object fragment (photograph and drawing by Letty ten Harkel); b) griffin disc from Wimborne St Giles, Dorset (photograph by Martin Green; previously published as Deckers 2012, 28, fig 10d. Reproduced with kind permission of Martin Green.); c) P70 ⟨ae171⟩, Catalogue **no. 91** (photograph by Letty ten Harkel).

including the aforementioned specimen from Wimborne St Giles.[87] This object – probably a pendant as well – seems to conform stylistically to a group of mostly eleventh-century bird brooches from Scandinavia, England and the nearby Continent, which Anne Pedersen has suggested expressed a Christian identity.[88] In addition, a number of eleventh-century metal-detected finds with broadly similar decoration, interpreted as depicting griffins, have since been published from coastal Flanders.[89] Pieterjan Deckers has argued that the griffin was essentially also a Christian symbol, referring to the dual nature of Christ, being at once human and divine.[90] Unlike the openwork discs from Lincoln, the Flemish objects were of smaller size and with attachment fittings suggesting that they were brooches. This demonstrates that similar decoration occurred on different types of ornaments, and – as we have already seen with simpler decorative styles – confirms the suggestion that specific combinations of decoration and ornament type may be regionally specific.

The interpretation of the elements of the Lincoln pendants is more complicated. Although a stylized wing extending upwards can be discerned, it lacks the bird-like tail and beak of the Wimborne St Giles example (compare Figs. 12b and 12c). The decoration is fairly abstract, like the Flemish brooches, and depicts a winged forward-looking quadruped with a tail curving back towards its head. The tail intersects at right angles with the raised wing and a backwards-extended leg, forming two rough cross-shapes that are reminiscent of the positioning of crosses on the Agnus Dei brooches. Its dragonesque features have something in common with depictions of *amphisbaena* – mythical two-headed serpent-like creatures – from the Bayeux Tapestry, who are also winged, with tails that curve back over their shoulders, although the similarities are superficial.[91] Although the Lincoln objects are unusual in their detail, they nevertheless fit with broader fashions that have been argued to express Christian identities.

Conclusions

In sum, there is little metalwork production evidence from Anglo-Scandinavian Lincoln – tentative or certain – that can be argued to indicate the deliberate creation of a Scandinavian identity. A similar lack of overtly ethnic styles has been noted for other small finds from Lincoln, made of different materials.[92] The evidence presented here is overwhelmingly fairly late, dating to the tenth to twelfth centuries rather than the initial period of Scandinavian settlement. Although the eleventh century undoubtedly also witnessed a strengthening of ties with the Scandinavian territories, especially during the reign of King Cnut, Scandinavia was becoming increasingly integrated with other parts of Europe by this stage, which may have rendered previous differences less pronounced. A driving force behind this integration was, of course, the spread of Christianity, and it is interesting to note that Tweddle has commented on a similar lack of 'classic Viking art' from York, instead interpreting the York assemblage as reflecting changes in the balance of power between secular and ecclesiastical magnates.[93] The Lincoln production evidence, with its recurring cross-shapes and other arguably Christian motifs, may reflect similar concerns. In this context it may also be worth drawing attention to the absence of Thor's Hammers from either Lincoln or York, in contrast to evidence from the later ninth-century Viking winter camp at nearby Torksey, indicating a clear difference in the character (and date) of occupation.[94] However, even more striking is the relative simplicity of decorative designs, allowing for fast and low-cost production techniques. The implications of this will be revisited further below, after a discussion of other decorative metalwork finds from Lincoln.

Other decorative metalwork from Lincoln

Introduction

The choices in terms of form and decoration that are made during the production of decorative metalwork – as with all types of objects – are the outcome of a complex interaction between supply and demand, embedded in the relationship between consumers and producers.[95] Put simply, a craftsperson is unlikely to make things that no one wants, but at the same time he or she might try to impress or influence prospective clients or patrons through the introduction of new elements or motifs. A craftsperson's repertoire was influenced by encounters with other craftspeople and also their products, and for that reason this paper will now turn to the analysis of other decorative metalwork from the city, to place the production evidence in its appropriate context. Rather than by object type, the discussion is organized chronologically, to chart changes in the decorative and stylistic tastes of Lincoln's population. Given the difficulties in dating metalwork on art-historical grounds and the stratigraphic complexities of the Lincoln excavations, the chronological divisions are necessarily fairly broad and overlapping.

Before the Scandinavian settlement (earlier ninth century)

The decorative metal artefacts that can broadly be dated to the period before the Scandinavian settlement in the later ninth century were part of the cultural and typological repertoire of the southern North Sea zone, in particular Anglo-Saxon England and the Low Countries. The largest quantity of ninth-century middle-Anglo-Saxon metalwork is from St Paul-in-the-Bail, consisting of a silver Anglo-Saxon Trewhiddle-style buckle and strap-end – a ubiquitous Anglo-Saxon art style – and a silver Carolingian buckle (nos. 117–18 and 124). Another probably ninth-century copper-alloy buckle with a triangular buckle-plate has been found at Michaelgate in the Lower City (no. 122).[96] The Trewhiddle style is better represented on finds from York, where their production has been argued to continue into the tenth century, after the initial Scandinavian settlement.[97]

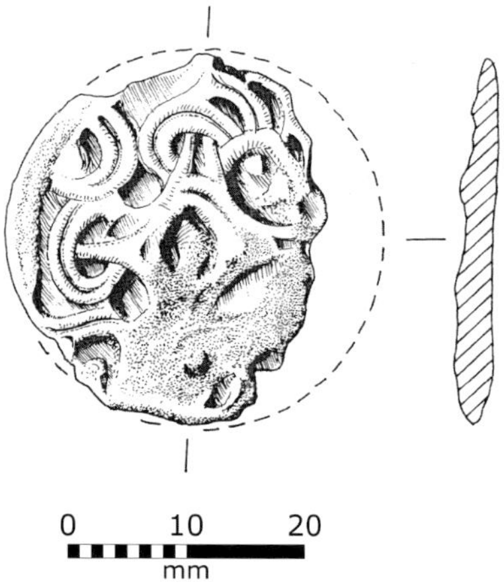

Fig. 13 Drawing of F72 ⟨ae302⟩, Catalogue **no. 81** (drawing by Dave Watt, copyright City of Lincoln Council).

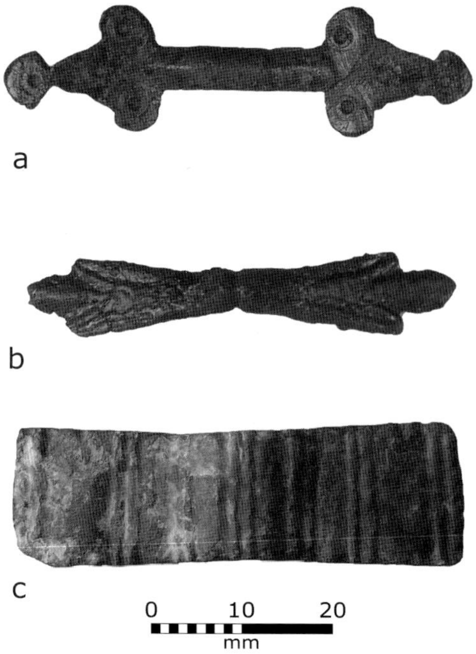

Fig. 14 Photograph of a) SM76 ⟨ae92⟩, Catalogue **no. 87**; b) F76 ⟨ae107⟩, Catalogue **no. 83**; and c) F72 ⟨ae23⟩, Catalogue **no. 79** (photographs by Letty ten Harkel).

Other early artefacts belong to generic types and their attribution to the middle Anglo-Saxon period is tentative. The corpus of dress pins from Lincoln reveals a variety of cultural influences. Many of the earlier copper-alloy pins – like their bone counterparts – are common types, also found at nearby Flixborough, typologically spanning the middle and late Anglo-Saxon periods.[98] Two are plain, with globular and biconical pinheads, which have a widespread distribution across England (nos. 94 and 99). In addition, there are three copper-alloy polyhedral-headed pins with ring-and-dot decoration from Lincoln, again with parallels from other Anglo-Saxon and Anglo-Scandinavian sites including York, although the corpus of metal dress-pins from York is substantially larger and more varied (nos. 93, 97 and 101).[99]

After the Scandinavian settlement (later ninth to tenth centuries)

From the later ninth and tenth centuries onwards, a greater variety of cultural influences becomes apparent, including artefacts that are distinctively 'Scandinavian' in style and/or decoration. A multi-headed copper-alloy strap-end in derived Scandinavian *Borre*-style, dated to the late ninth to tenth centuries, was found in Wigford (no. 125).[100] Parallels are known from across the Scandinavian homelands and diaspora, including an example from Fishergate in York.[101] In addition, a D-shaped buckle in Scandinavian *Borre*-style, with an outward facing stylized animal head *en face* protruding from the lip, was either manufactured in Scandinavia, or produced in England but overtly imitating contemporary Scandinavian buckles (no. 123).[102]

There are two probably tenth-century brooches from Lincoln that betray Scandinavian influences. They belong to fairly standard types. A convex disc-brooch decorated in *Jellinge*-style was found in Wigford (no. 88), from the same site that also yielded the aforementioned *Borre*-style buckle. Jane Kershaw has suggested that this type may be of southern Scandinavian manufacture.[103] The attachment fittings included a third attachment loop, a diagnostically Scandinavian trait.[104] The other example is a flat copper-alloy disc-brooch decorated in *Borre*-style from Flaxengate (no. 81; Fig. 13). This tenth-century brooch type – a common metal-detector find in East Anglia and Lincolnshire from after the Scandinavian settlement – was mass-produced in East Anglia.[105] It combines Scandinavian-derived decoration with an essentially Anglo-Saxon or Continental brooch form, the flat disc shape, and is often seen as expressing a hybrid Anglo-Scandinavian identity.[106]

Other brooches display Continental influences. The earliest brooches from Lincoln are ansate or equal-armed brooches. They are broadly dated to the seventh to tenth centuries, although the presence of broadly similar brooches in York at the Anglo-Scandinavian Coppergate site, and their absence from the earlier, predominantly Anglian Fishergate site, suggest that – in England at least – they belong to the later part of the period.[107] The Lincoln examples include two brooches from Flaxengate (nos. 79 and 83; Fig. 14b–c) and one, of the so-called Lincoln Type, from St Mark's Church in Wigford (no. 87; Fig. 14a). They are common on the Continent, and their distribution in England is distinctly eastern.[108] In his discussion of the York material, Dominic Tweddle has interpreted such brooches as evidence for continuing links with Continental Europe during the Anglo-Scandinavian period.[109]

A tenth-century polychrome enamelled disc brooch from Flaxengate, together with the majority of the hooked tags also found in association with Structure 20, probably represents a Continental import (no. 80; Fig. 15). It

Fig. 15 Photograph of F72 ⟨ae296⟩, Catalogue **no. 80** (photograph by Letty ten Harkel).

is only the third of its kind to have been recognized in England, and has been the subject of a separate publication.[110] Its most striking aspect was undoubtedly its colourful decoration depicting a bird holding a branch in its beak, which should be understood as Christian imagery, either reflecting Jesus' words in John 15:1 ('I am the true vine') or representing the dove that returns to Noah with an olive branch.[111]

Ringed pins are commonly regarded as indicating a Hiberno-Norse identity, based on their frequent occurrence in the Irish Sea region between the ninth and twelfth centuries. Two excavated examples from (near) the Lower City belong to Fanning's plain-ringed polyhedral-headed type, the most common type of ringed pin found in the British Isles between the early tenth and mid-eleventh centuries; another example is a parallel from Coppergate, York (nos. 96 and 100; Fig. 16).[112] A third pin, with a slightly flattened head but probably still belonging to the same broad group, was a casual find from Nettleham Road, roughly one mile to the north-east of the Upper City (no. 102; Fig. 17).

Four hexagonal bells with cusped bottom and ring-and-dot decoration are also known from Lincoln (nos. 133–6).[113] Commonly described as 'Norse bells', these are frequent finds on sites within areas of Scandinavian settlement, especially in England, but only outside Scandinavia, thus rendering the label 'Norse' somewhat misleading. Within England, their distribution is biased towards the east, concentrating particularly on East Yorkshire and Lincolnshire.[114] Their function is debated, including theories about their use for horse harness accessories, dog collars or falconry or as fashion accessories. Other suggestions, often highlighting their common occurrence in funerary contexts, have focused on more ritual/religious connotations, including the importance of bells in Christian worship.[115] On the basis of the occurrence of a bell in a possible female child burial from the Isle of Man, Deirdre McAllister has suggested that they may have been

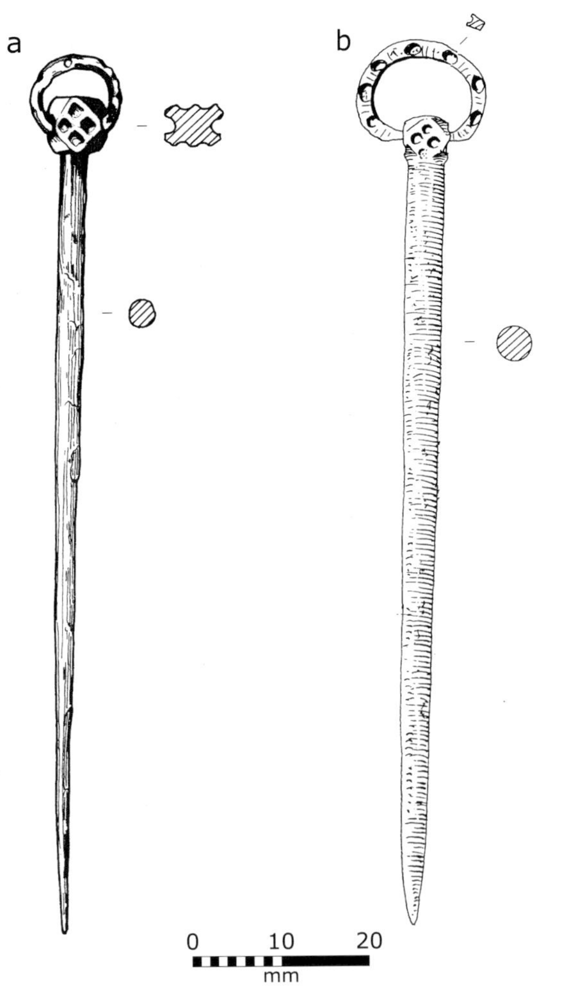

Fig. 16 Drawings of ringed pins from Lincoln: a) F72 ⟨ae290⟩, Catalogue **no. 96**; b) BE73 ⟨ae164⟩, Catalogue **no. 100** (drawings by Dave Watt, copyright City of Lincoln Council).

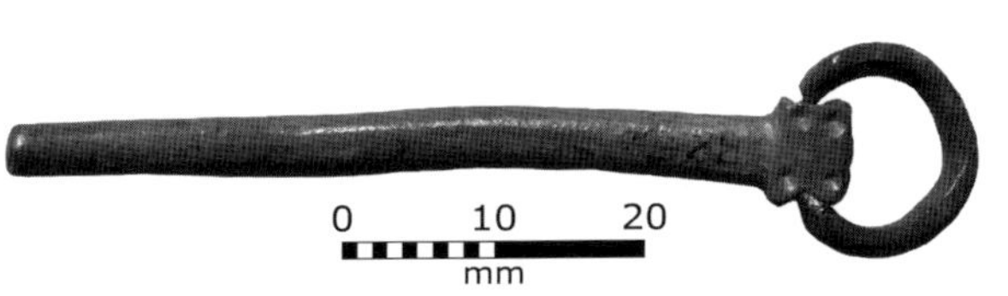

Fig. 17 Photograph of *The Collection* no ⟨88.52⟩, Catalogue **no. 102** (photograph by Letty ten Harkel).

toys; however, Meagan Schoenfelder and Julian Richards have emphasized the female (rather than juvenile) identity of the deceased, drawing attention to the fact that poor bone preservation made ageing of the skeletal remains impossible.[116]

A final object of interest is a crude zoomorphic iron-plated hasp or hinge from Grantham Place in the Lower City, possibly for a box (no. 137; Fig. 18). It was found in an eleventh-century pit, but in association with tenth-century pottery, making an earlier date not unlikely. This is the only piece of decorative metalwork from early medieval Lincoln that was almost certainly used for the decoration of furniture rather than for personal adornment,

Fig. 18 Photograph of GP81 ⟨57⟩, Catalogue **no. 137** (photograph by Letty ten Harkel).

Fig. 19 Photograph of F74 ⟨ae184⟩, Catalogue **no. 82** (photograph by Letty ten Harkel).

but it shares certain qualities, such as relative ease and low cost of production.

In sum, there is a clear increase in the circulation of objects with Scandinavian influences after the period of settlement in the later ninth century, some – like the soapstone mould discussed in the previous section – possibly representing the personal possessions of Scandinavian settlers. However, many of these link to other parts of the Viking diaspora, rather than directly to the Scandinavian homelands. Moreover, these objects only represent part of the overall assemblage, with additional evidence for the continued presence of Continental Frankish, or indeed Anglo-Saxon, influences (including some of the objects discussed in the previous section, which undoubtedly also belong to this period). Rather than suggesting an influx of distinctly 'Scandinavian' influences, the assemblage therefore points to a more general influence from a variety of geographical directions, a fact that might be overlooked when analysis is focused on specific artefact types rather than entire assemblages. The strongest evidence for Scandinavian imports (i.e. objects manufactured in Scandinavia) comes from Wigford, despite the fact that the largest quantity of metalwork overall has been found in the Lower City, which includes more hybrid forms as well as objects of possible Continental manufacture. This may indicate a possible difference in the ethnic composition of the inhabitants of various parts of the city, although the evidence is too thin to be definitive.

Fig. 20 Photograph of HG72 ⟨ae58⟩, Catalogue **no. 86** (photograph by Letty ten Harkel).

The eleventh century and later

The final part of this section turns to the eleventh century, which witnessed continued intermixing of different metalwork styles from across the southern North Sea zone, with forms that are now entirely hybrid. Two brooches belong to this period. A convex disc brooch with an irregular and unusual pattern of petal-like loops in high relief from Flaxengate bears superficial resemblance to the tenth-century Scandinavian Terslev-style, although it is much more devolved and should thus be placed in a slightly later time period (no. 82; Fig. 19).[117] The domed shape also suggests Scandinavian influence, but the attachment fittings are Anglo-Saxon.[118] This could be an Anglo-Saxon brooch inspired by Scandinavian prototypes, although parallels are known from the Continent, and it is uncertain whether the devolved decoration retained any Scandinavian connotations at this stage.[119]

Also somewhat reminiscent of the Terslev style in its placement of the four volutes or back-to-back C-shaped scrolls, but no longer comprising the actual ring-chain interlace characteristic of the style in its pure form, is a flat copper-alloy gilded disc brooch from Wigford (no. 86; Fig. 20). The flat shape suggests Anglo-Saxon or Continental influences but the decorative motif is common across Europe, also appearing on a tenth-century lead brooch from York.[120] Although this type of decoration first occurs in the tenth century, both the devolved adaptation and the slightly unusual brooch form suggest a slightly later, eleventh-century date.[121]

There are two pendants with possible Scandinavian parallels, although neither is decorated in what might be considered a 'Scandinavian' art style. A small lead-alloy pendant was found at St Mark's Station in Wigford (no. 92; Fig. 21a). The object is similar to a miscast found at Coppergate, York (Fig. 21b), as well as to a second example

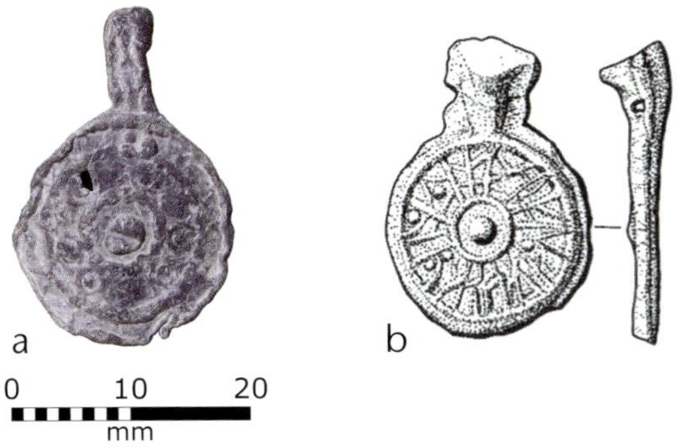

Fig. 21 Photograph of Z86 ⟨676⟩, Catalogue **no. 92** alongside a parallel from York, previously published in Bayley 1992, 780, fig 340 (photograph by Letty ten Harkel; drawing reproduced with kind permission of Christine McDonnell, York Archaeological Trust).

Fig. 22 Photograph of H83 ⟨455⟩, Catalogue **no. 90** (photograph by Letty ten Harkel).

Fig. 23 Photograph of CWG86 ⟨106⟩, Catalogue **no. 126** (photograph by Letty ten Harkel).

Fig. 24 Photographs of a) F72 ⟨ae243⟩, Catalogue **no. 130** and b) LIN73 ⟨44⟩, Catalogue **no. 131** (photographs by Letty ten Harkel).

from York with crescent-shaped motifs, and may represent evidence for York-produced metalwork circulating in Lincoln.[122] The York miscast bears a pseudo-runic inscription, possibly expressing Scandinavian associations, but the markings on the Lincoln pendant represent circles or crescent-shapes.[123] Possible parallels in lead- and silver-alloy are also known from Domburg, and similarities with silver pendants from graves in Birka (Sweden) have also been noted.[124] A similar object, although with a less protruding attachment fitting, was found in Mainz on the German Rhine as well, again emphasizing the widespread connections of many object types by this time.[125]

Finally, a possible gilded pendant was found at Hungate in the Lower City (no. 90; Fig. 22). Its interpretation as a pendant rests on comparison with a copper-alloy object found in the Danish Viking fortress of Aggersborg, although there is little about either of these objects that is distinctively Scandinavian.[126] The Scandinavian object was simpler in execution, the decoration applied in the so-called rocked-tracing technique rather than as applied strips, but it shares the small diameter, paper-thin quality and symmetrical decorative pattern with the Hungate object. The Aggersborg find was attributed to the eleventh to twelfth centuries, which is consistent with a renewed, more widespread use of gilding in England after the Norman Conquest.[127]

The most clearly Scandinavian-derived decorative elements from this period are found on mounts and studs. Two are executed in *Urnes*-style, including the published mount from Danes Terrace in the Lower City (executed in an insular adaption of this originally Scandinavian art style), as well as an unprovenanced openwork stirrup mound 'from Lincoln', now in the collection of the British Museum (nos. 128 and 132).[128] The *Urnes*-style decoration is also common on contemporary rural objects (recovered through metal-detecting) from Lincolnshire. Together with an almost complete absence of decorative horse-harness gear dating to the eighth, ninth and earlier tenth centuries, this suggests that a re-appreciation of equestrian activity occurred *after* the Scandinavian settlement, possibly as late as the eleventh century, during the reign of Cnut. By this stage, the 'Scandinavian' decoration may have become associated with a more generic 'elite' identity.

A third object, from the Castle Westgate site in the Upper City, was decorated with a gilded zoomorphic motif depicting two back-turned dragon-like winged creatures with intertwined tails (no. 126; Fig. 23). Although unusual, the design has certain parallels in Romanesque art and the wings display similarities to those of the aforementioned *amphisbaena* from the Bayeux Tapestry, although it is otherwise difficult to ascribe to a specific style. The rope-like border is reminiscent of the Lincoln-style stone grave-markers, suggesting that this piece may have more in common with other Lincoln products in a different medium than with metalwork from further afield.[129]

Other studs and mounts are executed in more neutral, geometric styles. These include another copper-alloy stud from Castle Westgate, similar to lead-alloy examples found in Domburg, Denmark and Norway, possibly representing a decorative stud for a saddle strap, and a small square-headed copper-alloy stud with crudely executed incised geometric decoration (nos. 127 and 130; Fig. 24a).[130] A similar example was found at nearby Saltergate (no. 131; Fig. 24b). Finally, two undiagnostic D-shaped buckles of probable eleventh-century date were found at Flaxengate (nos. 119 and 121; Fig. 25), as well as a

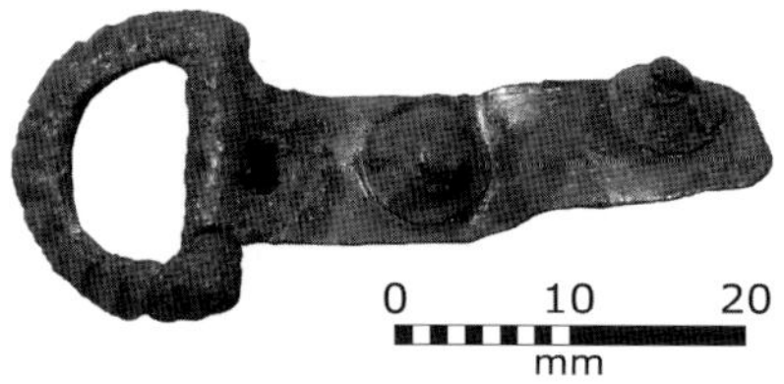

Fig. 25 Photograph of F72 ⟨ae44⟩, Catalogue **no. 119** (photograph by Letty ten Harkel).

more elaborate eleventh- or twelfth-century Romanesque buckle with two animal-head terminals biting the bar (no. 120; Fig. 26).[131] Finally, a simple copper-alloy strap-loop of slightly crude workmanship with incised decoration was found in an eleventh- or twelfth-century context at Flaxengate (no. 129), although the latter is more difficult to date on stylistic grounds.[132]

Metalworkers in London

A question that remains to be answered is, who were the metalworkers who produced this material? The social status of early medieval craftspeople, including smiths, has frequently been the subject of scholarly debate, and it is beyond the scope of the current paper to go into much detail. However, in the introductory sections to this paper I posed the question of to what degree changes in production mode – the emergence of mass-production in specialized workshops – affected the styles of the objects being produced. What, then, is the evidence that this was indeed the way in which metalworking activities were organized in early medieval Lincoln?

Different schemes for the classification of modes of production exist, although they tend to be variations on the same theme. A classification by Brandenburgh, proposed in the context of textile manufacture, likewise part of people's personal attire, distinguishes between household production, household industry, tethered specialization and workshop industry.[133] Of course, such categories are by their nature always overlapping, and the Lincoln evidence seems to have aspects of several of these. This includes the household level, on which crafts seem to have been organized – suggested by the combined living and working space in the craftsworkers' dwellings, mentioned previously, as well as the broad spread of often small amounts of metalworking debris and crucible sherds across different sites – but also workshop industries, of which the standardized efficiency of the finished products is characteristic.[134] The clearest evidence for the latter comes from the production evidence for the hooked tags, which were largely associated with a sequence of buildings (S13, S17 and S20) dating to the later tenth to eleventh centuries.[135] This might suggest a chronological development, whereby the organization of metalwork production increasingly moved into the category for workshop industries.

Another consideration that deserves mentioning is the question of to what degree craftspeople were sedentary.

Fig. 26 Photograph of F72 ⟨ae297⟩, Catalogue **no. 120** (photograph by Letty ten Harkel).

The notion of the itinerant artisan is persistent in considerations of Viking-Age craft production. Criteria for mobility have included smaller-than-expected workshop waste deposits – which is certainly not an issue at the Flaxengate site – as well as morphological and decorative homogeneity of finished products.[136] Although the latter can indeed be observed, itinerancy is of course not the only plausible explanation for the spread of ideas, and the superimposed nature of several metalworkers' workshops at Flaxengate would suggest that craft activities were passed down the generations in the same location. This would seem in line with evidence from contemporary settlement contexts in York and Dublin, although – as Ashby has highlighted – different craftsmen active in the same settlements might have different ways of living.[137]

Discussion: identities in Lincoln

To return to the question posed at the start of this paper, how important was ethnicity to the inhabitants of Anglo-Scandinavian Lincoln? The urban metalwork assemblage from Lincoln displays evidence for Anglo-Saxon, Frankish, Scandinavian and Irish (or Hiberno-Scandinavian) influences. Unsurprisingly, the latter two only occur from the period of Scandinavian settlement onwards. This is also true for the presence of other materials from Scandinavia, such as amber and Norwegian Ragstone, and the soapstone ingot mould of probable Swedish provenance.

Although some of the objects displaying Frankish influences do, on art-historical grounds, predate the Scandinavian settlement in the third quarter of the ninth century, there is nevertheless a possible 'Viking' explanation for their presence. The aforementioned Carolingian silver belt-buckle from St Paul-in-the-Bail may have been part of a dispersed Viking hoard.[138] Jane Young and Alan Vince have, furthermore, suggested that Lincoln's small assemblage of Continental pottery from the Rhineland and northern France was introduced 'during the early years of Anglo-Scandinavian settlement'.[139] What is more, a possible middle-Anglo-Saxon settlement core south of the Lower City, referred to above, is seemingly indicated by the presence of middle 'Anglo-Saxon' pottery only, with no published reference to imported Continental wares, as were common at *Eoforwic* in York or *Hamwic* near Southampton.[140] In this respect, then, pre-Viking Lincoln differed from York, which – as Tweddle has demonstrated – was already part of a broader North Sea world with connections to the Carolingian court.[141] The difference may be one of relative status: although Lincoln was not unimportant as an ecclesiastical centre, it did not have the same status (and therefore connections) as York – one of Britain's two archiepiscopal sees – either.

Did any of this represent the deliberate expression of ethnic identities, Scandinavian or otherwise? The answer to this question is surely scale-dependent. Even if we accept the possibility that (some of) the objects of Scandinavian manufacture were the personal possessions of Scandinavian settlers (and assume that these were understood to signal 'Scandinavian-ness' by the individual wearer and/or others) and that some of the metalworkers may have been of Scandinavian origin, there is no evidence at present that they were reproduced on a larger scale in Lincoln – in other words, that there was a market for these objects, aimed at promoting a more general 'Scandinavian' identity. This seems to exist in contrast to the more abundant evidence for the popularity of Scandinavian-derived styles in rural contexts in the East Midlands (recovered through metal detecting).[142] Why was this the case? A plausible explanation might be the pre-existing importance of Lincoln as a central place of some sort, as emphasized at the start of this paper. Even if economic activity was still limited, at the time of the Scandinavian settlement in the second half of the ninth century, Lincoln was a regional centre of considerable importance. The Scandinavian settlement was a factor in its growth, but not the only one. To depict the town as 'Anglo-Scandinavian' is therefore overly simplistic: it was a place where different agents coalesced and had to negotiate hybrid – or neutral – identities in order to coexist.

A possible exception to the lack of evidence for overtly 'Scandinavian' styles in Lincoln is the eleventh-century *Urnes*-style decorative mount, which fits in a broader eleventh-century 'fashion' of *Urnes*-style objects, also including horse harness accessories, although by this stage – the reign of the Danish King Cnut – Scandinavian-derived styles may have come to signify elite status rather than any 'ethnic' identity.[143] A similar caveat is relevant to Frankish-derived styles, which may have appealed to Christian identities instead. Indeed – as Thomas has argued – the cultural dynamics of Viking-Age England were highly fluent and adaptive, and so were the cultural repertoires from which they drew, both before and after the Scandinavian settlement.[144] What is more, meanings were also fluid, and we have to acknowledge the likelihood that the mixture of Anglo-Saxon, Scandinavian, Frankish and Hiberno-Norse styles that *we* can discern lost their ethnic significance soon after they started to be produced.[145]

So, ethnic identity or something else altogether? Perhaps the answer is ethnic identity *and* something else. Once we let go of the ethnically-focused culture-historical frameworks characteristic of many early medievalist approaches, the story actually becomes more interesting. Even within a single urban metalwork assemblage, different aspects of identity can be discerned in all their complexity, each with their own chronological trajectory. These may *include* ethnic identities, but also religious and regional ones, or identities specific to an even smaller locale, such as the city of Lincoln itself. Some objects, such as the openwork pendants, may have expressed multi-layered identities, combining references to Christianity (in the decoration) and Scandinavian-ness (in the pendant form), and perhaps lending a distinct Anglo-Scandinavian or even Lincoln-based twist in the specific combination of the two. In other cases, the messages that a single aspect of an object conveyed may have been deliberately or unavoidably ambiguous. Rather than the defining characteristic of an object being a reference to a 'Continental' or a 'Christian' identity, for example, both may have been inherently intertwined: the Continent *was*, after all, where Rome was located.

Again, different scales at which identities were played out can also be recognized, ranging from the possessions of individuals, via the products of workshops with regional distributions, to styles (often Christian) that enjoyed a pan-European currency. The scale at which a particular object type operated was context-specific: a product of a regional production centre in Lincoln (such as a hooked tag with rocked-tracer decoration) would become an individual curiosity in a different location, just as a *Jellinge*-style brooch common in Scandinavia was one-of-a-kind in Lincoln. Here, a contextual approach focusing on the relationship between (numbers of) artefacts in circulation and manufacturing evidence from sites or regions becomes particularly relevant, as this can shed light on the deliberate choices that were made with regards to expressing particular aspects of identities in particular locales.

A contextual approach also avoids cherry-picking particular object types that skew the picture. Looking at the Lincoln assemblage as a whole, it is evident that fairly plain objects without any clear ethnic or religious characteristics comprise the larger part of the production evidence. In some cases it is still possible to recognize locally-specific traits, as may be the case with the seeming preference for rocked-tracer decoration (instead of, for example, ring-and-dot motifs) in Lincoln.[146] The relatively simple decoration of these objects was a prerequisite for mass-production on a scale that allowed Lincoln to grow into a manufacturing centre of importance. It was therefore the production of these smaller, less interesting – from our perspective – and more easily produced artefacts that shaped the emerging urban identity of Lincoln.

Of course, much work remains to be done. The arguments presented here are based on a selection of material retrieved during generally small-scale excavations scattered across the settlement, and the possibility exists that a single site in the future may alter our understanding entirely. There is also much scope to compare different urban assemblages, or to link the evidence from urban assemblages more explicitly on a regional scale to the ever-growing corpus of metal-detected finds listed in the Portable Antiquities Scheme database. Finally, comparisons on an international scale may shed light on the relative representativeness of the Lincoln evidence on a broader level. It is hoped that this paper will inspire such undertakings. One thing is clear, however: our focus on early medieval ethnicities does insufficient justice to the multi-layered and complex nature of early medieval identities, which consisted of ethnicity *and* a lot else besides.

Acknowledgements

Many thanks must go to Anthony Lee of 'The Collection: Art and Archaeology in Lincolnshire' in Lincoln for his never-ending patience and cheer in dealing with many enquiries and museum visits over the years, and his permission to reproduce the photographs taken during a series of study visits. Jenny Mann also deserves special mention, as her enthusiasm and assistance in coming to grips with the material were invaluable, especially during the early stages of research. Without the assistance of James Graham-Campbell during the final writing-up stage, some major errors would have remained unchecked. Thanks must go as well to Michael J. Jones, whose knowledge about early medieval Lincoln is unparalleled, and who allowed me to read the drafts of the Lower City volume (Steane *et al.* 2016) well ahead of publication. Justine Bayley explained the science of metallurgy to me in the most lucid of ways. This paper ultimately derives from my AHRC-funded PhD research carried out at the University of Sheffield between 2006 and 2010, and has benefited greatly from the input of Dawn Hadley, my PhD supervisor, and Grenville Astill, my external examiner. As this paper has been many years in the making, many people have helped with artefact identifications or contributed in other ways; amongst those are (in no particular order) Jane Kershaw, Rosie Weetch, Gabor Thomas, Rob White, Kevin Leahy, Anne Pedersen, Pieterjan Deckers, Nicola Rogers, John Sheehan, Tim Pestell and Caroline Paterson. Christine McDonnell and Martin Green kindly permitted reproduction of the drawing of the lead seal pendant from Coppergate, York, and the photograph of the griffin disc from Wimborne St Giles respectively; Justine Bayley arranged permissions to reproduce the photograph of the stone brooch mould from Flaxengate. Many thanks must also go to Julia Warszewski for her help with some of the figures. The comments of an anonymous peer-reviewer has helped greatly to iron out some unhelpful generalizations and over-simplifications. Finally, a massive thank-you to Vicky and Jay for the use of their sofa and kettle.

CATALOGUE OF EARLY MEDIEVAL DECORATIVE METAL OBJECTS FROM LINCOLN

This catalogue lists decorative metalwork finds from Lincoln, referred to in the text. Finds are organized by finds type, main part of the city (Upper City, Lower City, Butwerk, Wigford, 'other'), and then alphabetically by site and numerically by excavation phase and small-find number. Finds from the Waterside excavations, located just to the south of the Lower City on the north bank of the river, are grouped with the Lower City finds. Unless otherwise indicated, information about find-spots is based on unpublished information held within the archives of the former City of Lincoln Archaeology Unit – now held by *The Collection: Art and Archaeology in Lincolnshire* – kindly provided by Jenny Mann or taken from Rob White's unpublished 1982 MSc dissertation. Objects without detailed information either could not be located during a visit to the stores of *The Collection* in July 2014, or (if indicated) were not removed from display cases for this study. Finds from excavations at *The Collection* were not available for study but are included in the list with relevant literature references.

HOOKED TAGS

Upper City

St. Paul-in-the-Bail (SP72)

1 SP72 ⟨ae46⟩ copper-alloy hooked tag.

2 SP72 ⟨ae170⟩ copper-alloy hooked tag.

West Bight (WB80)

3 WB80 ⟨ae13⟩ triangular piece of sheet metal; possible unfinished copper-alloy hooked tag. No attachment holes or hook. 46 × 13 mm. Fig. 8p.

Lower City

Danes Terrace (DT74i and DT74ii)

4 DT74i ⟨ae116⟩ copper-alloy hooked tag with triangular plate (on display).

5 DT74ii ⟨ae177⟩ corroded fragment of a copper-alloy hooked tag. Both attachment holes and hook broken off. 7.5 × 9 mm (including corrosion). Residual, from post-medieval context.

Flaxengate (F72; F73; F74; F76)

6 F72 ⟨ae15⟩ copper-alloy hooked tag with circular plate. One of two closely-spaced attachment holes damaged. Plate 11 mm diam.; surviving part of hook 8 mm long. Rocked-tracer

decoration on front of plate in cross-shape, and possibly around circumference of plate. Unstratified. Fig. 7a.

7 F72 ⟨ae45⟩ copper-alloy hooked tag with circular plate. Tip of hook broken off. Plate 14 mm diam.; surviving part of hook 4.5 mm. It has two attachment holes spaced rather far apart. Symmetrical, possibly abstract-zoomorphic decoration in broad black lines. Similar to a metal-detected find from Thimbleby (Lincs) (PAS NLM–E7A805). Deposited in Saxo-Norman building T24, dated to the early- to late-twelfth century. Fig. 9.

8 F72 ⟨ae213⟩ copper-alloy hooked tag with triangular plate. Hook mostly broken off and one of attachment holes damaged. Plate 14 × 12 mm (tapering towards 4 mm near hook); surviving hook 2.5 mm. Rocked-tracer decoration around circumference of plate, around attachment holes, and in horizontal line across middle of plate. Similar to BE73 ⟨ae37⟩ and F74 ⟨ae546⟩. Residual, from late-twelfth- to early-thirteenth-century pit. Fig. 10a.

9 F72 ⟨ae220⟩ two fragments of a heavily damaged and unfinished copper-alloy hooked tag made of copper-alloy. Fragment 1 part of sub-circular plate, 10.5 × 8 mm. Fragment 2 attachment hook, 11 × 2 mm.

10 F72 ⟨ae294⟩ copper-alloy hooked tag with roughly pear-shaped plate. Plate 15 × 13 mm; hook 4.5 mm. Rocked-tracer decoration on front of plate in cross-shape and around circumference. Included in Roesdahl *et al.* 1981, 101, G3 (with F74 ⟨ae169⟩). Residual, from late-twelfth- to thirteenth-century levelling dump. Fig. 7b.

11 F73 ⟨ae274⟩ unfinished copper-alloy hooked tag with a triangular plate, heavily corroded. No attachment holes or hook. 20 × 14 mm. Deposited in mid- to late-eleventh-century context. Included in White 1982, 51, F84 and (as F72 Ae274) in Bayley 2008b, 129, table 35, who identified metal composition as bronze.

12 F74 ⟨ae25⟩ unfinished copper-alloy hooked tag with a triangular plate. No attachment holes or hook. 18 × 10 mm. Residual, from late-fourteenth- to early-fifteenth-century layer. Included in White 1982, 51, F85 and Bayley 2008b, 129, table 35, who identified metal composition as brass.

13 F74 ⟨ae153⟩ fragmented copper-alloy hooked tag, heavily corroded. Only the hook and bottom of plate survive. 9 × 5 mm.

14 F74 ⟨ae163⟩ unfinished copper-alloy hooked tag with triangular plate, broken into three pieces. No attachment holes or hook. 24 × 10 mm. Traces of metallurgical analysis, but not included in Bayley 2008b, 129, table 35.

15 F74 ⟨ae164⟩ unfinished copper-alloy hooked tag with circular plate. No attachment holes. 21 × 14 mm. Included in White 1982, 52, F86, who concluded that it underwent a high degree of working, with little evidence for porosity or inclusions. Also included in Bayley 2008b, 129, table 35, who identified metal composition as copper/brass. Deposited in context dated to second half of eleventh century.

16 F74 ⟨ae165⟩ unfinished copper-alloy hooked tag with triangular plate. No attachment holes or hook. 21 × 7 mm. Included in White 1982, 52–3, F87 and Bayley 2008b, 129, table 35, who identified metal composition as copper/brass. Deposited in mid-eleventh-century context. Fig. 8a.

17 F74 ⟨ae166⟩ unfinished copper-alloy hooked tag with triangular plate. No attachment holes or hook. 19 × 12 mm. Included in White 1982, 53, F88 and Bayley 2008b, 129, table 35, who identified metal composition as bronze. Deposited in mid-eleventh-century context. Fig. 8d.

18 F74 ⟨ae167⟩ unfinished copper-alloy hooked tag with circular to oval plate. No attachment holes. Plate 12 × 15 mm; hook 25 mm. Included in White 1982, 53, F89 and Bayley 2008b, 129, table 35, who identified metal composition as copper/brass. Deposited in mid-eleventh-century context.

19 F74 ⟨ae169⟩ two unfinished copper-alloy hooked tags, both with sub-circular, teardrop-shaped plates. No attachment fittings. The hook of the smaller one is broken. 26 × 14 mm and 19 × 13 mm. Included in Roesdahl *et al.* 1981, 101, G3, together with F72 ⟨ae294⟩. Figs. 8k–l.

20 F74 ⟨ae170⟩ unfinished copper-alloy hooked tag with triangular plate. No attachment holes. 22 × 12 mm. Included in White 1982, 54, F90 and Bayley 2008b, 129, table 35, who identified metal composition as brass. From mid-eleventh-century context.

21 F74 ⟨ae183⟩ unfinished copper-alloy hooked tag with triangular plate. No attachment holes. 20 × 10 mm. Included in White 1982, 54, F91, and Bayley 2008b, 129, table 35, who identified metal composition as brass. Deposited in later-eleventh-century context.

22 F74 ⟨ae209⟩ unfinished copper-alloy hooked tag.

23 F74 ⟨ae216⟩ three fragments of copper-alloy hooked tag. 5 × 3.5 mm, 6 × 3.5 mm and 9 × 6 mm, the latter with part of attachment hole (diam. 2 mm).

24 F74 ⟨ae217⟩ unfinished copper-alloy hooked tag.

25 F74 ⟨ae240⟩ unfinished copper-alloy hooked tag with triangular plate. No hook, and top of plate damaged. 19.5 × 8.5 mm. Fig. 8b.

26 F74 ⟨ae241⟩ two unfinished copper-alloy hooked tags.

27 F74 ⟨ae242⟩ unfinished copper-alloy hooked tag with shield-shaped plate. No attachment holes or hook. 24 × 14 mm. Fig. 8i.

28 F74 ⟨ae254⟩ unfinished copper-alloy tag with shield-shaped plate. No attachment holes or hook. 25 × 16.5 mm. Included in White 1982, 54–5, F92 and Bayley 2008b, 129, table 35, who identified metal composition as brass. Deposited in a later-eleventh-century context. Fig. 8n.

29 F74 ⟨ae259⟩ unfinished copper-alloy hooked tag with coarsely shaped triangular plate. No attachment holes or hook. 22 × 11.5 mm. Fig. 8g.

30 F74 ⟨ae281⟩ unfinished copper-alloy hooked tag with shield-shaped plate. No attachment holes or hook. 21 × 11 mm. Included in White 1982, 55, F93 and Bayley 2008b, 129, table 35, who identified metal composition as brass. Deposited in a mid-eleventh-century context. Fig. 8h.

31 F74 ⟨ae286⟩ unfinished copper-alloy hooked tag with triangular plate. No attachment holes or hook. 20 × 12 mm. Included in White 1982, 55, F94, and Bayley 2008b, 129, table 35, who identified metal composition as brass. Deposited in a mid-eleventh-century context.

32 F74 ⟨ae289⟩ unfinished copper-alloy hooked tag with an asymmetrically shaped plate, rounded on one side and triangular on the other. No attachment holes or hook. 23 × 12 mm. Included in White 1982, 56, F95, and Bayley 2008b, 129, table 35, who identified metal composition as brass. Deposited in a context dated *c.* 1040–70. Fig. 8j.

33 F74 ⟨ae296⟩ unfinished copper-alloy hooked tag with shield-shaped plate, broken into three fragments. Traces of attachment hole visible but hook not yet bent. 14 × 11 mm, 5 × 4 and 6 × 4 mm.

34 F74 ⟨ae299⟩ unfinished copper-alloy hooked tag with triangular plate. No attachment holes or hook. 20 × 9 mm. Included in White 1982, 56, F96 and Bayley 2008b, 129, table 35, who identified metal composition as brass. Deposited in a context dated *c.* 1040–70.

35 F74 ⟨ae302⟩ unfinished copper-alloy hooked tag with triangular plate. No attachment holes or hook. Included in White 1982, 56–7, F97 and Bayley 2008b, 129, table 35, who identified metal composition as copper/brass. Deposited in a context dated *c.* 1040–70.

36 F74 ⟨ae306⟩ unfinished copper-alloy hooked tag with triangular plate. No attachment holes or hook. 27 × 12 mm. Included in White 1982, 57, F98 and Bayley 2008b, 129, table 35, who identified metal composition as copper/brass. Deposited in a context dated *c.* 1040–70.

37 F74 ⟨ae308⟩ unfinished copper-alloy hooked tag with triangular plate. No attachment holes or hook. 21 × 11 mm. Included in White 1982, 57, F99 and Bayley 2008b, 129, table 35, who identified metal composition as brass. Deposited in a context dated *c.* 1040–70.

38 F74 ⟨ae335⟩ two unfinished copper-alloy hooked tags with triangular plates. No attachment holes or hooks. 18 × 9 mm and 21 × 10 mm. Included in White 1982, 58, F100 and Bayley 2008b, 129, table 35, who identified metal composition as brass. Both from context dated *c.* 1040–70. Figs. 8c and e.

39 F74 ⟨ae354⟩ unfinished copper-alloy hooked tag with triangular plate. No attachment holes or hook. Upper right-hand corner damaged. 21 × 7 mm. Included in White 1982, 58, F101 and Bayley 2008b, 129, table 35, who identified metal composition as brass. Context dated *c.* 1040–70.

40 F74 ⟨ae385⟩ unfinished copper-alloy hooked tag.

41 F74 ⟨ae439⟩ two fragments of an unfinished copper-alloy hooked tag. No trace of attachment holes; hook not yet bent. 12 × 10.5 mm and 10 × 7 mm.

42 F74 ⟨ae484⟩ unfinished copper-alloy hooked tag.

43 F74 ⟨ae485⟩ unfinished hooked tag with a triangular plate. 22 × 11.5 mm. No attachment holes or hook. Included (as F75 ⟨ae485⟩) in Roesdahl *et al.* 1981, 101, G4 together with F74 ⟨ae546⟩. Fig. 8f.

44 F74 ⟨ae527⟩ unfinished copper-alloy hooked tag. No attachment holes or hook. 25 × 10 mm. Included in White 1982, 58–9, F102 and Bayley 2008b, 129, table 35, who identified metal composition as brass. Unstratified.

45 F74 ⟨ae529⟩ unfinished copper-alloy hooked tag.

46 F74 ⟨ae538⟩ copper-alloy hooked tag from eleventh-century context.

47 F74 ⟨ae546⟩ copper-alloy hooked tag with triangular plate. Attachment holes at opposite corners, *c.* 1 mm diam. Plate 17 × 12 mm (tapering to 6 mm); hook 9 mm long. Rocked-tracer decoration around circumference of plate, and forming inverted T-shape across plate. Included (as F75 ⟨ae546⟩) in Roesdahl *et al.* 1981, 101, G4. From eleventh-century layers. Fig. 10b.

48 F74 ⟨fe1443⟩ unfinished iron hooked tag.

49 F74 ⟨fe1620⟩ unfinished iron hooked tag with circular plate.

50 F74 ⟨fe1699⟩ unfinished iron hooked tag. No attachment holes or hook. 36 × 15 mm.

51 F74 ⟨fe1788⟩ unfinished iron hooked tag with a triangular plate, heavily corroded. 20 × 11 mm.

52 F74 ⟨fe1820⟩ two fragments of iron hooked tag, heavily corroded. First fragment with two attachment holes with diam. of 2.5 mm, spaced 2 mm apart. 19 × 18 mm. Second fragment part of attachment hook, 9 mm long.

53 F74 ⟨fe1934⟩ unfinished iron hooked tag with triangular plate. No attachment holes or hook. 31 × 10 mm.

54 F74 ⟨fe1969⟩ unfinished iron hooked tag with triangular plate.

55 F74 ⟨fe1984⟩ unfinished iron hooked tag with triangular plate, heavily corroded. No attachment holes or hook. 44 × 16 mm.

56 F74 ⟨fe1992⟩ unfinished iron hooked tag, heavily corroded. 27 × 18 mm.

57 F74 ⟨fe2163⟩ unfinished iron hooked tag, heavily corroded. 33 × 16 mm.

58 F74 ⟨fe2285⟩ unfinished iron hooked tag with triangular plate.

59 F74 ⟨fe2329⟩ unfinished iron hooked tag with triangular plate, heavily corroded. 26 × 20 mm.

60 F74 ⟨fe2431⟩ unfinished iron hooked tag with triangular plate.

61 F74 ⟨fe2524⟩ unfinished iron hooked tag with triangular plate, heavily corroded. 20 × 14 mm.

62 F74 ⟨fe2609⟩ unfinished iron hooked tag with triangular plate. No attachment holes. 22 × 10 mm. From early- to mid-eleventh-century context.

63 F76 ⟨ae85⟩ copper-alloy hooked tag with triangular plate. 6 × 12 mm. Included in Bayley 2008b (129, table 35), who identified metal composition as gunmetal.

64 F76 ⟨fe658⟩ unfinished iron hooked tag with triangular plate, heavily corroded. No attachment holes or hook. 27 × 9 mm.

Grantham Place (GP81)

65 GP81 ⟨147⟩ unfinished copper-alloy hooked tag with triangular plate. No attachment holes or hook. 37 × 15 mm. Fig. 8o.

Waterside (WO89, WNW88; WW89)

66 WO89 ⟨162⟩ unfinished iron hooked tag with triangular plate.

67 WO89 ⟨210⟩ unfinished iron hooked tag with triangular plate.

68 (WNW88) ⟨306⟩ unfinished iron hooked tag.

69 (WNW88) ⟨2116⟩ unfinished iron hooked tag.

70 WNW88 ⟨577⟩ copper-alloy hooked tag with shield-shaped plate. Two attachment holes with diam. of *c.* 1 mm, *c.* 4 mm apart. 16 × 12 mm.

71 WNW88 ⟨1225⟩ copper-alloy hooked tag.

72 WW89 ⟨193⟩ damaged and corroded copper-alloy hooked tag. Tip of hook broken. Outside of the plate damaged so that shape is hard to identity. 34 × 13 mm. Part of one attachment hole with diam. of 1.5 mm visible. Fig. 8m.

West Parade (WP71)

73 WP71 ⟨ae24⟩ unfinished copper-alloy hooked tag. Roughly cut to shape. No attachment holes or hook. Plate intended to be circular. 13 × 12 mm. Included in Colyer *et al.* 1999, 226, fig. 109. Found with twelfth-century hearth. Fig. 7d.

74 WP71 ⟨ae62⟩ silver hooked tag with circular plate. Two closely-spaced attachment holes with diam. of 2 mm. Tip of hook broken off. Plate 10 mm diam.; hook 4 mm. Included in Colyer *et al.* 1999, 226, fig. 109. From thirteenth-century pit.

Butwerk

Broadgate East (BE73)

75 BE73 ⟨ae10⟩ fragment of copper-alloy hooked tag with (probably) triangular plate. Only the hook and bottom of plate survive. 12 × 4 mm.

76 BE73 ⟨ae37⟩ copper-alloy hooked tag with triangular plate. Top right corner damaged. Two circular attachment holes in opposing corners. 20 × 12 mm. Possible traces of rocked-tracer decoration around circumference of plate. Similar to F72 ⟨ae213⟩. From post-medieval dumping layer. Fig. 7c.

Wigford

St Mark's Church (SM76)

77 SM76 ⟨fe365⟩ two fragments of iron hooked tag with triangular plate, broken between plate and attachment hook. Two attachment holes with diam. of 2 mm, spaced 3 mm apart. 28 × 14 mm.

170 High Street (HS90)

78 HS90 ⟨34⟩ unfinished copper-alloy hooked tag with triangular plate, heavily corroded. No attachment holes or hook. 19 × 11 mm.

BROOCHES

Lower City

Flaxengate (F72; F74; F76)

79 F72 ⟨ae23⟩ rectangular copper-alloy ansate brooch with a pronounced bow in the middle. Transverse ribbed decoration. 49 × 16 × 6 mm. Similar to Weetch Type XI A. Belongs to broad 'caterpillar' type, with terminals that do not expand beyond the width of the bow, but different sub-type from published Coppergate examples (Mainman and Rogers 2000,

2571; Tweddle 2004, 456–7, fig. 116). Parallel from Domburg (the Netherlands) published as Capelle 1976, table 5, no. 65. Fig. 14c.

80 F72 ⟨ae296⟩ polychrome enamelled copper-alloy disc brooch of so-called Kettlach-style; tenth century. Severely damaged. Diam. 43 mm. Ribbed border. Raised inner part (diam. 25 mm) with traces of polychrome enamel surrounding a bird-with-branch motif. Published separately in Ten Harkel *et al.* 2016. From eleventh- to twelfth-century levelling layer. Fig. 15.

81 F72 ⟨ae302⟩ flat copper-alloy *Borre*-style disc brooch of Kershaw's East Anglian group (Kershaw 2009, 319). Decorated with four symmetrical strands of knotted interlace emerging from a central lozenge. Catch plate and lug missing. Plate damaged. Diam. originally 32 mm; in current state 31 × 27 × 3 mm. Found associated with thirteenth-century road surface. Fig. 13.

82 F74 ⟨ae184⟩ convex copper-alloy disc brooch decorated in high relief, in possible devolved Terslev-style. Eleventh- or twelfth-century date. Decoration consists of central circle divided into three fields by raised cross-bars, surrounded by another concentric circle divided into twelve. Outside the second circle are twelve petal-shaped loops. Diam. 36 mm. Found associated with early- to mid-twelfth-century floor. Fig. 19.

83 F76 ⟨ae107⟩ copper-alloy ansate brooch with leaf-shaped terminals. 45 mm long, 8 mm wide at each terminal, 5 mm wide in the middle, and 5 mm thick in the centre. Weetch Type XII Aii (Weetch 2013, 172, 250, fig. 35), with a production centre in East Anglia. Fig. 14b.

Grantham Street (SW82)

84 SW82 ⟨386⟩ cast lead-alloy flat disc-brooch decorated with stylized curved-armed cross-design. At the centre of the cross is a pellet within a lozenge-shaped decoration with a double border. The curved arms of the cross are decorated with a ladder pattern. In each of the spaces between the arms are two raised pellets. Outer rim of brooch decorated with ladder pattern as well. Diam. 20 mm; thickness 1 mm. A small hole is visible next to one of the pellets between the cross-arms. Weetch Type 4C (Weetch 2013, 76–7, fig. 3.11C). Included in Mann 1999, 156–7. From post-medieval context. Identical to P70 ⟨pb13⟩ (cat. no. 85). Fig. 11b.

The Park (P70)

85 P70 ⟨pb13⟩ identical to SW82 ⟨386⟩ (cat. no 84), although one of the pellets between the cross arms is missing. Previously published in Mann 1999, 156–7, fig. 75, and Ten Harkel 2013a, 183, fig. 11.7a. Unstratified. Fig. 11a.

Wigford

181–3 High Street (aka Holmes Grainwarehouse) (HG72)

86 HG72 ⟨ae58⟩ gilt copper-alloy flat disc brooch. Volute decoration reminiscent of Terslev style, consisting of four back-to-back C-shaped scrolls arranged in a cross-shape in low relief around a lozenge-shaped centre with an incised cross. Border plain. No sign of attachment fittings. 27.8 × 27.2 × 1 mm. Weetch Type 6 (Weetch 2013, 79–81). Fig. 20.

St Mark's Church (SM76)

87 SM76 ⟨ae92⟩ copper-alloy ansate brooch of so-called Lincoln Type, dated to seventh to ninth centuries. 80 mm in length. Weetch Type VII B (Weetch 2013, 155, fig. 29), with parallels from London, East Anglia, Lincolnshire and Yorkshire. Included in Vince 2003a, 154, fig. 8.15. Parallel from Domburg (the Netherlands) published as Capelle 1976, table 6, no. 67. From thirteenth-century pier base in north of nave. Fig. 14a.

St Mark's Station (ZEB95)

88 ZEB95 ⟨442⟩ copper-alloy convex disc brooch with *Jellinge*-style interlace decoration, dated to ninth or tenth centuries. Not cleaned/conserved. Attachment fittings include a third loop intended for suspension of beads, chains or pendants. 32 × 33 × 6 mm. Deposited in eleventh-century context.

PENDANTS

Lower City

Grantham Place (GP81)

89 GP81 ⟨44⟩ copper-alloy openwork disc with plain border, dated to tenth or eleventh centuries. Not cleaned/conserved. Roughly circular. Decoration consisting of winged back-turned quadruped gripping border. Diam. 44 mm; thickness *c.* 5 mm. Protruding lug for attachment as pendant. Identical to P70 ⟨ae171⟩ (cat. no. 91). Found associated with eleventh-century building phase.

Hungate (H83)

90 H83 ⟨455⟩ gilded wafer-thin copper-alloy disc, possibly used as pendant. Damaged. Circular and slightly convex. Decorated with punched applied strips of gilt copper-alloy in a geometric pattern radiating out from centre in fake filigree effect. Diam. 17 mm. Unstratified. Fig. 22.

The Park (P70)

91 P70 ⟨ae171⟩) identical to GP81 ⟨44⟩ (cat. no 89), but cleaned. Damaged, missing a rear leg and adjacent portion of frame. Slightly convex. Diam. 40 mm; thickness c. 3 mm. Included in Mann 1999, fig. 67 and Ten Harkel 2013a, 180, fig. 11.5. Fig. 12c.

Wigford

St Mark's Station (ZEB95; Z86)

92 Z86 ⟨676⟩ small lead-alloy pendant. Roughly circular. 18 × 20 × 1 mm, with 9 mm protrusion with square cross-section and pierced hole. Decorated with three concentric rings around a central pellet, with markings between them possibly representing garbled runes. Attachment protrusion decorated with parallel lines. Similar to miscast from York with runic inscription (Bayley 1992, 780, fig. 340). From late-eleventh- to early-twelfth-century pit containing a high percentage of tenth-century pottery. Fig. 21a.

PINS

Upper City

St Paul-in-the-Bail (SP74)

93 SP74 ⟨ae120⟩ polyhedral-headed pin with ring-and-dot decoration. Included in Roesdahl *et al.* (1981, 51, C16).

Lower City

Flaxengate (F72; F76)

94 F72 ⟨ae67⟩ copper-alloy pin with plain globular head. Head 10 × 11 mm. Shaft broken; surviving length 11 mm. Circular cross-section *c.* 3 mm. Uncollared. Flixborough Type 100 (Rogers 2009, 33–4, 47). Parallels from *Hamwic*, the Anglian settlement at Fishergate, York and the earliest Anglo-Scandinavian layers at Coppergate (Hinton 1996, 14–21; Rogers 1993, 1361–3; Mainman and Rogers 2000, 2577). Unstratified.

95 F72 ⟨ae197⟩ copper-alloy wire-like pin with globular green glass head. Head 8 × 5 mm. Cone-shaped on top, tapering towards a central ridge, with flat base. Wire-like shaft is bent, *c.* 42 mm. Similar to MH77 ⟨ae2⟩ (cat. no. 98). Parallels from Winchester (Biddle 1990, 556–7). From twelfth- to thirteenth-century building phase.

96 F72 ⟨ae290⟩ ringed pin of Fanning's plain-ringed polyhedral-headed type. 94 mm long. Head 6.0 × 5.0 × 6.5 mm. Front and back faces lozenge-shaped, decorated with four lozenge-shaped depressions arranged in cross-shape. Shaft 88 mm; circular cross-section 3 mm at the top, gradually tapering towards point. Uncollared. Diam. of undecorated ring 10.5 mm, with circular cross-section measuring *c.* 1.5 mm. From twelfth-century context. Fig. 16a.

97 F76 ⟨ae64⟩ copper-alloy pin with polyhedral head of rectangular cross-section, hexagonal facets on the sides and triangular corner facets, and a deeply stamped dot on each side. Head 6 × 7 × 4 mm. Circular shaft, diam. 2 mm. Bent, tip broken; surviving length 42 mm. No collar. Flixborough Type 221 (Rogers 2009), found in contexts spanning the middle and late Anglo-Saxon periods. Previously published (not illustrated) in Vince 2003a, 154. From early- to mid-tenth-century levelling dump containing much residual earlier pottery.

Motherby Hill (MH77)

98 MH77 ⟨ae2⟩ copper-alloy wire-like pin with globular opaque light brown glass head, speckled with pale greenish and blueish grey and mid-brown. Head 7.9 × 7.4 × 4 mm. Wire-like shaft bent, measuring 29.3 mm. Similar to F72 ⟨ae197⟩ (cat. no. 95).

Steep Hill (SH74)

99 SH74 ⟨ae144⟩ copper-alloy bi-conical pinhead. Head 12 × 14 mm. Shaft broken; surviving length 4 mm. Circular cross-section of shaft 4 mm. No obvious medial band. Collared. Flixborough Type 310, of later-ninth- to early-eleventh-century date (Rogers 2009, 34, 55–6.). Found in association with residual late-ninth- to early-tenth-century pottery.

Butwerk

Broadgate East (BE73)

100 BE73 ⟨ae164⟩ ringed pin of Fanning's plain-ringed polyhedral-headed type. 91 mm in length. Head 6 mm × 5 mm; lozenge-shaped front and back faces decorated with four recessed holes arranged in a cross-shape. Shaft 86 mm long with circular cross-section, measuring *c.* 4 mm, gradually tapering towards point. Faint collar, *c.* 1 mm wide. Ring is rectangular in cross-section, *c.* 1.7 × 1.5 mm. Ring decorated with 7 recessed oval holes, each *c.* 1.5 × 1.0 mm. Found associated with a thirteenth-century building. Fig. 16b.

Wigford

St Benedict's Square (SB85)

101 SB85 ⟨64⟩ copper-alloy pin with polyhedral head of square section, with lozenge-shaped facets on the sides and triangular corner facets. Decoration damaged by surface corrosion, but seems to consist of regularly spaced punched dots on the side facets. Head 4 × 4 × 4 mm. Length of pin 60.9 mm. Shank circular in section and swollen near head. Collared. Flixborough Type 232, of mid-eighth- to eleventh-century date (Rogers 2009). From early- to mid-tenth-century context.

Other (casual find)

Nettleham Road (northeast of Upper City, outside early medieval walled town)

102 *The Collection* ⟨88.52⟩ ringed pin, probably a crude version of Fanning's plain-ringed polyhedral-headed type (Fanning 1994). 99.5 mm long. Head broad and slightly flattened, measuring 7.5 × 11.5 mm. Decoration consists of four evenly-spaced circular depressions on each of the flat sides. Vertical narrow sides deeply indented (rather than perforated) to attach ring. Uncollared. Pin 86.5 mm long with oval cross-section of *c.* 3.5 mm, tapering to point. Ring plain and roughly circular, with sub-rectangular cross-section *c.* 18 × 22 mm. Fig. 17.

RINGS

Lower City

The Collection

103 Plain copper-alloy ring of circular-sectioned wire with knotted terminals. Described and illustrated in Mann 2009.

Flaxengate (F72, F74)

104 F72 ⟨ae203⟩ plain copper-alloy wire ring, circular cross-section, *c.* 2.5 mm. 24 × 21 mm. Found associated with late-twelfth- to early-thirteenth-century building.

105 F72 ⟨ae250⟩ plain copper-alloy wire ring. Found in late -eleventh- to early-twelfth-century pit.

106 F72 ⟨ae259⟩ plain copper-alloy wire ring, circular cross-section, *c.* 2 mm. 23 × 20 mm. Associated with early- to mid-twelfth-century building T25.

107 F72 ⟨ae262⟩ plain copper-alloy wire ring, circular cross-section, *c.* 2.5 mm. 22 × 20 mm. From late-eleventh- to early-twelfth-century layer.

108 F74 ⟨ae66⟩ plain copper-alloy wire ring. Found in mid-eleventh- to mid-twelfth-century levelling dump.

109 F74 ⟨ae221⟩ plain copper-alloy wire ring with knotted ends, square cross-section, *c.* 1.5 mm. 14 × 14 mm. From mid- to late-eleventh-century context.

110 F74 ⟨ae470⟩ plain copper-alloy wire ring with knotted ends, circular cross-section, *c.* 1 mm. 19 × 19 mm. From early- to mid-tenth-century context.

111 F74 ⟨ag3⟩ plain copper-alloy wire ring with knotted ends, square cross-section, *c.* 1.5 mm or less. Damaged; originally *c.* 17 mm diam. From early- to late-tenth-century context.

Hungate (H83)

112 H83 ⟨733⟩ plain copper-alloy wire ring, circular cross-section, *c.* 1.5 mm. 21 × 19 mm.

West Parade (WP71)

113 WP71 ⟨ae41⟩ copper-alloy finger-ring formed from a tapering strip decorated with three parallel rows of punched decoration. Ring 12 × 16 mm in diam.; width of strip 5.5 mm or less, thickness less than 1 mm. Included in Mann 1999, 226, fig. 109(4). From late-eleventh- to twelfth-century pit.

114 WP41 ⟨ae55⟩ plain copper-alloy wire ring, *c.* 13 mm diam. Included in Mann 1999, 226, fig. 109(5).

Wigford

181–3 High Street (aka Holmes Grainwarehouse) (HG72)

115 HG72 ⟨ae12⟩ unfinished copper-alloy finger ring. Tapering strip less than 1 mm thick, broken into four pieces (8 × 2 mm, 6 × 3 mm, 12 × 4 mm and 16 × 4 mm). From early- to mid-eleventh-century context.

116 HG72 ⟨ae50⟩ unfinished copper-alloy finger ring. Tapering strip, 43 × 4.5 × ⟨1 mm. From early- to mid-eleventh-century context.

BUCKLES

Upper City

St Paul-in-the-Bail

117 Silver Trewhiddle-style buckle of ninth-century date, published in Vince 2003a, 151, fig. 8.10.

118 Silver Carolingian buckle of ninth-century date, published in Vince 2003a, 151, fig. 8.9.

Lower City

Flaxengate (F72; F74)

119 F72 ⟨ae44⟩ copper-alloy D-shaped buckle with associated buckle-plate. Undiagnostic, probably eleventh century or later. Buckle 17.5 × 13.5 mm. Top of buckle with segmented decoration. Buckle-plate consists of double copper-alloy sheet, 32 × 9 mm. Two of three boss-capped rivets still in place. Rivets 9.5 mm diam., 5.5 mm in height and their flat, circular top *c.* 2.5 mm diam. Deposited in a twelfth-century levelling dump. Fig. 25.

120 F72 ⟨ae297⟩ copper-alloy D-shaped buckle; part of the pin still attached to the bar. Romanesque zoomorphic decoration with two animal heads in profile facing each other, biting the bar. Buckle loop segmented with incised ribbing. Eleventh- or twelfth-century date. 27 × 21 × 4 mm. Fig. 26.

121 F74 ⟨ae346⟩ copper-alloy D-shaped buckle. Undiagnostic type. Damaged, broken in three pieces. Whole object 30 × 26 mm. Incised radial decoration. Associated with eleventh-century building T20.

Michaelgate

122 Ninth-century copper-alloy buckle with a triangular buckle-plate, published in Vince 2003a, 153, fig. 8.14.

Wigford

St Mark's Station (ZEB95)

123 ZEB95 ⟨443⟩ copper-alloy D-shaped buckle in *Borre*-style, with an animal head with a rounded snout, beady eyes and looping ears on the lip. Not cleaned/conserved. Buckle 33 mm × 29 mm; buckle plate measures 25 × 24 mm × 10 mm. Traces of iron pin remain as corrosion near the buckle plate. From ninth- to tenth-century layer.

STRAP-ENDS

Upper City

St Paul-in-the-Bail

124 Silver Trewhiddle-style strap-end of ninth-century date, published in Vince 2003a, 151, fig. 8.10.

Wigford

181–3 High Street (aka Holmes Grainwarehouse) (HG72)

125 HG72 ⟨ae5⟩ copper-alloy strap-end of Thomas Class B, type 4 (multi-headed strap-ends), similar to Thomas cat. no. 1009 from York (Rogers 1993, 1351, fig. 652, 5320). 51 × 11 × 4 mm. Published as Steane *et al.* 2001, 130, fig. 8.33. From early- to mid-eleventh-century dump.

MOUNTS, STUDS AND STRAP-LOOPS

Upper City

Castle Westgate (CWG86)

126 CWG86 ⟨106⟩ rectangular copper-alloy stud with zoomorphic gilt inlay decoration. Object 34 × 18.5 × 2 mm; protruding stud on reverse with circular cross-section of *c.* 5 mm, and *c.* 10.5 m long. Decoration depicts two symmetrical beasts with intertwined tails, ribbon-like bodies and back-turned heads facing each other, inside a 2-mm-wide twisted rope-like decoration. Animal heads display certain similarities to those on the eleventh- to twelfth-century Sutton Brooch (Wilson 1964, pl. 83). Residual, from a modern levelling layer. Fig. 23.

127 CWG86 ⟨1384⟩ decorative copper-alloy stud, possibly part of horse harness gear, with traces of gilding, formed of four hollow lobes. 31 × 27 × 17 mm. Heavily corroded.

Lower City

Danes Terrace (DT74)

128 DT74 ⟨ae108⟩ copper-alloy openwork mount in eleventh-century Scandinavian-derived insular *Urnes*-style. Sub-rectangular, measuring 62 × 31 mm. Openwork decoration executed to high level of craftsmanship, incorporating five intertwined animals with fine tendrils and canine heads. Separately published as Owen 2001. Found associated with high- to late-medieval building phase.

Flaxengate (F72)

129 F72 ⟨ae234⟩ irregularly shaped copper-alloy strap-loop. Decorated with simple incised parallel lines. 19 × 18 × 2 mm. Included in Ten Harkel 2013a, 185–6, fig. 11.8; 2013b, 167–8, fig. 4a. From late-eleventh- to early-twelfth-century pit.

130 F72 ⟨ae243⟩ square-headed copper-alloy stud with crude geometric decoration and traces of gilding. Convex head, 7 × 6.5 mm; length of stud 7.5 mm. Eleventh or twelfth century; found in a mid-twelfth- to mid-thirteenth-century levelling dump. Fig. 24a.

Saltergate (LIN73)

131 LIN73 ⟨44⟩ copper-alloy stud with convex head and incised geometric decoration. Head 14.5 × 13 × 5.5 mm. Stud *c.* 20 mm long, with square cross-section; diam. *c.* 3 mm but tapering towards tip. Fig. 24b.

Other (casual find)

132 BM ⟨1867,0320.20⟩ openwork copper-alloy stirrup mount with a zoomorphic pattern, sub-triangular in shape and decorated with niello. Full description of the object available on http://www.britishmuseum.org/research/collection_online/collection_object_details.aspx?objectId=65239&partId=1. Included in Wilson 1964, 167–8.

BELLS

Lower City

Flaxengate (F72; F76)

133 F72 ⟨ae166⟩ well-preserved copper-alloy hexagonal bell with cusped bottom. 32 mm high; base diam. *c.* 29 mm. Clapper missing. Ring-and-dot decoration along cusped bottom and near attachment loop. Included as *Flaxengate 1* in Richards and Schoenfelder 2011, 164. From fourteenth- to fifteenth-century deposit containing much residual twelfth-century material.

134 F76 ⟨ae72⟩ damaged copper-alloy hexagonal bell with cusped bottom. 30 mm high; base diam. *c.* 29 mm. Heavily-corroded

iron clapper inside. Attachment loop broken off. Corrosion too heavy for decoration to be visible. Included as *Flaxengate 2* in Richards and Schoenfelder 2011, 164. From tenth-century context.

Wigford

181–3 High Street (aka Holmes Grainwarehouse) (HG72)

135 HG72 ⟨ae49⟩ complete copper-alloy hexagonal bell with cusped bottom. 29 mm high; base diam. *c.* 23 mm. Iron clapper corroded but still present. Double row of ring-and-dot decoration along cusped lower edge. Attachment loop measuring 7 × 6 mm separated from bell by a 2 mm wide collar. Included as *Wigford 1* in Richards and Schoenfelder 2011, 165. From eleventh-century context.

St Mark's Station (Z86)

136 Z86 ⟨82⟩ complete hexagonal copper-alloy bell with cusped base. Published as Vince 2003b, 296, fig. 9.122; drawing suggests it was undecorated. Included as *Wigford 2* in Richards and Schoenfelder 2011, 165. Residual find from much later context.

MISCELLANEOUS

Lower City

Grantham Place (GP81)

137 GP81 ⟨57⟩ iron-plated hasp or hinge, possibly for a box, with rough zoomorphic terminal decorated with silvery lines. 71 × 22 mm. Corroded remnants of two iron attachment bands run across the object, both *c.* 15 mm wide. From earlier-eleventh-century levelling layer containing tenth-century pottery. Fig. 18.

Hungate (H83)

138 H83 ⟨269⟩ possible copper-alloy *stylus*-fragment, representing the splayed terminal (eraser) with short length of *stylus* still attached. Heavily corroded. 34 × 12 mm. From early- to mid-eleventh-century pit. Fig. 2.

Notes

1 Hadley and Richards 2000, 10.
2 See, for example, Kershaw 2013; Thomas 2012.
3 *Ibid.*, 486.
4 *Ibid.*, 487.
5 Hadley and Richards 2000, 4.
6 Pohl 2013, 13.
7 Steane, Darling, Jones, Mann, Vince and Young 2016, 56, 486.
8 Ten Harkel 2006.
9 E.g. Kershaw 2013; Thomas 2000b; 2012; Weetch 2013.
10 Røstad 2012.
11 Steane *et al.* 2016, 56–7.
12 Mann 1982.
13 But see Ten Harkel 2013a; Ten Harkel, Weetch and Sainsbury 2016 for selective aspects of this assemblage. The catalogue accompanying this paper represents the fullest catalogue of the Lincoln material that is available in print.
14 Bayley 1992; Mainman and Rogers 2000; Rogers 1993; Tweddle 2004, esp. 453, 456–8.
15 Steane *et al.* 2016, 56.
16 Ten Harkel 2013c.
17 Steane *et al.* 2016.
18 Bayley 2008a; 2008b; Mann 1982; Perring 1981; Steane *et al.* 2016, 11–62, 488–90; Vince 2003b, 284; Young and Vince 2005.
19 E.g. Bayley 2008b.
20 E.g. Steane *et al.* 2016, 84, 145, 199, 246.
21 In particular Steane, Darling, Mann, Vince and Young 2001; Steane, Darling, Jones, Mann, Vince and Young 2006; Steane *et al.* 2016.
22 E.g. Pohl 2013.
23 Burke and Stets 2000.
24 Ten Harkel 2013a, 172–3, 178–9; see also Davis 1992, 16–17.
25 Skre 2011, 418.
26 Ten Harkel 2013a; Mainman and Rogers 2000, 2478–9.
27 Thomas 2000a, 284–5.
28 The most comprehensive and up-to-date overview is still Stocker 2003.
29 For a discussion of the political relationship between Lincoln and York, based on coin evidence, see Ten Harkel 2013c.
30 Williams 2013, 26–9 for a recent discussion of the significance of this passage for the political status of the five towns mentioned.
31 E.g. Roesdahl, Graham-Campbell, Connor and Pearson 1981, 95.
32 Jones and Stocker 2003; Mann 1982, 46; Vince 2003b, 196, 235–42.
33 Vince 2003a, 141.
34 Gilmour 2007; Steane *et al.* 2006; Vince 2003a, 144–50.
35 Bede, *HE* II, 16, 18; for discussion of possible contenders for Paulinus' church, see Vince 2003a, 144–5.
36 *Ibid.*, 144–5.
37 Pestell, Brown, Okasha, Ottaway and Rogers 2009, 124–38; Pestell *pers. comm.*
38 Lincolnshire HER number 71064, available on http://www.heritagegateway.org.uk/Gateway/Results_Single.aspx?uid=MLI97571&resourceID=1006 (information last checked on 24 March 2015); Steane *et al.* 2016, 485.
39 Bayley 1991; Bayley, Crossley and Ponting 2008, 52; Rogers 1993, 1239.
40 See *ibid.*, 1232–8; Mainman and Rogers 2000, 2475–9; Bayley 1992.
41 Adams Gilmour 1988, 59; Mann 1982, 4; Perring 1981, 4–5; Ten Harkel *et al.* 2016.
42 Hadley 2006, 145; see also Astill 2009, 265.
43 Blackburn 2011a; 2011b; 2011c; Ten Harkel 2013c.
44 Vince 1993, 156; Kilmurry 1980; Blinkhorn 2013.
45 Bayley 2008b.
46 Forster, Thomas and Driscoll 2004; Bayley 2008b, 20, fig. 18.
47 Skre 2011, 431–2.
48 Bayley 1992, cat. no. 4001; see also cat. nos. 3990, 3998 and 4000.
49 Mann 1982, 20–1, 42; Mainman and Rogers 2000, 2541–4; Steane *et al.* 2016, 57.
50 Bayley 2008b, 20.
51 Steane *et al.* 2016, 57.
52 Bayley 2008b, 20. For the Lincoln hones, see Mann 1982, 27–30, 47.
53 Sketch drawings of some of the larger fragments have been included in Bayley 2008b, 96–7, and some of the better-preserved examples with traces of decorative elements have been included on p. 16.
54 Mainman and Rogers 2000, 2569–70, figs. 1265, 10421–2; Tweddle 2004, 447, fig. 105.
55 Thomas *pers. comm.*; Thomas 2000a, 186–8.
56 Bayley 2008b, 17, fig. 10.
57 Capelle 1976, no. 88; Weetch 2013, 78–9, 122–3, cat. nos. 809–17.
58 *Ibid.*, 123–5.
59 Ten Harkel 2013a; Mainman and Rogers 2000, 2478–9.
60 Heighway and Bryant (1999, 138) suggest they were meant for fastening heavier clothing than the lighter copper-alloy variants.
61 Mann 1982, 4; 1999, 226–7; Perring 1981, 41. For discussion of a production centre for hooked tags from Lund, Sweden, see Cinthio 1999.
62 Bayley 2008b.

63 Mann 1982, 1.
64 Tweddle 2004, 455–6, fig. 115; Mainman and Rogers 2000, 2576, fig. 1273, no. 10437.
65 Tweddle 2004, 456.
66 Mainman and Rogers 2000, 2576, fig. 1273, no. 10684; Biddle 1990, 550, fig. 148, no. 1423; Heighway and Bryant 1999, 136, fig. 3,14, no. 40; Shoesmith 1985, 8–11, figs. 4.5 and 6.
67 Mainman and Rogers 2000, 2576, fig. 1273, no. 10435.
68 Ten Harkel 2013a, 176–8, fig. 11.3.
69 Mainman and Rogers 2000, 2585–6, fig. 1279, cat. nos. 10515 and 10517.
70 Mann 1982, 5–6, fig. 3, cat. no. 4.
71 Bayley 2008b.
72 Rogers 1993, 1370–4; Mainman and Rogers 2000, 2584–6.
73 Mann 1982, 11.
74 Mainman and Rogers 2000, 2591; Mann 1982, 47.
75 Bayley 2008a; 2008b.
76 Biddle 1990, 556–7, fig. 150, nos. 1440–1.
77 Ten Harkel 2013c, 21, table 7.
78 Bayley 2008a, 17, fig. 10; Mann 1999, 157–8.
79 Bayley 2008b, 35.
80 Kershaw 2009, 300–1.
81 Weetch Type 4C: Weetch 2013, 76–7; Ten Harkel 2013a, 181–3.
82 For the York material, see Mainman and Rogers 2000, 2571–4; Tweddle 2004, 452–3.
83 Mann 1999, 152, fig. 67.
84 Ten Harkel 2013a, 180–1, fig. 11.5; Leahy and Paterson 2001, 195.
85 Mann 1982, 11–12; Mainman and Rogers 2000, 2588–91.
86 Mainman and Rogers 2000, 2589–90.
87 Deckers 2012, 28, fig. 10d; Mann 1999, 152; Ten Harkel 2013a, 180.
88 Deckers 2012, 30; Pedersen 2001.
89 Deckers 2012, 27–34.
90 *Ibid.*, 32–4.
91 Hicks 1993, 255, fig. 5.2.
92 Mann 1982, 42.
93 Tweddle 2004, 456–8.
94 Blackburn 2011d.
95 Davis 1992, 16–17; Ten Harkel 2013a.
96 Vince 2003a, 151, 153, figs. 8.9, 8.10, 8.14; but see Steane *et al.* 2006, 201–2.
97 Tweddle 2004, 450–1.
98 For the bone pins, see Mann 1982, 8–11. For the Flixborough corpus, see Rogers 2009.
99 The polyhedral-headed pins from Lincoln belong to Coppergate Type 2: Mainman and Rogers 2000, 2577. See also *ibid.*, 2576–80; Rogers 1993, 1361–7.
100 Steane *et al.* 2001, 130, fig. 8.33; Thomas 2000a, 102–4, 204.
101 Rogers 1993, 1351, fig. 652, 5320.
102 Paterson *pers. comm.*
103 See Kershaw 2009, 317, fig. 11 for a decorative parallel.
104 *Ibid.*, 310, 317, fig. 11.
105 *Ibid.*, 319; Richardson 1993, 31–2.
106 Kershaw 2009, 318–9; Margeson 1997, 23; Richardson 1993, 31–2.
107 Mainman and Rogers 2000, 2571.
108 See, for example, Capelle 1976, table 5, no. 65 and table 6, no. 67; Mann 1986, 41.
109 Tweddle 2004, 457.
110 Weetch Type 21: Weetch 2013, 114–16; Ten Harkel *et al.* 2016. See Hinton 1990, 636–9; Alexander 1987, 102 for other specimens from England.
111 Ten Harkel *et al.* 2016.
112 Mainman and Rogers 2000, 2581–2, fig. 1275, 10477; Fanning 1994, 10, 25, 28 and 70–88; Steane *et al.* 2016, 57.
113 Richards and Schoenfelder 2011, 157, 164–5; Vince 2003b, 295–6.
114 Richards and Schoenfelder 2011, 154–7, fig. 2.
115 *Ibid.*, 157–9.
116 Freke 2002, 70; McAllister 2013, 90; Richards and Schoenfelder 2011, 159.
117 Kershaw 2013, figs. 3.27, 3.29, 3.31, 3.33, 3.36, 3.38, 3.40; *pers. comm.*
118 *Ibid.*, 24, fig. 2.2.
119 *Ibid.*, map 3.9; Capelle 1976, no. 404.
120 Weetch 2013, 79–81; Mainman and Rogers 2000, 2573, fig. 1268.
121 Weetch 2013, 80.
122 Bayley 1992, 780, fig. 340; Mainman and Rogers 2000, 2588, fig. 1282, 10615.
123 Roesdahl *et al.* 1981, 118.
124 Capelle 1976, nos. 271 and 278; Bayley 1992, 780; Mainman and Rogers 2000, 2588.
125 Wamers 1994, 39, fig. 23 no. 073.
126 Eriksen, Egeberg, Olesen and Rostholm 2009, 260, fig. K32–4; Pedersen, Roesdahl and Graham-Campbell 2014, 288, fig. 6.112.
127 *Ibid.*, 288.
128 Owen 2001, 212–3; Steane *et al.* 2016, 145; Wilson 1964, 33.
129 Everson and Stocker 1999; Ten Harkel 2013b, fig. 2a.
130 Capelle 1976, nos. 320–5.
131 Caroline Paterson *pers. comm.*
132 Ten Harkel 2013a, 185–6, fig. 11.8; 2013b, 167–8, fig. 4a.
133 Brandenburgh 2010, 47.
134 Bayley 2008b.
135 Perring 1981, 41; Steane *et al.* 2016, 28–31; Ten Harkel *et al.* 2016.
136 For a critique, see Ashby 2015.
137 *Ibid.*, 5, 22–3.
138 Vince 2006, 529; Steane *et al.* 2016, 486.
139 Young and Vince 2005, 34.
140 Lincolnshire HER number 71064, available on http://www.heritagegateway.org.uk/Gateway/Results_Single.aspx?uid=MLI97571&resourceID=1006 (information last checked on 24 March 2015); Mainman 1993; Brown 1997.
141 Tweddle 2004.
142 Leahy 2007; Kershaw 2013.
143 Sheeran 2009.
144 Thomas 2012, 486.
145 Tweddle 2004, 456–8.
146 Ten Harkel 2013a, 176–8, fig. 11.3.

Abbreviations

HE Bede, *Historia ecclesiastica gentis anglorum*

Bibliography

Primary sources

Bede, *Historia ecclesiastica gentis anglorum*, in McClure, J. and Collins, R. (trans.) 1999. *The Ecclesiastical History of the English People*, Oxford: Oxford University Press.

Secondary sources

Adams Gilmour, L. 1988. *Early Medieval Pottery from Flaxengate, Lincoln*, The Archaeology of Lincoln, 17 (2), London: CBA for the Trust for Lincolnshire Archaeology.

Alexander, M. 1987. 'A "Viking-Age" grave from Cambois, Bedlington, Northumberland', *Medieval Arch.*, **31**, 101–5.

Ashby, S. P. 2015. '"With staff in hand, and dog at heel"? What did it mean to be an "itinerant" artisan?', in G. Hansen, S. P. Ashby and I. Baug (eds.), *Everyday Products in the Middle Ages: Crafts, Consumption and the Individual in Northern Europe c. 800-1600*, 1 27, Oxford: Oxbow

Astill, G. G. 2009. 'Medieval towns and urbanization', in R. Gilchrist and A. Reynolds (eds.), *Reflections: 50 Years of Medieval Archaeology,*

1957–2007, 255–70, Society for Medieval Archaeology Monograph, 30, Leeds: Maney Publishing.

Bayley, J. 1991. 'Anglo-Saxon non-ferrous metalworking: a survey', *World Archaeology*, **23 (1)**, 115–30.

Bayley, J. 1992. *Anglo-Scandinavian Non-Ferrous Metalworking from 16–22 Coppergate*, The Archaeology of York, 17 (7), London: CBA.

Bayley, J. 2008a. *Lincoln: Evidence for Glass-working on Flaxengate and Other Sites in the City: Technology Report*, unpublished EH Research Department Report 68-2008.

Bayley, J. 2008b. *Lincoln: Evidence for Metalworking on Flaxengate and Other Sites in the City: Technology Report*, unpublished EH Research Department Report 67-2008.

Bayley, J., Crossley, D. and Ponting, M. 2008. *Metals and Metalworking: A Research Framework for Archaeometallurgy*, The Historical Metallurgy Society Occasional Publication, 6, London: Historical Metallurgy Society.

Biddle, M. 1990. *Object and Economy in Medieval Winchester. Part II: Artefacts from Medieval Winchester*, Oxford: Clarendon Press.

Blackburn, M. 2011a. 'The coinage of Scandinavian York', in M. Blackburn, *Viking Coinage and Currency in the British Isles*, 281–307, London: Spink for the British Numismatic Society.

Blackburn, M. 2011b. 'Currency under the Vikings. Part 1: Guthrum and the earliest Danelaw coinages', in M. Blackburn, *Viking Coinage and Currency in the British Isles*, 2–31, London: Spink for the British Numismatic Society.

Blackburn, M. 2011c. 'Currency under the Vikings. Part 2: the two Scandinavian kingdoms of the Danelaw', in M. Blackburn, *Viking Coinage and Currency in the British Isles*, 32–58, London: Spink for the British Numismatic Society.

Blackburn, M. 2011d.'The Viking winter camp at Torksey, 872–73', in M. Blackburn, *Viking Coinage and Currency in the British Isles*, 221–48, London: Spink for the British Numismatic Society.

Blinkhorn, P. 2013. 'No pots please, we're Vikings: pottery in the southern Danelaw, 850–1000', in D. M. Hadley and L. ten Harkel (eds.), *Everyday Life in Viking-Age Towns: Social Approaches to Towns in England and Ireland, c. 800–1100*, 157–71, Oxford: Oxbow.

Brandenburgh, C. R. 2010. 'Early medieval textile remains from settlements in the Netherlands: an evaluation of textile production', *Journal of Archaeology in the Low Countries*, **2 (1)**, 41–79.

Brown, D. 1997. 'The social significance of imported medieval pottery', in C. G. Cumberpatch and P. W. Blinkhorn (eds.), *Not So Much a Pot, More a Way of Life*, 95–112, Oxford: Oxbow.

Burke, P. J. and Stets, J. E. 2000. 'Identity theory and social identity theory', *Social Psychology Quarterly*, **63**, 224–37.

Capelle, T. 1976. *Die frühgeschichtlichen Metallfunde von Domburg auf Walcheren*, 2 vols., Amersfoort: Rijksdienst voor het Oudheidkundig Bodemonderzoek in collaboration with the Koninklijk Zeeuwsch Genootschap der Wetenschappen.

Cinthio, M. 1999. 'Guldsmed i Lund', in G. Fellows-Jensen and N. Lund (eds.), *Beretning fra Attende Tværfaglige Vikingesymposium*, 35–52, Højbjerg: Forlaget Hikuin og Afdeling for Middelalderarkaeologi.

Colyer, C., Gilmour, B. J. J. and Jones, M. J. 1999. *The Defences of the Lower City: Excavations at The Park and West Parade 1970–2, and a Discussion of Other Sites Excavated up to 1994*, York: Council for British Archaeology for the City of Lincoln Archaeological Unit.

Davis, F. 1992. *Fashion, Culture and Identity*, Chicago: The University of Chicago Press.

Deckers, P. J. 2012. '"Productive" sites in the polders? "Griffin brooches" and other early medieval metalwork from the Belgian coastal plain', *Medieval and Modern Matters*, **3**, 21–43.

Eriksen, P., Egeberg, T., Olesen, L. H. and Rostholm, H. 2009. *Vikinger i vest: vikingetiden i Vestjylland*, Moesgaard: Jysk Arkaeologisk Selskab.

Everson, P. and Stocker, D. 1999. *Corpus of Anglo-Saxon Stone Sculpture*, Vol. 5 *Lincolnshire*, Oxford: Oxford University Press.

Fanning, T. 1994. *Viking Age Ringed Pins from Dublin*, Medieval Dublin Excavations 1962–81, Ser. B Vol. 4, Dublin: Royal Irish Academy.

Forster, A. K., Thomas, J. and Driscoll, S. J. 2004. 'Spatial analysis and cultural indicators: Viking settlers at old Scatness Broch, Shetland?', in J. Hines, A. Lane and M. Redknap (eds.), *Land, Sea and Home: Settlement in the Viking Period*, 219–34, Society for Medieval Archaeology Monographs, 20, Leeds: Maney.

Freke, D. 2002. 'The cemeteries: the excavated evidence', in D. Freke (ed.), *Excavations on St Patrick's Isle, Isle of Man, 1989–1992: Prehistoric, Viking, Medieval and Later*, 58–82, Liverpool: Liverpool University Press.

Gilmour, B. 2007. 'Sub-Roman or Saxon, pagan or Christian: who was buried in the early cemetery at St Paul-in-the-Bail, Lincoln?', in L. Gilmour (ed.), *Pagans and Christians from Antiquity to the Middle Ages: Papers in Honour of Martin Henig, Presented on the Occasion of his 65th birthday*, 229–56, BAR International Ser., 1610, Oxford: Archaeopress.

Hadley, D. M. 2006. *The Vikings in England; Settlement, Society and Culture*, Manchester: Manchester University Press.

Hadley, D. M. and Richards, J. D. 2000. 'Introduction: interdisciplinary approaches to the Scandinavian settlement', in D. M. Hadley and J. D. Richards (eds.), *Cultures in Contact: Scandinavian Settlement in England in the Ninth and Tenth Centuries*, 3–15, Turnhout: Brepols.

Heighway, C. and Bryant, R. 1999. *The Golden Minster: The Anglo-Saxon Minster and Later Priory of St Oswald at Gloucester*, CBA Research Report, 117, York: CBA.

Hicks, C. 1993. *Animals in Early Medieval Art*, Edinburgh: Edinburgh University Press.

Hinton, D. 1990. 'Disc and rectangular brooches', in M. Biddle (ed.), *Object and Economy in Medieval Winchester*, 636–63, Oxford: Clarendon Press.

Hinton, D. 1996. *The Gold, Silver and Other Non-Ferrous Alloy Objects from Hamwic, Southampton*, Southampton Archaeological Monographs, 6, Stroud: Allan Sutton.

Jones, M. J. and Stocker, D. 2003. 'Geological and topographical background', in D. Stocker (ed.), *The City by the Pool: Assessing the Archaeology of the City of Lincoln*, 13–18, Lincoln Archaeological Studies, 10, Oxford: Oxbow.

Kershaw, J. 2009. 'Culture and gender in the Danelaw: Scandinavian and Anglo-Scandinavian brooches', *Viking and Medieval Scandinavia*, **5**, 295–325.

Kershaw, J. 2013. *Viking Identities: Scandinavian Jewellery in England*, Oxford: Oxford University Press.

Kilmurry, K. 1980. *The Pottery Industry of Stamford, Lincs, c.* AD *850–1250: Its Manufacture, Trade and Relationship with Continental Wares, with a Classification and Chronology*, BAR British Ser., 84, Oxford: BAR.

Leahy, K. 2007. *The Anglo-Saxon Kingdom of Lindsey*, Stroud: Tempus.

Leahy, K. and Paterson, C. 2001. 'New light on the Viking presence in Lincolnshire: the artefactual evidence', in J. Graham-Campbell, R. Hall, J. Jesch and D. N. Parsons (eds.), *Vikings and the Danelaw: Select Papers from the Proceedings of the Thirteenth Viking Congress*, 181–202, Oxford: Oxbow.

Mainman, A. 1993. 'Imported wares in York', in D. Piton (ed.), *Travaux du Groupe de Recherches et D'Etudes sur la Céramique dans le Nord – Pas-de-Calais: actes du Colloque D'Outreau (10–12 Avril 1992)*, 189–93, Numéro hors-série de Nord-Ouest Archéologie, Berck-sur-Mer: CRADC.

Mainman, A. J. and Rogers, N. 2000. *Craft, Industry and Everyday Life: Finds from Anglo-Scandinavian York*, The Archaeology of York, 17 (14), York: CBA.

Mann, J. 1982. *Early Medieval Finds from Flaxengate I: Objects of Antler, Bone, Stone, Horn, Ivory, Amber, and Jet*, The Archaeology of Lincoln, 14 (1), London: CBA for the Lincoln Archaeological Trust.

Mann, J. 1986. 'Small finds', in B. J. J. Gilmour and D. A. Stocker (eds.), *St Mark's Church and Cemetery*, 41–3, The Archaeology of Lincoln, 13 (1), London: CBA for the Trust for Lincolnshire Archaeology.

Mann, J. 1999. 'Other artefacts', in C. Colyer, B. J. J. Gilmour and M. J. Jones (eds.), *The Defences of the Lower City: Excavations at The Park and West Parade 1970–2 and a Discussion of Other Sites Excavated up to 1994*, The Archaeology of Lincoln, 7 (2), 146–69 and 224–36, York: CBA for the City of Lincoln Archaeology Unit.

Mann, J. 2009. 'Some finds from the site of the new City and County Museum, Flaxengate, Lincoln (LDG03)', in S. Malone, *Excavations at the Site of The Collection, Danes Terrace, Lincoln*, unpublished Archaeological Project Services report 20/09.

Margeson, S. M. 1997. *The Vikings in Norfolk*. Norfolk: Norfolk Museums Service.

McAllister, D. 2013. 'Childhood in Viking and Hiberno-Scandinavian Dublin, 800–1100', in D. M. Hadley and L. ten Harkel (eds.), *Everyday Life in Viking-Age Towns: Social Approaches to Towns in England and Ireland, c. 800–1100*, 86–102, Oxford: Oxbow.

Owen, O. 2001. 'The strange beast that is the English Urnes style', in J. Graham-Campbell, R. Hall, J. Jesch and D. N. Parsons (eds.), *Vikings and the Danelaw: Select Papers from the Proceedings of the Thirteenth Viking Congress*, 203–22, Oxford: Oxbow.

Pedersen, A. 2001. 'Rovfugle eller duer: fugleformede fibler fra den tidlige middelalder', *Aarbøger for Nordisk Oldkyndighed og Historie*, **1999**, 19–66.

Pedersen, A., Roesdahl, E. and Graham-Campbell, J. 2014. 'Dress accessories and personal ornaments of metal: amulets', in E. Roesdahl, S. M. Sindbæk, A. Pedersen and D. M. Wilson (eds.), *Aggersborg: the Viking-Age Settlement and Fortress*, 279–89, Jutland Archaeological Society Publications, 82, Aarhus: Aarhus University Press.

Perring, D. 1981. *Early Medieval Occupation at Flaxengate, Lincoln*, The Archaeology of Lincoln, 9, London: CBA.

Pestell, T., Brown, M., Okasha, E., Ottaway, P. and Rogers, N. 2009. 'Artefacts relating to specialist activities', in D. H. Evans and C. Loveluck (eds.), *Life and Economy at Early Medieval Flixborough, c. AD 600–1000: The Artefact Evidence*, 122–42, Excavations at Flixborough, 2, Oxford: Oxbow.

Pohl, W. 2013. 'Introduction. Strategies of identification: a methodological profile', in W. Pohl and G. Heydemann (eds.), Strategies of Identification: Ethnicity and Religion in Early Medieval Europe, 1–64, Turnhout: Brepols.

Richards, J. D. and Schoenfelder, M. 2011. 'Norse bells: a Scandinavian colonial artefact', *ASSAH*, **17**, 151–68.

Richardson, C. 1993. 'The Borre Style in the British Isles and Ireland: A Reassessment', unpublished MA dissertation, University of Newcastle.

Roesdahl, E., Graham-Campbell, J., Connor, P. and Pearson, K. 1981. *The Vikings in England and in their Danish Homeland*, London: The Anglo-Danish Viking Project.

Rogers, N. 1993. *Anglian and Other Finds from Fishergate*, The Archaeology of York, 17 (9), London: York Archaeological Trust and CBA.

Rogers, N. 2009. 'The pins', in D. H. Evans and C. Loveluck (eds.), *Life and Economy at Early Medieval Flixborough, c. AD 600–1000: The Artefact Evidence*, 32–78, Excavations at Flixborough, 2, Oxford: Oxbow.

Røstad, I. M. 2012. 'En fremmed fugl: "Danske" smykker og forbindelser på Østlandet I overgangen mellom vikingtid og middelalder', *Viking*, **75**, 181–210.

Sheeran, H. 2009. 'Artefact distribution case study: equestrian equipment', *Internet Archaeology*, **25** (http://intarch.ac.uk/journal/issue25/2/3.4.3.html; consulted 13 June 2017).

Shoesmith, R. 1985. *Hereford City Excavations*, Vol. 3 *The Finds*, CBA Research Report, 56, London: CBA.

Skre, D. 2011. 'The inhabitants: origins and trading connexions', in D. Skre (ed.), *Things from the Town*, 417–41, Kaupang Excavation Project Publication Ser., 3, Norske Oldfunn XXIV, Oslo: Aarhus University Press and the Kaupang Excavation Project.

Steane, K., Darling, M. J., Jones, M. J., Mann, J., Vince, A. and Young, J. 2006. *The Archaeology of the Upper City and Adjacent Suburbs*, Lincoln Archaeological Studies, 3, Oxford: Oxbow.

Steane, K., Darling, M. J., Jones, M. J., Mann, J., Vince, A. and Young, J. 2016. *The Archaeology of the Lower City and Adjacent Suburbs*, Lincoln Archaeological Studies, 4, Oxford: Oxbow.

Steane, K., Darling, M. J., Mann, J., Vince, A. and Young, J. 2001. *The Archaeology of Wigford and the Brayford Pool*, Lincoln Archaeological Studies, 2, Oxford: Oxbow.

Stocker, D. (ed.) 2003. *The City by the Pool: Assessing the Archaeology of the City of Lincoln*, Lincoln Archaeological Studies, 10, Oxford: Oxbow.

Ten Harkel, L. 2006. 'The Vikings and the natives: ethnic identity in England and Normandy c.1000', *The Medieval Chronicle*, **4**, 175–88.

Ten Harkel, L. 2013a. 'Of towns and trinkets: metalworking and metal dress-accessories in Viking-Age Lincoln', in D. M. Hadley and L. ten Harkel (eds.), *Everyday Life in Viking-Age Towns: Social Approaches to Towns in England and Ireland, c. 800–1100*, 172–92, Oxford: Oxbow.

Ten Harkel, L. 2013b. 'Urban identity and material culture: a case study of Viking-Age Lincoln, *c.* AD 850–1000', *ASSAH*, **18**, 157–73.

Ten Harkel, L. 2013c. 'The urbanization of Viking Age Lincoln: a numismatic perspective', *The Mediaeval Journal*, **13 (1)**, 1–48.

Ten Harkel, L., Weetch, R. and Sainsbury, V. 2016. 'An early medieval polychrome-enameled brooch from Flaxengate, Lincoln: continental fashions in an Anglo-Scandinavian town', *Medieval Arch.*, **60 (1)**, 57–71.

Thomas, G. 2000a. 'A Survey of Late Anglo-Saxon and Viking Strap-ends from Britain', unpublished PhD thesis, University College London.

Thomas, G. 2000b. 'Anglo-Scandinavian metalwork from the Danelaw: exploring social and cultural interaction', in D. M. Hadley and J. D. Richards (eds.), *Cultures in Contact: Scandinavian Settlement in England in the Ninth and Tenth centuries*, 237–55, Turnhout: Brepols.

Thomas, G. 2012. 'Carolingian culture in the North Sea world: rethinking the cultural dynamics of personal adornment in Viking-Age England', *European Journal of Archaeology*, **15 (3)**, 486–518.

Tweddle, D. 2004. 'Art in pre-Conquest York', in R. A. Hall (ed.), *Aspects of Anglo-Scandinavian York*, 446–58, The Archaeology of York, 8 (4), London: CBA.

Vince, A. 1993. 'Forms, functions and manufacturing techniques of late ninth- and tenth-century wheelthrown pottery in England and their origins', in D. Piton (ed.), *Travaux du Groupe de Recherches et D'Etudes sur la Céramique dans le Nord – Pas-de-Calais: actes du Colloque D'Outreau (10–12 Avril 1992)*, 151–64, Numéro hors-série de Nord-Ouest Archéologie, Berck-sur-Mer: CRADC.

Vince, A. 2003a. 'Lincoln in the early medieval era, between the 5th and 9th centuries', in D. Stocker (ed.), *The City by the Pool: Assessing the Archaeology of the City of Lincoln*, 141–56, Lincoln Archaeological Studies, 10, Oxford: Oxbow.

Vince, A. 2003b. 'The new town: Lincoln in the high medieval era (*c.* 900 to *c.* 1350)', in D. Stocker (ed.), *The City by the Pool: Assessing the Archaeology of the City of Lincoln*, 159–296, Lincoln Archaeological Studies, 10, Oxford: Oxbow.

Vince, A. 2006. 'Coinage and urban development: integrating the archaeological and numismatic history of Lincoln', in B. Cook and G. Williams (eds.), *Coinage and History in the North Sea World, c. AD 500–1250: Essays in Honour of Marion Archibald*, 525–43, Leiden: Brill.

Wamers, E. 1994. *Die frühmittelalterlichen Lesefunde aus der Löhrstrasse (Baustelle Hilton II) in Mainz*, Mainzer Archäologische Schriften 1, Mainz: Landesamt für Denkmalpflege Rheinland-Pfalz.

Weetch R. 2013. 'Late Anglo-Saxon Brooches within their Northwest European Context: A Study of Social Identities Between the Eighth and Eleventh Centuries', unpublished PhD thesis, University of Reading.

White, R. 1982. 'Non-Ferrous Metalworking on Flaxengate, Lincoln, from the 9th–11th Centuries', unpublished MSc dissertation, Institute of Archaeology, UCL.

Williams, G. 2013. 'Towns and identities in Viking England', in D. M. Hadley and L. ten Harkel (eds.), *Everyday Life in Viking-Age Towns: Social Approaches to Towns in England and Ireland, c. 800–1100*, 14–34, Oxford: Oxbow.

Wilson, D. M. 1964. *Anglo-Saxon Ornamental Metalwork, 700–1100, in the British Museum*, London: Trustees of the British Museum.

Young, J. and Vince, A. 2005. *A Corpus of Anglo-Saxon and Medieval Pottery from Lincoln*, Lincoln Archaeological Studies, 7, Oxford: Oxbow.

What was the basis for Bede's list of overlords in *Historia Ecclesiastica* 2.5?

Richard Shaw

Abstract
Bede's list of overlords in Historia ecclesiastica 2.5 has inspired much academic commentary. Many now hold the catalogue to be Bede's invention. Examination, however, shows the arguments for this are not convincing. Rather, the evidence points to Bede's possession of a written source from which he copied the list.

Introduction

Attempts to understand seventh-century Anglo-Saxon politics by necessity depend on the account in Bede's *Historia ecclesiastica* [*HE*].[1] Each passage in that work of potential relevance to the subject has been scrutinized in order to extract every possible implication. It is no surprise therefore that Bede's list of overlords in *HE* 2.5 is among the most frequently examined passages in the entire book.[2] The catalogue is part of one of the central chapters in the *History*. The first half of 2.5 records Æthelberht's death and provides a eulogistic account of the king and his reign, summarizing some key pieces of information that Bede possessed about the monarch. In the second half Bede moves on to the 'apostasy' that followed under Eadbald, Æthelberht's son and successor. The list of hegemons comes in the first part of the chapter, in the context of Bede's celebration of King Æthelberht of Kent's memory and achievements:

> He [Æthelberht] was the third of the kings of the English people who ruled [*imperauit*] all their southern kingdoms [*prouinciis*], which are divided from the northern ones by the river Humber and its adjacent territory; but he was the first of them all to enter the kingdom of heaven. The first king to gain authority [*imperium*] of this kind was Ælle, king of the South Saxons; the second was Cælin, king of the West Saxons, who was called Ceawlin in their own language; the third, as we have said, was Æthelberht, king of the *Cantware*; the fourth was Rædwald, king of the East Angles, who even while Æthelberht was living was providing the leadership [*ducatum*] for his own people;[3] the fifth was Edwin, king of the Northumbrian people, that is the one which inhabits the district to the north of the River Humber. Edwin had still greater power and ruled over all the peoples who live in Britain, English and British alike, except only the Kentish. He even subjected to the authority [*imperio*] of the English [*Angli*] the Mevanian Islands [Anglesey and Man] of the Britons which lie between Ireland and Britain. The sixth to hold rule [*regnum*] within the same bounds was Oswald, who was indeed the most Christian king of the Northumbrians. The seventh was his brother Oswiu who for some time held rule [*regnum*] over almost the same frontiers. For the most part he subjugated and made tributary the peoples of the Picts and also the Irish who hold the northern parts of Britain. But these things will be dealt with later.[4]

In this passage, Bede is setting out a list of seven hegemons in order:[5] Ælle, of the South Saxons, Cælin, of the West Saxons, Æthelberht of Kent, Rædwald of the East Angles, and Edwin, Oswald and Oswiu of the Northumbrians. Details are interspersed among the names: for instance, the description of Oswald as *rex Christianissimus*; or the peoples Oswiu 'subjugated and made tributary'; or the demarcation of the basic borders of the overlordship as being south of the Humber. Nonetheless, these details should not distract from a consideration of the list on its own terms. At the heart of the extract from 2.5 is a catalogue of rulers wielding overlordship over Anglo-Saxon kingdoms and in some cases more widely.

Taken at face value, therefore, this hegemon list could cast great light on the situation in the seventh century. But can it be taken at face value? Given that Bede was at best a secondary source for most of the events in the

History, it cannot be assumed that he was well informed about all the incidents he records. The question here, as elsewhere, is whether Bede possessed an earlier and reliable source upon which he based his account in the *HE*. If Bede did have access to such a text then, even though it does not survive today, the basic outlines of it are probably reconstructable from the list he gives. This reconstruction would provide a rare direct, contemporary insight onto Anglo-Saxon politics for some of the seventh century that could prove a vital basis for examining the period. If, however, Bede's list was not based on a source, then it tells us nothing about the 600s, but only about Bede, his perspectives and potentially his authorial intentions.

Thus, identifying whether or not Bede was using a source in this passage is crucial not only for determining what use can be made of this section, but also for interpreting the work as a whole. Given how reliant historians studying the Middle Ages continue to be on Bede and his *History*, this is a key question affecting the use of the book both to understand Anglo-Saxon England, and as evidence for the nature of the early medieval world in general. Discerning the reality behind *HE* requires a careful examination of Bede's sources for his statements and an attempt to assess their relative credibility.

The search for the sources of *HE*, however, has not attracted much academic attention recently. Historians' focus – with many very fruitful results – has been on discerning the various assumptions and even agendas that arguably lay behind Bede's writing of *HE*.[6] This research has shown that despite Bede's scholarship, his reliability cannot be taken for granted. The impressions he wanted to leave on his audience inevitably affected his presentation of material.

In this context, perhaps unsurprisingly, it now tends to be presumed that Bede did not have a source for his list of hegemons in *HE* 2.5. Instead there is a growing academic consensus that the catalogue was Bede's own creation, either intended as a summary of his understanding of the situation a century before he was writing, or designed with more specific rhetorical purposes in mind.[7] If true, this conclusion has significant implications for how we view *HE*. If Bede fabricated the list, then, as noted above, it cannot be used to provide evidence for the political situation in the seventh century. Indeed, it is not possible to accept that Bede created the list *ex nihilo* and yet treat the rest of *HE* as if the value of its evidence for Anglo-Saxon England and for the early Middle Ages as a whole was unaffected.

The present essay seeks to re-examine the basis for Bede's list of hegemons in *HE* 2.5. It begins by assessing how scholars have come to the view that Bede invented the list and shows that the arguments have all started by assuming that he did not have a source, thereby begging the question. It will then be shown how the assumption of invention has subsequently been used as the basis for creative explanations of what Bede must have been trying to achieve by fabricating the catalogue and inserting it into the *HE*. These explanations, however, are inconsistent internally and tend to presume that Bede was acting here in ways that can be shown to be uncharacteristic of his practices in the rest of the *HE*. Furthermore the rationales offered fail to deal with problems which are all better resolved by concluding that Bede did indeed possess a source for the passage.

Unfortunately, the issue of whether Bede used a source or invented the list has been unnecessarily confused by two separate issues: first, the question of the existence or not of the so-called 'Bretwalda' (or better, 'Brytenwalda'),[8] a term initially found in the *Anglo-Saxon Chronicle* (*ASC*) 827, *recte* 829, as part of a repetition (in translation) and minor extension of Bede's list; and second, the assumption that Bede's list must be associated with his problematic description of the boundaries of the rulers' hegemony – that is, 'all their southern kingdoms [*prouinciis*], which are divided from the northern ones by the river Humber and its adjacent territory'.[9] As will be seen, these are discrete issues without relevance to Bede's basis for the list. In short, this is because, on the one hand, the errors and assumptions of the ninth-century chronicler do not cast any light either way on the question of whether Bede possessed a source for his catalogue; while, on the other, Bede's description of the boundaries of the powers of these overlords reflects contemporary descriptions of the current hegemon, Æthelbald of Mercia,[10] and is therefore most simply explained as Bede's instinctive projection of the situation in his own time on to the past.[11] Once these confusing elements have been removed, it becomes easier to see that the natural explanation for Bede's catalogue of the names of hegemons in *HE* 2.5 is his use of a source.

Indeed, when examined in context in *HE* 2.5, careful textual analysis can show that there are several strong reasons to conclude that Bede was working from a written document which he had in front of him as he wrote and which he utilized in a manner closely paralleled by his practice elsewhere in the same section of the same chapter. The basic content of this source can be recovered and it will be possible to make some suggestions about its nature, origins, provenance and possible connections. There is no space in this paper to pursue the potential implications of Bede's possession of such a source for reconstructing the political shape of early Christian Anglo-Saxon England. Nonetheless, if it is accepted that an early text did indeed lie behind Bede's account, then this putative document can provide both a better foundation for interpretation of seventh-century politics and also clearer insights into Bede's methods. Such a conclusion is a reminder of the value of searching for sources in the works of medieval authors like Bede, alongside an emphasis on understanding their agendas.

The emergence of the view that the hegemon list was Bede's invention

As noted above, modern historians have frequently concluded that the hegemon list in *HE* 2.5 was Bede's invention and that he did not base his catalogue on a written source. When this case has been made, however, it tends to represent purely the first stage in a wider argument. The conclusion is treated as an assumption. Nicholas Higham was quite upfront about the fact he was doing this: 'In offering his list of 'overkings' there are no indications that Bede was quoting from some pre-existing (but now lost) text ... Without far clearer evidence to the contrary we should assume that Bede compiled his list ....'[12] Others have made the same presumption more subtly.[13]

Once these scholars have assumed that Bede did not possess a source and must have invented the catalogue, they subsequently set out to explain why Bede carried out the fabrication. Again, Higham was most explicit about his process. To continue the earlier quotation: '... we should assume that Bede compiled his list and that he did so with the same clear intelligence which is discernible elsewhere in his work. There must, in other words, be a logic to this list: it is our task to identify that logic as the first stage in interpreting its contents in an appropriate context.'[14] This same two-stage process is also found in the works of others.[15]

Perhaps these explanations could be seen as serving to argue for Bede's invention of the list. If they, or any of the varying individual explanations offered, were accepted then it could be claimed they provide a case for Bede's invention of the list. If the list could be shown to fulfil a Bedan purpose then, implicitly, there would be no reason to expect a source. Is it really likely that Bede would have access to a text that was so perfectly aligned with his own attitudes?

This is a perspective, however, that has only been reached by presuming the outcome from the start. Nor, as will be seen below, do the explanations so far provided by historians do enough either to justify the conclusion or to show that they are consistent with Bede's ideas and practices. Indeed, they raise their own problems, problems which are more satisfactorily resolved by accepting that Bede did have a source for his list.

The explanations historians have offered for Bede's invention of the list vary significantly, but they fall broadly into two main types. The first type claims that the list marks personal reflection on Bede's part: it is taken to be Bede's view of how things were in the seventh century based on the other information at his disposal.[16] The second type of explanation suggests that the list served a rhetorical or ideological purpose of Bede's. Within this latter group the range of explanations is understandably wide. On examination, it can be seen that there are difficulties with both types of rationalization.

Does the list represent Bede's own considered view of the past?

The idea that the list represents, in Simon Keynes' words, the 'exercise of his [Bede's] judgment as a historian',[17] is undermined by the inconsistency of its content with other material in the *HE*. If Bede had been producing the list based on his own knowledge, then we must wonder why Bede's reflection and his judgment here were so uncharacteristically in error, since his version of power politics in the catalogue does not line up with other information in the *HE*. This is demonstrated both by the individuals on the list and by those missing. Bede knew enough to extend the list much further, even up to his own day, mostly with Mercian names.[18] King Ecgfrith of Northumbria's power, for instance, was comparable to, and perhaps for a time greater than, those Northumbrian rulers who preceded him,[19] yet he is not mentioned in the catalogue, while Edwin, Oswald and Oswiu are.[20] Additionally, in *HE* 5.23, Æthelbald of Mercia's power is described in similar terms to those of the rulers in 2.5, but his name is not included on the hegemon list.

Bede, therefore, knew of overlords beyond those enumerated in 2.5 and he had no reservations about using that knowledge elsewhere in the *HE*. Despite this, he inserts the list of overlords as if it were complete. This does not make sense if the list were his own reflection on the past, summarizing his considered view as a historian. Nor can this 'choice' be dismissed as 'naked Northumbrian chauvinism'[21] on Bede's part, as Dumville rightly showed.[22] Both the above examples – Ecgfrith and Æthelbald – demonstrate that it was not blind jingoism or hatred of Mercians that limited Bede's list to seven. Ecgfrith was Northumbrian, and the patron or even founder of Bede's own monastery,[23] so his absence from the list can hardly be explained as a consequence of Bede's desire to celebrate only Northumbrian rulers. Moreover, Bede's mention of Æthelbald's overlordship in 5.23,[24] which was not demanded by the context, includes no criticism of the Mercian monarch; thus, the evidence shows Bede was not trying to disguise or downplay the realities of Mercian power.

It is not only the omission of later names which undermines the theory that Bede was producing the list based on his own knowledge. The inclusion of the earliest hegemons seems to be equally inconsistent with such a hypothesis. It is not possible to demonstrate that Bede knew nothing about Ælle or Cælin except their names, but they do not feature anywhere else in the *HE*. Perhaps one should not put too much weight on such an argument from silence; even so, their absence from the work does require emphasis, since some scholars have attempted to use these individuals as evidence for invention. In reality, however, there is no positive reason to think Bede inserted the names of Ælle or Cælin because these figures were well known to him, as Higham believed.[25] Nor is there anything to support Keynes' view that they played 'a particularly important role in his [Bede's] story'.[26] Earlier kings who do feature with relative prominence in *HE*, such as Hengist or Æthelfrith, are not found in the list.[27] If the catalogue were really Bede's own 'private scheme',[28] he was in no way compelled to include Ælle and Cælin. He could have chosen whomsoever he wished.

Therefore, the evidence of the list – both the rulers omitted and those included – argues against taking the catalogue as representative of Bede's knowledge or raw historical reflection.[29] In short, if Bede had produced a list of overlords based on his own knowledge, he would have done a better job. In contrast, the inconsistencies between the list and the other information that the rest of the *HE* shows was at Bede's disposal would be naturally explained by his possession of a written source – so too would the inclusion of surprising names. If the basic structure of the *HE*'s list was simply Bede's repetition of a text in front of him, then it would make perfect sense that the material in this passage did not cohere precisely with details found elsewhere in the *HE* and that were based on other sources of information. Over-reliance on a written document meant Bede included material he had other reasons for doubting.

This type of error on Bede's behalf – and its explanation – are quite characteristic of his ways of working in the *HE*. It is analogous to his inclusion through repetition of textual errors in other written sources he was copying: the papal letters, and especially the *Libellus Responsionum* in *HE* 1.27, are the most obvious examples.[30] The mistakes were not Bede's fault; they were the fault of his sources. In other words, the very inconsistencies which undermine the theory that the list represents Bede's invention based on his own view of the past, quietly support the view that he was drawing from a written source in front of him.

Before moving on, it is necessary to address another problem with the claim that Bede invented the list as a summary of how he saw earlier shifts in hegemonic power. There are no other examples of Bede compiling similar catalogues from scratch in the *HE*. It is worth emphasizing, therefore, how uncharacteristic it would have been for Bede to concoct a set of office holders in *HE* 2.5. Perhaps this instance represents an exception, but we need to acknowledge that it would be an exception; as a result, the burden of proof is on those arguing for the fabrication of the catalogue to justify why Bede here adopted a different practice from usual.

Keynes believed there was a parallel that supported his case for invention. He felt Bede's invention of the catalogue mirrored the lists of bishops in the *HE*. The hegemon list was 'a secular counterpart to the numerous passages where Bede is concerned to establish the order of succession to a particular episcopal see'.[31] According to such a view, the idea that Bede built up the catalogue of overlords from other information he possessed would be completely in line with his practice elsewhere, because that is precisely what Bede did with passages like the following description of the succession of Mercian bishops:

> The first bishop in the kingdom of Mercia, of Lindsey, and the Middle Angles was Diuma: as has already been said, he died and was buried among the Middle Angles. The second bishop was Ceollach, who resigned his bishopric before his death and returned to Ireland, for both he and Diuma were Irish. The third bishop was Trumhere, an Englishman but educated and consecrated by the Irish. He was abbot of the monastery called Gilling.[32]

This short list is indeed very much like that of the hegemons in *HE* 2.5: both are catalogues of names interlaced with whatever additional information about the individuals Bede possessed. But this does not prove that the hegemon list was Bede's invention, or that it was Bede's standard practice to compile lists of office holders from disparate information at his disposal.[33] Quite the opposite. This kind of list is very unlikely to be the product of deductions on Bede's behalf. Most would accept that the basic structures of such catalogues of bishops in the *HE*, while interspersed with other information, derive from episcopal lists.[34] No manuscripts with Anglo-Saxon episcopal lists survive from the period before Bede was writing;[35] but the content of the *HE* shows that they did exist and that Bede used them.[36] Bede utilized episcopal lists in a similar way to how he employed regnal lists and genealogies, such as that for the Kentish kings given in *HE* 1.15 and 2.5, or that for Rædwald given in *HE* 2.15. Sometimes Bede drew details from these lists to add to his narrative; at others, as with the example of the episcopal list quoted above, he used the content of these catalogues as the basic structure of a more extended passage, weaving in other information around them.[37]

Lists like that in *HE* 3.24 do not represent Bede's collation of material he had compiled from a variety of different sources into a single catalogue produced by himself. They are drawn from written texts – episcopal lists, regnal lists and genealogies – that he had in front of him. Thus, the similarities between the treatment of bishops in passages like *HE* 3.24 and that of hegemons in *HE* 2.5 point not to Bede's invention of the catalogue, or deduction of the list from other information he had compiled, but to his use of a source. Such a use of a source is characteristic of Bede's methodology: inventing a list is not. This conclusion does not only affect the claim that Bede's list represented his view of the past; it also undermines those arguments that Bede invented the catalogue of hegemons for ideological purposes, to which we must now turn.

Does the list represent Bede's attempt to advance a certain ideological agenda?

While the idea that the list represented Bede's perspective on the past has been influential, more of the resistance to the idea that Bede possessed a source for the list of hegemons has come from those who would see the catalogue as an invention to serve Bede's ideological purposes. The purposes proposed vary from attempts to fulfil a 'Eusebian function',[38] to emphasizing the power of Æthelberht,[39] or competing with British tradition represented by the later *Historia Brittonum*.[40] Several theories have placed emphasis on the fact that there are seven hegemons in Bede's list. As noted above, all the arguments begin by assuming that the catalogue was Bede's invention and then set out to explain why he would have done such a thing. Each explanation comes with its own individual problems, although some, especially pertaining to numerology, are shared.

According to Henry Mayr-Harting, Bede introduced the list because he conceived of the overlords 'as vital instruments in the spread of Christianity among the English beyond the confines of their own kingdoms, on the Eusebian analogy of Constantine in the Roman Empire'.[41] As evidence of this, Mayr-Harting pointed to the ways in which Bede drew out distinctively Eusebian elements in his portrayals of the three Northumbrian hegemons in the *HE*: the peace of Edwin's reign;[42] the connection for Oswald of the cross and successful battle;[43] and the major *synodus* under Oswiu.[44] There is no reasonable doubt that when Bede comes to treat of these moments he is reflecting a Eusebian model.[45] This makes these kings, in those instances, seem very Constantinian.

Moving beyond these acknowledged Eusebian elements in those specific examples, however, none of the three kings is otherwise or consistently presented as Constantinian in the *HE*.[46] Nor do any of the individual 'distinctively Constantinian' examples occur in the context of, or connected to, the hegemon list in *HE* 2.5.[47] In other words, while there is a Eusebian/Constantinian character to specific tales about Edwin, Oswald and Oswiu (one for each), this attitude does not dominate or shape Bede's characterization of the kings in question taking *HE* as a whole. The mere mention of their names in the hegemon list therefore cannot be assumed to represent a reference to a Eusebian intention.

The other names in the list are even less convincing examples of a 'Eusebian function'. As Mayr-Harting acknowledged, the pagans, as well as Rædwald, who added an altar to Christ to the others in his temple,[48] do not seem to be consistent with such an explanation. Mayr-Harting sought to resolve this difficulty by equating the pagans with the 'powerful pagan emperors before Constantine, of whom Eusebius wrote';[49] while Rædwald was explained away as Bede's attempt to provide a Maxentius, or a Maximinus figure.[50] These ambiguous identifications are not very persuasive. Moreover, returning to the reason Mayr-Harting gave for the invention of the list, it is difficult to see how Bede can conceivably have seen these outliers as 'vital instruments in the spread of Christianity among the English'.[51] The first two hegemons, Ælle and Cælin, were pagan: they played no role at all in spreading the faith. The fourth, Rædwald, was an apostate, whose attitude to Christianity is specifically condemned by Bede.[52]

Indeed, if establishing this 'Eusebian function' was Bede's intention, we would expect to see it set out in a more instrumental way within the narrative of the entire work: but it is not. The role of the leaders of the united English in spreading the faith across the Anglo-Saxon kingdoms is not the, or even a, central organizing principle of *HE*'s narrative.[53] This explanation, therefore, raises more questions than it answers.

The same can be said for the rationales others have given for Bede's invention of the list. For Higham the context was not Eusebius, it was military success. The purpose of creating the list was to place Æthelberht in the company of monarchs famous for their military prowess. These individuals were remembered, Higham contended, because: 'In all instances known to us, those chosen were victors in memorable battles'.[54] But this claim is not in fact borne out by the names on the list: it does not apply either to Ælle or to Cælin,[55] or even to Æthelberht.[56]

For Eric John the decision to include seven hegemons represented Bede's 'riposte' to the British tradition preserved in *Historia Brittonum* that spoke of seven emperors ruling in Britain.[57] Most of John's piece was dedicated to sketching out the powers of hegemons, and particularly to claims about the 'Bretwalda'. The argument for Bede's fabrication of the catalogue was not structural to the rest of his case; nor did he develop it very far,[58] and, clearly, in this instance his view has been overtaken by more modern research. Most would now accept that if any influence did operate between Bede and *Historia Brittonum*, then, chronologically, we should expect to see it being exercised the other way round: that is, the *Historia Brittonum* was competing with Bede, rather than Bede with an ancient British tradition.[59]

Thus, in all instances, the arguments for what was in any case an assumption – that Bede did not possess a source for his hegemon list, but invented it himself – are undermined by the evidence and are so fraught with internal contradictions that they do not make sense even on their own terms. In every case, a simpler solution is that Bede was dependent on a written document.

Before progressing, however, it is necessary to consider one further element that has been at the heart of several of the ideological arguments for Bede's invention of the list: the number of hegemons on it. Those claiming Bede fabricated the catalogue have frequently seen meaning in the fact that it includes seven overlords. Seven, so the argument goes, is obviously a sacred or meaningful number for exegetes, and Bede was an exegete par excellence.[60] Therefore, the claim is that Bede must have invented the list. This point has been important in the emerging academic consensus that the list could not have come from a source and must have been Bede's invention.[61]

There are several problems with arguments that rely on this element. The first is that every scholar advocating the meaningfulness of the number seven has proposed a different way in which to interpret it.[62] Moreover, the variety of explanations lies not only between scholars' interpretations, but also sometimes within each one. To demonstrate the importance of 'seven', Mayr-Harting included an example where Bede, in his commentary *On the Temple*, had drawn out the significance of the number; even within the short paragraph quoted, however, Bede offers two different meanings for the use of seven.[63] If the idea is that the list was invented because of the meaningfulness of the number seven, then that meaning must be clear for the hypothesis to make sense.[64] This is not the case, however, even in Mayr-Harting's own carefully constructed argument;[65] others have been much less cautious with numerological theories.[66]

Criticism of this kind of approach to textual analysis was provided by Mayr-Harting himself, who drew attention to Aldhelm's discussion of the importance of the number seven at the start of the *Epistola ad Acircium*, and noted that the 'plethora of [Aldhelm's] points' meant they lost their saliency for interpreting specific examples.[67] In other words, it is not that the number seven cannot be meaningful, it is simply that in light of all the interpretations assigned to 'seven' for the hegemon list, the figure has become meaningless.[68] Therefore, there is no good reason to think that the number of hegemons is evidence that Bede invented the list of overlords.

Moreover, if the number of hegemons – or any ideologically driven significance at all – was so important for Bede and his authorial purposes, it is surprising that he does not draw more attention to it. Bede enumerates the hegemons as he includes their names in order; but, beyond that, he places no emphasis on their number. He does not introduce the list by setting out how many overlords he is about to catalogue, nor does he repeat the figure in a summary of the list at the end to underline its importance. Even Keynes, who raised the possibility of the significance of the number of the overlords, acknowledged that, 'it would have to be said that he [Bede] did not make much of the point.'[69] The number of the hegemons can hardly be said to have been among Bede's rhetorical priorities in this passage – any more than was explaining the meaning that number should possess.

The latter point is particularly important. It is true that Bede could include numbers in *HE* that he intentionally imbued with significance. The best example of such a practice, however, contrasts starkly with how he presents the hegemon list. In *HE* 1.1, Bede notes that there are five languages in Britain, and, unlike in 2.5, draws attention to the significance of the number.[70] Five is certainly a number with many potential meanings for an exegete. Nonetheless Bede does not leave readers to sort through the possibilities and interpret according to their own lights. He specifically directs them to the external reference he has in mind, stating that the five languages match the five books of the *lex diuina*.[71] Bede shows the numerological meaning he wants his readers to take away. There is no parallel explanation in the hegemon list in *HE* 2.5. Thus, the best example of Bede's intentional use of a numerologically significant figure in *HE* should warn us against assuming that any number in *HE* should be treated as significant unless Bede points out the meaning himself.[72] Scholars who would like to force a meaning on to the fact that there are seven hegemons again have to assume Bede was here acting uncharacteristically compared to his behaviour and practice discernible in the rest of *HE*.[73]

As a result, no weight can be placed on the claim that the fact that there are seven hegemons on the list shows that Bede cannot have copied the catalogue from a source and must have invented it himself. A simpler explanation for the presence of seven overlords on Bede's list is that there were seven in his source. This is also the obvious solution to another significant difficulty with asserting that the number of hegemons is the reason he invented the list – and indeed with all the ideological arguments for Bede's fabrication of the catalogue: its location in *HE*. If the list and the number of rulers on it, are supposed to have been conveying authorial intent, then we should expect this to be fulfilled in the later names, which represent the culmination of the group. The catalogue comes as part of the description of Æthelberht on his death, however. This is a real obstacle to accepting the claim that Bede invented the list to convey purposes in context. If, for example, the 'Eusebian function' of Bede's list were indeed best realized by 'the three Christian Northumbrians',[74] why is it here in the eulogy for Æthelberht? If Bede wanted to emphasize the seven hegemons and Oswiu, as the seventh, was the consummation of the list,[75] the perfect number for the perfect king, then the natural place to put the catalogue would be after treating Oswiu's reign, not here in concluding Æthelberht's.[76]

Thus, the position of the list in the *HE* further undermines the claim that Bede invented the list for ideological reasons and especially in order to place seven overlords in it. Higham implicitly recognized this challenge. As he noted, the first half of *HE* 2.5 is undoubtedly designed for rhetorical effect to praise Æthelberht.[77] This is why Higham placed such emphasis on Æthelberht's position – third – in the list and on the potential significances of that number.[78] This explanation, however, does nothing to avoid the obvious difficulty that Æthelberht's name is buried in the middle of the list, while the climax of the catalogue is clearly the Northumbrian overlords, not Æthelberht at all. Their power is described in terms showing that it dwarfed that of Æthelberht. It is therefore difficult to see how inventing the hegemon list might have served to bolster Æthelberht's wider reputation.[79] If the list was invented to praise Æthelberht, then why does it show how easily superseded his reach was by Northumbrian hegemons? But if one imagines that Bede's overall aim in creating the catalogue was instead to praise Oswald and Oswiu, then why is it here, rather than in his treatment of those monarchs? If the list was Bede's invention, it reads very oddly in this context.

On the other hand, including a list from a source he possessed makes perfect sense of all these problems. If Bede was copying the basic frame of his catalogue of hegemons from a text in front of him, then this would not only account for the tension between the list and his knowledge as demonstrated by the content of the rest of the *HE*, it would also explain why, as seen above, no clear and consistent ideological purpose emerges from the list. Bede did not have a grand masterplan for including these names: he was taking them from his source. In addition, use of a written source would at last provide a credible rationale for the location of the list in the work. In the first half of *HE* 2.5, as will be discussed in more detail shortly, Bede was collecting the material he possessed that related to Æthelberht and including it in his summary of the monarch and his rule. The proposed hegemon list document would have fitted neatly among these materials since it mentioned the king. Thus, if the list is from a source, one can accept that Bede *included* the catalogue to praise Æthelberht, while recognizing that the placement and content of the list itself show that he did not *invent* it for that purpose.

This view is supported by how artificially the catalogue appears in context. As David Dumville noted, Bede ended the section including the hegemon list abruptly – 'but of these things more later'[80] – as if he had gone on too long and needed to drag the narrative back to its real focus.[81] Thus, the next section begins effectively back at the same point as the beginning of the chapter – with Æthelberht's death – almost ignoring the interruption the digression on hegemons had caused.[82] This is scarcely the action we should expect were the list of hegemons supposed to represent the fulfilment of one of Bede's authorial agendas. On the other hand, it is exactly what one would anticipate if Bede were copying from a source. If Bede was dependent on a source then it is no surprise that the content breaks the flow of the narrative. Inserting the content and commenting on it took him away from the point with which he started – Æthelberht – and to which he had to return.[83] Bede's catalogue in *HE* 2.5 did not stop at Æthelberht, because his source did not. The list in Bede's source went beyond Æthelberht: it went up to Oswiu. So too, therefore, did Bede; but he had to return to Æthelberht, because that king was the focus of the first half of the chapter.[84] It was not ideal, but it was what he had. Furthermore, as will be seen below, this kind of practice is precisely consistent with Bede's approach elsewhere in this section of the *HE* chapter.

Two issues clouding the question: Bretwaldas and borders

Before considering the hegemon list in context, it is important to consider two separate issues, discussion of which has often unnecessarily confused the question of whether Bede possessed a source for his list and which have been used, unfairly, to deny that he used such a document and to argue instead for invention. These issues were briefly mentioned in the introduction. First, examination of the basis of the hegemon list in 2.5 has been unprofitably tied up with the vexed question of the existence of the so-called 'Brytenwalda', or as earlier historiography called it, 'Bretwalda'. The second point confusing consideration of the question is the assumption that if the set of hegemons came from a source, then so too must have Bede's description of the Humber as the border of the authority of these overlords.[85]

The word Brytenwalda appears in the *Anglo-Saxon Chronicle* (*ASC*) as part of a description of the achievements of Ecgberht, king of Wessex.[86] The Chronicler first notes that Ecgberht conquered the Mercians and ruled everything south of the Humber, before claiming that the king was the eighth Brytenwalda. The *ASC* then repeats the list from *HE* 2.5, adding Ecgberht at the end. Unfortunately, this repetition of Bede's list has led to confusion in the search for the roots of Bede's catalogue. Some scholars have attempted to use the unreliability of the *ASC* account to undermine Bede's.[87] But this is to mix together two separate issues: on the one hand, the basis of Bede's statement, and, on the other, the nature, or even existence, of a hegemonic office/institution called the 'Bretwaldaship'. Criticisms of this term and the assumption that it represented a reality have been, and remain, very valid. In earlier historiography the 'Bretwaldaship' tended to take on a life of its own, quite separate from any evidence for it or its functions.[88] Previous generations of historians had at times constructed vivid, not to say fanciful, depictions of the nature of the office, imbuing it with powers and insignia. In such scholarship, other evidence was often interpreted in the light of a theory about the supposed institution rather than on its own terms. The treatment of the discoveries at Sutton Hoo is the most obvious example of such a practice, with various items in Mound One at times identified as the regalia of a 'Bretwalda'.[89]

The arguments of Keynes and others, showing how weak is the case for an office called the Brytenwalda, have provided a much-needed counterweight to such imaginative theories. There is no reason to believe the term had any currency even at the time the *ASC* was written, let alone that Ecgberht of Wessex was called by the title during his reign. In Keynes' famous words, 'the time has come to Ban the Bretwalda'.[90]

None of this has any relevance to the basis of Bede's list, however. As Keynes himself noted: 'No one would doubt for a moment that this list [in the *ASC*] is directly dependent on Bede's *Ecclesiastical History*, and no one would argue, therefore, that the chronicler could be said to corroborate Bede's testimony'.[91] In the same way, the *ASC* cannot be said to undermine Bede's testimony. The term Brytenwalda may be a phantom, but since Bede does not mention the word or suggest that there was a title this cannot reflect negatively on the basis of his list. Nor is there even any reason to believe Bede knew the term or to think that such a word was current in Old English in Bede's time. We can hardly criticize Bede, therefore, for the use of the word by a ninth-century chronicler. The evidence of that later text has no relevance to the question of whether or not Bede had a source for the list he included in the *HE*.

Indeed, one possible explanation of the word Brytenwalda, meaning 'Britain ruler',[92] not previously raised, is worth suggesting here. The word may represent no more than a translation of a phrase like *rex/rector Britanniae*, or similar terminology used in Mercian diplomas.[93] The occurrence of such titles in charters like S89 from the eighth century show that the Latin term was evidenced before the Old English word brytenwalda whose first appearance was in the late ninth century. At one level the *Anglo-Saxon Chronicle* account certainly represents a translation – the list of overlords it gives is a mere translated replication of Bede's, a rendering in Old English of a Latin original. Perhaps brytenwalda is the Chronicler's attempt at a version of *rex/rector Britanniae*.[94] In that context, it may be telling that the only other occurrence of the word, in the form 'brytænwalda', is also as a translation of a Latin phrase. This comes in an Old English version of the charter S427. The Latin original includes the phrase, 'rex et rector totius huius britannie insule', which the translator renders, 'cyning 7 brytænwalda eallæs ðyses Iglandæs'.[95] Here, therefore, the Old English term brytenwalda is definitely a translation of a Latin phrase – specifically, *rector britanniae*. Perhaps the same is true, *mutatis mutandis*, for the *ASC*'s use of the word. Rather than *rex/rector Britanniae* being a Latin translation of a supposed earlier Old English title for a hegemonic office,[96] arguably 'brytenwalda' was merely a translation of phrasing like *rex/rector Britanniae*, one of the titles used in the eighth and early ninth centuries for Mercian kings, and also employed by Asser to describe Alfred.[97]

Whether or not such a theory be accepted, it is clear that there is no independent evidence, outside translated sources, for an Old English word brytenwalda, let alone an office with that name. Bede's list is no evidence in support of the latter. Equally, the non-existence of a 'Bretwaldaship' is no evidence against Bede's possession of a source with a list of putative hegemons. Attempts to prove the non-existence of a hegemonic institution cannot prove the list was Bede's invention. The non-existence of a brytenwalda institution, or even of a word in common use in the ninth century, are not arguments against Bede in the eighth century having possessed a written source with a list of seventh-century hegemons. The ninth-century source, the *Anglo-Saxon Chronicle*, should not be allowed to obscure our analysis of Bede's eighth-century use of a seventh-century source in the *HE*, especially when that ninth-century source was doing little more than mechanically copying out Bede's list of hegemons and adding Ecgberht of Wessex. Much had changed in Anglo-Saxon England between the early seventh century and the ninth – and even between the early seventh century and Bede's composition of the *HE*. Earlier imaginative conceptions of 'Bretwaldaship' are sufficiently behind us to be able to treat Bede's evidence independently. The list must be looked at on its own terms, separate from the 'Bretwalda', which – even if Bede did possess a written source – can safely remain 'banned'.

A similar situation pertains to the second area of unnecessary confusion. Bede's view that the Humber represented the border of the hegemony exercised by these overlords has sometimes been taken as integral to the list and has been implicitly used to argue against Bede having a source for the passage.[98] If one assumes a connection between the list and the description of the frontier then this is a valid point. Our limited knowledge of the vagaries of seventh-century politics suggests that these bounds were not as static as Bede implies. Bede's own descriptions of the extent of the power of people on the list – Edwin, Oswald and Oswiu, for instance – contradict it in the very same passage in *HE* 2.5.[99] Archaeology seems to confirm that the Humber was not a border until the later seventh century and indeed suggests that the river served more to unite than divide in the earlier period.[100] Thus, presuming an association of the description with the list argues against the catalogue coming from a pre-existing, seventh-century source, which would not be expected to include such an anachronism.

There is no reason to think that the list and the frontiers are connected, however, except by Bede. A much simpler explanation is available. The Humber was the boundary of hegemonic authority in Bede's own day, at least at the time of the completion of *HE*. This is how Bede describes Æthelbald's power in 5.23.[101] This is also shown by independent, contemporary descriptions of the hegemonic power of Æthelbald of Mercia, as found, for instance, in the Ismere charter and several other diplomas.[102] The Ismere charter, S89, refers to Æthelbald as: 'rex non solum Marcersium sed et omnium provinciarum quæ generale nomine Sutangli dicuntur'.[103] The 'Whitby' *Life of Gregory* uses a similar term for the power of the earlier Mercian king, Æthelred.[104] Bede's description of the reach of these overlords is too close to these to be a coincidence. This points to the most reasonable explanation for why Bede believed the Humber represented the ancient border of overlords' power. He was, in good faith, anachronistically reading back the situation in his own day, with the contemporary, accepted, bounds of Anglo-Saxon overlordship, as if they also represented the reality for earlier periods. Nevertheless, his teleological view of seventh-century conditions is likely to have been based on no more evidence than the current claims of Mercian kings.[105] That Bede was apparently well aware of such statements concerning the boundaries of Æthelbald's overlordship seems clear, given how close is his description of Æthelbald's power in 5.23 to claims such as those in S89.[106]

Bede's description of the boundaries of the hegemons' overlordship, therefore, represents the usage of his own day and has no validity for the time of rule of the individuals in the list – the seventh century or before. His explanation cannot be relied upon; but that does not affect the standing of the list or the question of whether the names on it came from a source. If Bede did indeed have a source for his catalogue of hegemons, as seems increasingly likely based on our discussion so far, then by including a description of the frontiers of their power extrapolated from the contemporary political situation, Bede was merely adding a gloss, as it were, to the list he was repeating. Bede intersperses the set of names with various other pieces of information;[107] the description of (his view of) the borders of the overlordship should simply be considered another added element. Faced with a list of earlier hegemons, it would have been natural for Bede to assume that their power should be conceived of in the same, contemporary terms as were at the time of writing currently in place.[108]

The list is not a list of English hegemons who held power south of the Humber.[109] It is just a list of English hegemons. It was Bede who assumed that hegemony meant power south of the Humber, because that is what it represented in his own time. The core list of the names of the seven hegemons must be assessed on its own terms, aside from such accretions.[110]

Therefore, neither of the perceived difficulties with accepting the existence of a source for Bede's list stands up to scrutiny. Instead, clarifying these issues permits a clearer assessment of the question. It is possible to see how the lack of proper distinctions in the past has unnecessarily clouded the issue, distracting scholars from the substantial difficulties that, as we have seen, undermine the case for Bede's invention of the list. In reality, not only do the arguments for Bede's invention of the list leave unsolved several serious questions, but the examples intended to prove the case actually point to Bede's possession of a source for the list. This conclusion becomes even clearer through examining Bede's use of the list in 2.5 in the context of what else he is doing in that chapter.

The hegemon list in context: Bede's methods and sources in 2.5

By watching Bede at work in *HE* 2.5, it is possible to gain a valuable insight into how he used his sources to construct his narrative both here and more widely in the work, since this section is a good example in microcosm of Bede's methods in putting together much of *HE*. The result strengthens the case for seeing the catalogue of hegemons as deriving from a documentary source, since examination shows that all the material around the list in 2.5 also comes from written documents Bede possessed.

In order to understand this, it is necessary to unpack Bede's account in *HE* 2.5 step-by-step, showing how he built up the section piece-by-piece.[111] As noted at the start of this essay, the first half of 2.5 relates to Æthelberht, giving a summary of information about the king in the context of his death; the second half begins the description of the period of the 'apostasy' under Æthelberht's successor Eadbald. At the start of the chapter, after giving the year of Æthelberht's death, his years of reign and the years since the dispatch of Augustine from Rome,[112] Bede enters into the list of overlords quoted in full at the start of this article. Following this excursus, Bede returns to Æthelberht's death: he gives the calendar date of Æthelberht's passing and the number of years since he had accepted the faith, noting the location of his tomb and stating that it was in the same church as his wife Bertha's.[113] Bede then moves on to a description of Æthelberht's law code,[114] followed by part of Æthelberht's genealogy, taking his line back to Hengist.[115] Thereafter follows the second half of the chapter with the account of the 'apostasy' of Eadbald and of the East Saxons, which is only completed in the subsequent chapter, 2.6. The two halves of 2.5 are essentially discrete sections. The first part of the chapter is designed rhetorically to praise and emphasize the rule of Æthelberht, the first Christian Anglo-Saxon king, and includes links back to *HE* 1.23, the description of the dispatch of the Gregorian missionaries, to which this chapter provides something of a bookend.

Although the purpose of the first half of the chapter is rhetorical, the information Bede uses to create this picture is taken from identifiable sources. Taking only the first half of 2.5, and leaving the hegemon list aside for a moment, it is possible to deduce most of Bede's sources of information for the content he includes. The incarnational year of Æthelberht's death is probably Bede's calculation based on his knowledge of the precise date of King Eorcenberht's death, 14 July 664,[116] combined with the information from the Kentish king list he possessed, which, as was frequently the case, seems to have included regnal years.[117] The dates in these written sources would have enabled him to work back to 616 for the death of Æthelberht.[118] The regnal years provided by the Kentish king list would also have been the basis for Bede's statement about Æthelberht's fifty-six years of reign.[119]

The calendar date of Æthelberht's death, 24 February, probably came from a copy of the text of Æthelberht's epitaph. Given Bede's reference to the location of the king's tomb, it is clear that there must have been some sort of epitaph associated with the sepulchre, even if it had only identified the incumbent. A calendar date of death is given in the comparable Canterbury epitaph that Bede does include in full – that for Augustine.[120] The tangential note here in 2.5 that Bertha's tomb was, like Æthelberht's, in the church of SS Peter and Paul at Canterbury is probably a sign that her epitaph was also known to Bede. Again, knowledge of the identity of the individual in the tomb must imply some form of inscription even if it had included little more than the name.[121] Thus, documentary texts once more lay behind Bede's content in this passage.

Æthelberht's epitaph is also the most likely source for Bede's statement that the king died twenty-one years since an event. Interestingly, this figure – twenty-one years – occurs twice in the first half of 2.5, but the reference point is different on each occasion: either the sending of Augustine,[122] or the king's conversion.[123] The repetition of the figure suggests that both mentions have the same basis. Since the reference point changes, however, this basis is unlikely to be Bede's invention or calculation, or we should expect him to be more consistent. The question therefore is what the original context for the figure was. The first indication is that, whatever the source was that provided the details about the king's death, in such a notice, a reference to Æthelberht's conversion is intrinsically more likely than one to the date of the departure of Augustine and his companions from Rome. The second clue lies in the context of the reference to Æthelberht dying twenty-one years after his conversion. This comes in the same sentence as – indeed, immediately after – the Julian date of the king's death, and is directly before the detail about where he was buried. Both those pieces of information, as we have seen, probably derived from the text of the king's epitaph. It seems most likely, therefore, that, as with the calendar date of death, the twenty-one years (since Æthelberht's conversion), was originally in the text of the king's epitaph and that Bede has again derived his information from a written source in front of him.[124]

After recording the place of burial of Æthelberht and Bertha, Bede, as noted earlier, turns to the king's law code. Since the text of this code survives and since Bede makes reference to the first articles of the law – those concerning theft from the church and clergy – the obvious conclusion is that Bede possessed a copy of the laws.[125] Thus, this written text lies behind his statement here, just as the epitaph and the Kentish regnal list lay behind his earlier statements discussed above.

The mention of the law code is followed by part of Æthelberht's genealogy, taking his line back to Hengist. This list ties up with that in *HE* 1.15, of which it is a continuation. In that chapter Bede gave the first half of the *Oiscingas* family genealogy leading back from Hengist and Horsa to Woden: 'They [Hengist and Horsa] were the sons of Wihtgisl, whose father was Witta, whose father was Wecta, whose father was Woden'.[126] These two parts of the genealogy then – that in 1.15 and that in 2.5 – would almost certainly have been connected in the text in front of Bede, forming a single, unified list, the content of which Bede separated for his own purposes, using one section for his narrative about Hengist and leaving the other for his treatment of Æthelberht. As discussed earlier, such a family tree is not likely to represent a compilation of a series of deductions by Bede from originally separate sources. The two parts of the Kentish royal genealogy in the *HE* would have been taken from a single written source – a genealogy.[127]

At this point, having taken the Kentish royal genealogy back to Hengist, Bede turns away from Æthelberht to an account of the 'apostasy' in Kent under Eadbald and in Essex under the sons of Sæberht. Taking the first half of 2.5 as a discrete whole, however, Bede's process and his sources are fairly clear. The very extent of the treatment of the king is intended to draw laudatory attention to Æthelberht and to emphasize his role as the first English king to welcome Christianity. Even so, while Bede's purposes may be rhetorical, his material is not invented: it is based directly on documents. In the entire section surrounding the hegemon list, Bede is putting together his account from details in written sources to which he had access. It is effectively possible to reconstruct the contents of the desk in front of Bede: first, a Kentish king list with regnal years to calculate Æthelberht's year of death and provide his years of rule; second, the text of an epitaph for Æthelberht, for his calendar date of death, the years since conversion and implicitly the location of his remains; third, another epitaph for Bertha to provide the position of her tomb; fourth, Æthelberht's law code for the references to his legislative activity; and finally, fifth, the Kentish royal genealogy for Æthelberht's family tree.[128]

The entire account, therefore, shows Bede the historian at work, reconstructing the past from the material at hand in much the same way as modern historians do. All that is missing are the footnotes. Assembling the information compiled from documentary sources, Bede was able to construct an impressive overview of Æthelberht, underlining the king's importance. The passage is a good introduction to the way Bede often worked in the *HE*, filling in the bare bones of his documentary sources with information gained from elsewhere, even including references to discussion in other places in the *HE*. This is not to say that he used his sources without deductions or without agendas, or that none of these distorted the reality of the past; but the basis of his statements lay in the sources, and written sources at that, in front of him. The information is carefully linked together to create a magisterial narrative appearance, but the sections remain distinct enough that their origins are sufficiently traceable to allow us to see that separate documentary texts underlie each Bedan claim.

Thus, in this context – that is in the context in which the hegemon list actually appears – the theory that the catalogue of overlords was Bede's invention seems even less likely. If the hegemon list were a Bedan creation, it would stand out as unique in the first half of this chapter, and apparently, as we have already seen, in *HE* as a whole. Just as none of the other elements in this section of 2.5 is a fabrication by Bede, neither is the list of overlords. Much more probably, it is derived, as is the rest of the information in this part of the chapter, from a written source. Thus, the hegemon list, the basic structure of which can be recreated, as will shortly be seen, can be added to the materials on Bede's desk as he was preparing this part of *HE* 2.5. This text need not be from Canterbury, of course,[129] despite the list occurring in a discussion of events in Kent and surrounded by information from sources probably supplied by Nothelm and Albinus. Once sources were in Bede's possession there is no reason to doubt that Bede could work with material from different places present at the same time in front of him. As will be discussed in more detail below, given the form of the list, concluding as it does with the names of three Northumbrians, the document – at least in the form Bede knew it – is much more likely to have come from more local (for Bede), Northumbrian, sources, thus helping to explain his access to such a text.

Examination of the context for the hegemon list in the *HE* therefore supports the conclusion to which this investigation was already pointing: Bede's catalogue came from a written source. The arguments against his possession of such a text and for his invention of the list rest on circular assumptions and contradict themselves and each other; they also require us to believe that Bede was acting here in a way quite inconsistent with his practice anywhere else in the *HE*, without providing a sufficiently obvious or coherent purpose that would justify Bede's making an exception. There are no signs that Bede inserted other comparable, invented lists into the *HE*. In short, the argument for invention raises a series of problems which are all resolved by accepting that Bede's information was based on a written text in front of him.

Leaving aside these unsupported claims for the fabrication of the list, Bede's possession of a source for the catalogue seems simple common sense: from where else would he have obtained the surprising details such as the names of Ælle and Cælin? Why else, if he was not following a source, would he take the narrative off on a tangent, beyond the focus of the chapter on Æthelberht, with no identifiable ideological purpose? One explanation cuts through the Gordian knot of these questions at a single stroke: Bede's list, and its oddities, come from a source in front of him. Furthermore, the use of a documentary source as the basis of his narrative is consistent with Bede's practice in the *HE*, for example with episcopal lists, and in the very same section of 2.5 itself. This meant that as he was composing this section of *HE*, just as he had the epitaphs, the regnal list, the genealogy and the law code in front of him, so too he had a hegemon list document.

Bede's hegemon list document: reconstruction, nature, origins and provenance

The conclusion from the previous sections seems fairly clear: Bede had a hegemon list document, the basic structure of which he interlaced with other details he had gathered about the various monarchs. Stripped down to simply the list of hegemons, Bede's source can effectively be reconstructed in modern English translation.[130] Thus, the basic core of the source would have read more or less as follows:[131]

> Ælle;
> Cælin [known in their language as Ceawlin];[132]
> Æthelberht;
> Rædwald;
> Edwin;
> Oswald;
> Oswiu.[133]

The natural next questions to ask concern the list's origins and provenance. Bede's access to the source might mean that it derived from Canterbury, as did most of the other sources that Bede drew on in constructing this section of 2.5; equally, it might be a local source – something obtained from Northumbria. Looking at the form of the list and the names and kingdoms included suggests an answer. In the form in which Bede knew the text, and as reproduced above, it looks like a Northumbrian text, ending with three Northumbrian overlords.[134] Other than Æthelberht there is no name on the list associating the text with Kent, nor is there any other reason to believe that it would have been stored and maintained at Canterbury. On the other hand, the three Northumbrian kings at the end of the catalogue would make perfect sense if it had been updated and preserved in that kingdom.[135]

Northumbrian origins and provenance for the text would also, as noted above, most easily explain Bede's access to it. Thus, Bede's source was probably a locally-preserved record, rather than something sent to him. The list might well have been preserved very locally indeed. Ian Wood has made a compelling case for the use King Ecgfrith made of Wearmouth-Jarrow as a treasury and archive.[136] In that light, given that the last name on the hegemon list was Ecgfrith's father and predecessor, Oswiu, perhaps Ecgfrith stored the list in Bede's monastery for safekeeping. Even if Ecgfrith deposited the source, however, the fact that his name is not on the list makes it more likely that the document, in the form Bede knew it, dated from Oswiu's reign – presumably from some stage after his 655 victory over Penda at Winwæd.[137]

One other intriguing piece of evidence seems to point in the same direction: the apparent connections between this text and Bede's source for the larger hidage figures he gives in the *HE*.[138] Bede's references to hides in the *HE* neatly divide into two groups: a 'charter type', in which Bede sets out the amount of land gifted to an individual or a monastery and where Bede's information was often derived from charters or similar documentary sources;[139] and a 'tribute type',[140] where the references cover larger areas, either kingdoms or territorial units within them.[141] In the latter case, Bede's knowledge is most easily explained by presuming his access to a single document that contained the hidages of all the places Bede mentions and which would not have been dissimilar to the surviving 'Tribal Hidage'.[142] Such a document, by its very nature, assumes a hegemony,[143] and Bede's access to it means it is likely to be a record from the period of the seventh-century Northumbrian hegemony, rather than a more recent Mercian one. Analysis of the places named points in the same direction, with locations in areas that Bede specifically claims as falling under the power of Northumbrian hegemons: for instance, Anglesey and Man, which he associates with Edwin,[144] and Iona – in the Irish part of Britain, which he connects with Oswiu.[145] Indeed, taken as a whole, the areas with hidages given by Bede from this putative source are most consistent with our understanding of the wider power wielded by Oswiu.[146]

The coverage of Bede's 'tribal hidage' type document therefore looks like a record whose text would be consistent with a dating in Oswiu's reign, presumably, again, subsequent to his defeat of Penda in 655.[147] This has potential implications for our understanding of Bede's hegemon list document. Bede had a seventh-century text with a list of hegemons that, as we have seen, may well have come from Oswiu's reign. He also had a seventh-century document, which probably served as a tribute list – thereby implying hegemony – which again makes most sense as deriving, in the form Bede knew it, from the time of King Oswiu.

This may be more than mere coincidence. Two of Bede's hidage references of the 'tribute type' appear in association with his claims about Northumbrian hegemony and in particular that of Edwin. Bede's enumeration of the hidages of the Mevanian islands of Man and Anglesey in *HE* 2.9 are linked to his notice of Edwin's overlordship, where he notes that the king *imperio subiugauit Anglorum* the islands. That Bede directly specifies these islands implies that he was working from a source which had done the same. Bede notes in 2.9 that he had mentioned them earlier and the context of that earlier reference provides a good indication of what Bede's source was for his mention of Edwin's control over Anglesey and Man, since it occurs in 2.5 in the section including the hegemon list. In describing Edwin's power in 2.5, Bede notes: 'He even subjected to the authority of the English the Mevanian islands of the Britons'.[148] Again, the specific mention of the islands strongly suggests that Bede's statement was based on a source. Indeed, the repetition of the claim, in 2.9, along with precise hidages, makes this almost certain.

That the first mention of the islands, in 2.5, occurs in Bede's list of overlords raises the possibility that the claim about Edwin's authority over Man and Anglesey may well have been simply copied over from Bede's source for that catalogue.[149] Thus, this text, the hegemon list document, would also have been Bede's source for the statement in 2.9 that Edwin had subjected both islands to his *imperium* which Bede goes on to link with the details about their hidage assessments. This association looks like more than just chance. The connection of the details in 2.9 may suggest the connection of the information in the texts from which Bede was working. Or, to put it in terms of sources: Bede's association of the information taken from his hidage document of the 'tribute' type with that taken from his hegemon list document might well imply that the texts themselves were related, or that they were present in the same manuscript. In other words, perhaps the hegemon list document and the 'tribal hidage' type text, which, as we have already seen, apparently share a context and, probably, a provenance, were part of the same document, or were at least connected.[150]

Certainty is impossible. The subtle signs of connections between the two texts may not bear sufficient weight for firm conclusions; but it seems plausible that Bede's two sources – one a 'tribute list', implying overlordship, and one a hegemon list text, spelling out those who possessed that overlordship – may well have been part of the same, single, larger document, or associated in some way in the manuscript in front of Bede. If the two sources – the hegemon list document and Bede's 'tribal hidage' – were connected, or even in some way united, then it makes sense for the former to be from the same period as the latter. Thus, the apparent dating of Bede's hidage document of the tribute list type to the reign of Oswiu would help confirm the case made in this article for dating the hegemon list document to the same reign. Even so, it probably remains most likely that it was actually Ecgfrith who deposited the text(s) in the archives at Wearmouth-Jarrow.

Conclusions and implications for future work

Whether or not the latter conclusion concerning connections with Bede's 'tribute list' is accepted does not affect the main argument presented here: Bede possessed a written source which served as the basis for his list of hegemons in *HE* 2.5. The arguments for Bede's invention of the catalogue and against his access to such a text were never much more than assumptions and collapse on careful examination. Following the case presented above, the burden of proof now rests with those who would claim the list was Bede's invention. Use of a source explains the oddities in the passage and is consistent with Bede's behaviour in comparable places elsewhere in the *HE*, and indeed in the very same section of the very same chapter. The hegemon list document Bede drew on seems to date from Oswiu's reign – specifically, between that king's victory over Penda in 655 and his death in 670 – and was perhaps preserved at Wearmouth-Jarrow, having been left there by Ecgfrith.

The direct implications of Bede's possession of this hegemon list document are beyond the scope of the present paper. The consequences of the existence of such a text for our understanding of politics and power shifts in the seventh century require further investigation that is not possible here. Such investigation need not revive debate over the existence of the Brytenwalda or the Brytenwaldaship. There is no such title in Bede and there is no foundation in the argument in this essay to begin to believe in one again. In fact, as proposed above, rather than ever having a separate existence, the Old English term may represent no more than a translation of Latin titles that we know did exist.

It might be argued that if Bede possessed a seventh-century document with a list of overlords then this implies the existence of an office. As Dumville put it, if Bede's list came from a source, 'then there is an institution to be explained'.[151] This is possible, although the list could equally be nothing more than the attempt of someone in Oswiu's reign to associate his overlordship with the rule of other, earlier kings. Even if there were an institution to be explained, future work undertaking such an exploration needs to begin on the basis that this potential evidence for the institution is as a seventh-century one, with no inherent connection to the reference to brytenwaldas in the *Anglo-Saxon Chronicle*. Whatever the implications of the existence of such a source, effectively preserved in the pages of the *HE*, we have therein what seems to be a text from the seventh century. Thus, however difficult to interpret, it represents more primary, and presumably less anachronistic, evidence for Anglo-Saxon politics in the seventh century than Bede's own secondary account of the period.

There are lessons in this specific example, therefore, that are relevant to historians' use of the *HE* as a whole and for the treatment of Bede and similar authors from the period more broadly, which bring us back to where this article started. Bede's *History* has long been our main evidence for seventh-century England, but it is not monolithic. Not all of the content of the *HE* is of equal value in understanding the Anglo-Saxon kingdoms and their politics. Bede was a great scholar, but his writings were suffused with agency and his materials were of greatly varying quality. It is incumbent on historians to delve beneath the surface of the text of the *HE* to understand the basis of Bede's statements. Why has Bede said what he has said in each individual place? Where, and to what extent, does it reflect rhetoric or agenda? Where does it represent information from a source? And, in the latter case, what were the origins and provenance of that source? Through such an exercise – however painstaking the process sometimes needs to be – we can separate Bede's deductions from his sources. This enables historians to make more informed choices about which sources to use in reconstructing the events and world of the seventh century. In that way, it will become possible to base conclusions about the seventh century not on the *HE per se*, but on the sources, carefully analyzed, which underlie that work.

Such an examination can also cast light on Bede's methods of constructing his *History*. Given how reliant we continue to be on works like the *HE*, not only for details about the political narrative in the kingdoms upon which they focus, but also for guiding our appreciation of the early medieval world as a whole, the question of whether Bede is the sort of author who invented material is a central one. In that sense, this exercise points towards a more complicated picture of early medieval authorship, even as Bede's process has become clearer. Bede made genuine attempts to understand the past, not least through use of the sources in his possession. This should affect our treatment of the work and of apparent difficulties within it. Bede wrote with purposes in mind, and, at times, even he nods. The above discussion of the hegemon list in *HE* 2.5, however, suggests that when Bede appears to contradict himself in his *History*, a better solution is normally found by asking questions about the materials in front of him. In other words, when we find inconsistency in Bede's presentation of events, people or institutions, our first instinct should not be to blame Bede, but to try to identify his methods and sources at the same time as we are looking for his aims in writing. The more seriously we treat early medieval authors like Bede the better we will appreciate them, their histories and the worlds they were attempting to describe.

Acknowledgements

I am grateful to Alexander Callander Murray, Michael D. Elliot, Alexander Andrée, Henrietta Leyser and Henry Mayr-Harting for their comments on earlier versions of this paper, although they are not to be held responsible for the arguments, conclusions or any errors. This essay is dedicated to the memory of James Campbell.

Notes

1 Colgrave and Mynors 1991. Translations from the *HE* are my own, based on the version in that edition. See also Lapidge and Chiesa 2008–10.

2 For instance: John 1966; Vollrath-Reichelt 1971; Yorke 1981; 2009; Fanning 1991; Keynes 1992; Mayr-Harting 1994; Higham 1995, 47–73; Foot 1996; Dumville 1997; Woolf 2000; Kirby 2000a, 14–19; and Wormald 2006.

3 The translation of the latter clause is much debated; since, however, the exact import of the phrase is not relevant to the current inquiry, the present translation is intended to remain ambiguous. For views on the question see Wallace-Hadrill 1988, 59; T. Charles-Edwards in Wallace-Hadrill 1988, 220–2; Keynes 1992, 106–7; Higham 1995, 58; Brooks 1984, 63 and 341; Vollrath-Reichelt 1971, 80–8; etc.

4 *HE* 2.5: 'Qui tertius quidem in regibus gentis Anglorum cunctis australibus eorum prouinciis, quae Humbrae fluuio et contiguis ei terminis sequestrantur a borealibus, imperauit; sed primus omnium caeli regna conscendit. Nam primus imperium huiusmodi Aelli rex Australium Saxonum; secundus Caelin rex Occidentalium Saxonum, qui lingua ipsorum Ceaulin uocabatur; tertius, ut diximus, Aedilberct rex Cantuariorum; quartus Reduald rex Orientalium Anglorum, qui etiam uiuente Aedilbercto eidem suae genti ducatum praebebat, obtenuit; quintus Aeduini rex Nordanhymbrorum gentis, id est eius quae ad borealem Humbrae fluminis plagam inhabitat, maiore potentia cunctis qui Brittaniam incolunt, Anglorum pariter et Brettonum, populis praefuit, praeter Cantuariis tantum, necnon et Meuanias Brettonum insulas, quae inter Hiberniam et Brittaniam sitae sunt, Anglorum subiecit imperio; sextus Osuald, et ipse Nordanhymbrorum rex Christianissimus, hisdem finibus regnum tenuit; septimus Osuiu frater eius, aequalibus pene terminis regnum nonnullo tempore cohercens, Pictorum quoque atque Scottorum gentes, quae septentrionales Brittaniae fines tenent, maxima ex parte perdomuit ac tributarias fecit. Sed haec postmodum'.

5 Terms in this paper such as 'list' and 'catalogue' are not intended to indicate different entities: variety is purely for the sake of the reader. The same is also true for words such as 'hegemons', 'overlords' and the like.

6 Examples are too numerous to cite comprehensively, but important critiques include: Campbell 1986a and 1986b; Markus 1975; Thacker 1983; Goffart 1988; Mayr-Harting 1991, 43–5; Higham 2006; DeGregorio 2010a; together with the chapters in Lebecq, Perrin and Szerwiniack 2002; DeGregorio 2006; 2010b; and many others.

7 Probably the most influential contribution has been Keynes' rhetorically masterful piece, Keynes 1992. See also John 1966; Mayr-Harting 1994; and Higham 1995. Fanning (1991) was an exception to this general rule, believing the evidence pointed to Bede's use of a source. Barbara Yorke initially leaned towards the same conclusion (Yorke 1981), although later seemed to change her mind (Yorke 2009).

8 Dumville 1997, 353; Wormald 2006, 131–2, additional note 1. Because of the unhelpfulness of this apparently artificial term, unattested before the ninth century, its use will be avoided here in describing the hegemons listed in Bede's catalogue.

9 *HE* 2.5: 'cunctis australibus eorum prouinciis, quae Humbrae fluuio et contiguis ei terminis sequestrantur a borealibus'.

10 As found in charters from his reign such as the famous Ismere charter, S89. (Charters are referred to by Sawyer number [S] from the updated electronic version produced by Simon Keynes and Susan Kelly at esawyer.org.uk. Quotations from the charters are taken from the same website.) Other charters of Æthelbald with a similar usage include: S94, S101 and S103. See also Wormald 2006, 125, n. 32.

11 In other words, as will be shown in more detail below, even though Bede did not modify the basic content of the list from the text he found in front of him, in inserting the catalogue into the *HE*, he framed it and interpreted it according to his anachronistic understanding of the political map.

12 Higham 1995, 49.

13 For instance, Simon Keynes, after quoting the passage in *HE*, stated without qualification that in including the list, 'Bede is making a statement about shifts in the balance of power among the various kingdoms of early Anglo-Saxon England' (Keynes 1992, 105). It was only after introducing the topic and dealing with problems of language in the passage over the next couple of pages that Keynes began to consider the question of the basis of the list, but from the start he had presumed intent on Bede's behalf – and thus implicitly Bede's creation of the list. Explaining the inclusion of the first two, pagan, kings, Keynes was explicit: 'one can only suppose that Bede included them to honor their memory and perhaps carry a sense of political continuity way back to the fifth century' (Keynes 1992, 107). Henry Mayr-Harting, at the start of his consideration of the question, rejected the existence of the 'bretwaldaship', and pivoted from this to dismissal of the idea that Bede can have had a source for his list (Mayr-Harting 1994, 369). Eric John ignored all possibility of a source behind the catalogue (John 1966, 12).

14 Higham 1995, 49.

15 For instance, Mayr-Harting, after he had assumed that Bede invented the list, asked: 'what function in his [Bede's] thinking was served by this formal list of rulers having widespread *imperium*?' He offered an explanation in the next sentence: 'Surely the answer is that he conceived the bretwaldas (to use the term of the Anglo-Saxon Chronicle) as vital instruments in the spread of Christianity among the English, beyond the confines of their own kingdoms, on the Eusebian analogy of Constantine in the Roman Empire.' Mayr-Harting 1994, 369.

16 This is the attitude of Keynes 1992. It is also the approach that Mayr-Harting assigns to Patrick Wormald (Mayr-Harting 1994, 369, citing an earlier version of Wormald 2006). Despite this, Wormald's view on the issue was more nuanced, at times even implying acceptance of a source (Wormald 2006, 132, additional note 2).

17 Keynes 1992, 115.

18 As John put it: 'Bede knew perfectly well there were more than seven [hegemons], probably several more' (John 1966, 12).

19 This is also evidenced by Stephen, *Life of Wilfrid*, 20, Colgrave 1927.

20 Yorke 2009, 84.

21 Mayr-Harting 1994, 370. Or 'Northumbrian pride', in the words of Wormald (2006, 116), who also called the list 'patriotically Northumbrian' (*ibid.*, 117).

22 Dumville 1997, 352. See also Yorke 2009, 84–5.

23 In a series of connected pieces Ian Wood has made a strong case for the role of Jarrow in particular as a house designed by Ecgfrith for his own benefit: Wood 2008a; 2008b; 2010.

24 As well as, implicitly, at the end of the *recapitulatio* annals in *HE* 5.24.

25 Higham claimed that Ælle, Cælin, and even Rædwald were included by Bede because their 'reputations were still high as late as the eighth century': Higham 1995, 53 (for Ælle and Cælin) and 56 (for Rædwald). But his only evidence for this was that the kings feature in the list of overlords in 2.5. Since Higham assumed that Bede created this list himself, he could conclude that the figures must have been famous (otherwise, so the argument goes, Bede could not have known enough about them to include their names in his invented list). There is, however, no reason to think Bede knew anything else about either Ælle or Cælin (as a result, it is hardly likely that Bede included their names 'to honor their memory': Keynes 1992, 107); nor is there anything even in Bede's treatment of Rædwald elsewhere in the *HE* to suggest that he had separate grounds for believing that the king controlled anywhere other than East Anglia, let alone that he had an eighth-century reputation for wielding a broad overlordship. These facts are not, as Higham (1995, 52) claimed, 'irrelevant' to his own argument since he made claims about these figures' reputations in the eighth century based simply on their presence in the *HE* in the hegemon list. The argument for Bede's invention of the list turns out to be circular, and we are thrown back on to the apparently unanswerable question of why Bede would invent a list in the first place, and one at odds with his other information. Where there are contradictions like this in the *HE* a much more plausible explanation is that Bede, respecting the evidence of a written source, has simply retained its structure and content, than that he has invented the material himself.

26 Keynes 1992, 110.

27 A similar point was made by Wormald (2006, 132, additional note 2).

28 Keynes 1992, 110.

29 Other perceived inconsistencies between the catalogue and information elsewhere in the *HE* have frequently been commented on: see, for instance, Plummer 1896, 2.86. See also Yorke 1981, 195–6, n. 19. Fanning called it a 'tangled passage' and a 'jumble of inconsistent information' (Fanning 1991, 16). Keynes felt it verged at times on 'nonsense' (Keynes 1992, 109). The specifics of these claims of confusion are not directly relevant to the issue at hand and so will not be discussed here; suffice it to say, however, that this type of lack of coherence is not what the evidence of the rest of the *HE* would lead us to expect from Bede. Furthermore, as noted above, the passage is not written with Bede's customary clarity, a sign perhaps that Bede himself was not very convinced of the list's consistency with the other information he possessed. This would be very surprising if the catalogue were indeed Bede's creation. Such signs do, however, make sense on the view that Bede based his list on a documentary source offering a picture which conflicted with that emerging from his other evidence and which he thus felt needed to be augmented or qualified. Keynes used the inconsistencies in Bede's account to bolster an argument against the existence of an early Anglo-Saxon hegemonic office. That is a question beyond the scope of this paper. For present purposes, it is enough to repeat that any such inconsistencies do not support the theory that Bede invented the list, but rather point in the opposite direction.

30 See the comment in the textual introduction to Colgrave and Mynors 1991, xxxix: 'In the whole work, as it appears in the consensus of our oldest and best copies, there are perhaps thirty-two places (in nearly 300 printed pages) where some defect of sense or syntax suggests that correction is required. But even this small quantum of error is not what it seems. In twenty-six of these places, Bede is transcribing from an earlier source: there are four, for example, in i. 17 and 20 where he is drawing on the *Vita sancti Germani*, four in i. 27 the *Libellus Responsionum* of St. Gregory, fourteen in the various papal letters which he has incorporated.'

31 Keynes 1992, 109. The examples he gave were *HE* 3.20; 3.24; 4.5; and 4.12 (Keynes 1992, 119, n. 42).

32 *HE* 3.24: 'Primus autem in prouincia Merciorum, simul et Lindisfarorum ac Mediterraneorum Anglorum, factus est episcopus Diuma, ut supra diximus, qui apud Mediterraneos Anglos defunctus ac sepultus est; secundus Cellach, qui relicto episcopatus officio uiuens ad Scottiam rediit, uterque de genere Scottorum; tertius Trumheri, de natione quidem Anglorum, sed edoctus et ordinatus a Scottis, qui erat abbas in monasterio quod dicitur Ingetlingum'. Bede then goes on to repeat the story of the foundation of that monastery (first told in 3.14).

33 In fact, this is a somewhat strange example for Keynes to use, given that the whole focus of his argument was to reject the idea that there was a hegemonic office, whereas it is quite clear there was an office of bishop.

34 See, for instance, Jones 1947, 46, 82, 88 etc; Harrison 1976, 97; Kirby 2000b, 72 and 77; Wallace-Hadrill 1988, 4; etc.

35 For background on Anglo-Saxon episcopal lists, including analysis of some of the few surviving examples, see Page 1965–66.

36 In the *HE* Preface, Bede seems to be making explicit reference to his access to episcopal lists, explaining that he learned about 'episcopal succession' (*successio sacerdotalis*) in Lindsey thanks to Bishop Cyneberht. Bede also claims in the Preface that his knowledge of the early bishops of Kent, Essex, Wessex and East Anglia came from Albinus, abbot of SS Peter and Paul's monastery at Canterbury: again, this is most naturally understood as a reference to

Albinus' provision of episcopal lists for the sees in question. The maintenance of episcopal lists in the Anglo-Saxon church is also apparently mandated by canon VIII of Theodore's 672 Council of Hertford: *HE* 4.5.

37 As Barbara Yorke put it: 'There are a large number of lists in the history, chiefly regnal and episcopal, but no one has suggested that Bede was responsible for drawing them all up' (Yorke 1981, 195, n. 19).

38 Mayr-Harting 1994.

39 Higham 1995.

40 John 1966.

41 Mayr-Harting 1994, 369.

42 *HE* 2.16.

43 *HE* 3.2.

44 Mayr-Harting 1994, 370–1.

45 This is not to suggest that Bede fabricated these stories. I take it as read that there was a proverb about peace under Edwin in Bede's time, that Oswald did set up a cross at Heavenfield, and that Oswiu did oversee a synod.

46 Furthermore Oswiu, at least, comes in for some Bedan criticism elsewhere, for instance in *HE* 3.14, for *miserrima* ('most wretchedly') killing the saintly Oswine.

47 Nor, of course, is there any comparable list in Eusebius' own *History*.

48 *HE* 2.15.

49 Mayr-Harting 1994, 370.

50 *Ibid.*, 370.

51 *Ibid.*, 369.

52 *HE* 2.15. The best that can be said for him in this context is that his victory over Æthelfrith permitted Edwin to become king of Northumbria, but this does not make him a champion of spreading the faith for Bede: overall Rædwald's rule clearly slowed the progress of conversion.

53 Fanning 1991, 20.

54 Higham 1995, 52.

55 As Higham himself acknowledged in an endnote (Higham 1995, 70, n. 22).

56 Or even perhaps Edwin, given that Bede credits Rædwald with the victory over Æthelfrith (*HE* 2.12); although Edwin did defeat the West Saxons (*HE* 2.9). One might also note that, for the comparable period, Penda's victories were probably the most impressive, yet he was not on the list.

57 John 1966, 12.

58 Indeed, John left implicit and unresolved the apparent tension in his case between arguing for the reality of the office while rejecting Bede's list as an invention.

59 Wormald 2006, 107–8. On the *Historia Britonnum*, see, for instance, Dumville 1975–76.

60 There is a good introduction to the use of numerological theory in Anglo-Saxon England, including an extensive bibliography, in Major 2010. See now also Major 2013.

61 This seems to have been behind the shift in Barbara Yorke's position. Together with Steven Fanning, Yorke had been one of the few to suggest that Bede's catalogue depended on a source (Yorke 1981). In her later work, however, she accepted that Bede was responsible for the form of the list and specifically cited the numerological issue and Mayr-Harting's arguments for its importance as evidence (Yorke 2009, 85).

62 Mayr-Harting saw Bede's choice of seven figures as underpinning the 'Eusebian function', since, so he argued, for Bede, as for Gregory the Great, 'the number seven is the height of perfection'. The number seven represented the 'universal validity' that, on the alleged analogy of Constantine, these rulers were supposed to have possessed. Mayr-Harting (1994, 372) went on to show how Gregory used the figure seven to represent both universality and perfection. As will be seen below, however, the quotes Mayr-Harting gave from Bede's own exegesis to demonstrate the same point do not make it nearly so well. Eric John, as noted above, took the seven as a deliberate attempt on Bede's behalf to match a British tradition represented by an allegedly similar list in the *Historia Brittonum* (John 1966, 12). For Higham, the relevance of the seven was that it was 'a number of very special significance in the early Church, for the creation of the world was complete on the seventh day which God blessed' (Higham 1995, 55).

63 One sense is completion and the other is spiritual grace, understood as the gifts of the Holy Spirit (Mayr-Harting 1994, 372). Neither meaning is identical to that Mayr-Harting cited Gregory the Great as favouring (see previous note).

64 One can envisage a situation where a number was used for rhetorical effect, because of the echoes of significance it might inspire in readers, rather than requiring a fully worked out specific meaning. But that is not relevant here. Such an implicit effect would not justify inventing the entire list simply to achieve it. Given that the argument is that Bede invented the list and that the evidence of this is that there are seven names on it, there must be some clear and comprehensible meaning of the number seven in this context that Bede intends. In reality, the varying interpretations by modern commentators show that this is not the case and that, therefore, the simple fact that there are seven overlords on the list is no evidence for Bede's invention of it.

65 Despite the weaknesses in Mayr-Harting's numerological arguments – and despite how influential his use of them has been – it should be noted in Mayr-Harting's defence that much of the numerological case was not part of the paper as it was initially delivered, but was only added later: see Mayr-Harting 1994, 367, n. 1.

66 Higham claimed that Æthelberht's position – third on the list – was also exegetically significant. He suggested that this may have been a sign of Bede's intention to associate Æthelberht with the coming of the Holy Spirit to the English. Or a reminder of the number of ships that carried the Saxons to Britain. Or the claim that three tribes had migrated from Germany. Or something unexplained to do with the 'Tribal Hidage' (Higham 1995, 55). In other words, there is no identifiable meaning. The idea that the number of ships and the Holy Spirit might be equally valid interpretations of the fact that Æthelberht is third reveals the weakness of the theory as an explanation.

67 Mayr-Harting 1994, 372, n. 20.

68 Furthermore, for a medieval exegete every number was full of significance: had there been six or eight, or however many hegemons, the figure could still be claimed to have been significant to Bede. Only, the same question would remain: what significance? In exegetical terms, there is nothing of particularly royal or imperial implication about the number seven.

69 Keynes 1992, 120, n. 47.

70 *HE* 1.1: 'Haec in praesenti iuxta numerum librorum quibus lex diuina scripta est, quinque gentium linguis unam eandemque summae ueritatis et uerae sublimitatis scientiam scrutatur et confitetur (At the present time, there are five languages in Britain, just as the divine law is written in five books, all devoted to seeking out and setting forth one and the same kind of wisdom, namely the knowledge of sublime truth and of true sublimity)'.

71 Moreover, there is no question here about the artificiality of the number, simply because Bede plays on its numerology; no one would deny that these five languages were used in Britain at the time. Bede later refers to the speakers of four languages in Britain (*HE* 3.6); but there the context is different. In *HE* 1.1 the reference is to the languages used in Britain; in *HE* 3.6, the languages refer to the peoples (*nationes*) speaking them who were under Oswald's hegemony. This does not exclude Latin (the fifth language) being spoken among all of these peoples, the point Bede is making in 1.1.

72 None of this, of course, is to deny the potential presence in the *HE* of 'Easter eggs', to use the terminology of modern computer programmers: that is, numbers hidden in the *HE* with alternative references to which Bede did not draw attention – such as the description of the synod of Whitby in 3.25, mirroring the incarnational year, 325, of the Council of Nicaea. This is quite a different situation from the seven hegemons listed in 2.5, however. There is no thought that Bede is inventing the synod of Whitby, as historians have claimed he is doing with the list of hegemons.

73 Indeed, there is good reason, as Timothy Furry has shown, to treat suggestions of allegorical intention in the *HE* with extreme caution: Bede neither offers figural exegesis of history in the *HE*, nor presents the work as material for exegesis by others (Furry 2013, 44–63). The underlying reason for this is clear. History and exegesis represent quite different genres. Bede's exegesis was commentary on the Word of God, not a history. There is no reason to believe Bede considered his *History* to be equatable to God's words, whose symbolic interpretation – whatever that interpretation – would be an asset to the audience. In contrast, in his *Commentary on Genesis*, Bede specifically warns anyone who had devoted 'attention to the allegorical sense, how far he may have forsaken the manifest truth of history by allegorical interpretation' (Bede, *On Genesis*, I, 25–31: 'Sed diligenter intuendum ut ita quisque sensibus allegoricis studium impendat, quatenus apertam historiae fidem allegorizando derelinquat'. Translation from Kendall 2008, 69).

74 Mayr-Harting 1994, 370.

75 Called the 'climax and endpoint' by Higham (1995, 62).

76 Although – and this is a further difficulty for such interpretations – Bede's treatment of Oswiu in the rest of the *HE*, as noted above, does not actually reflect a vision of that monarch as the model of perfection.

77 As he put it: to 'write up Æthelberht's reputation' (Higham 1995, 58).

78 Higham 1995, 55. See note 66 above.

79 For Higham (1995, 65), resolution of this difficulty lay in 'Bede's own Bernician prejudices'. But how then can it be argued that the list was only invented in order to praise Æthelberht? Higham's explanation fails to satisfy: 'At this point his [Bede's] purposes transcended those which had led him to start the list'. A reader perhaps might ask, rather, whether the evidence had not transcended the argument.

80 *HE* 2.5: 'sed haec postmodum'.

81 Dumville 1997, 352.

82 Peter Hunter Blair noted that the passage with the hegemon list, 'interrupts the flow of his [Bede's] narrative' (Hunter Blair 1977, 199), and called it a 'digression' (p. 200).

83 As Yorke pointed out, this is a good example of how Bede 'inserted such lists into the text somewhat awkwardly, taking the mention of a prominent member of the list as an opportunity to reproduce part or all of the rest of it' (Yorke 1981, 195, n. 19).

84 Indeed, the fact that he includes more overlords than are relevant in the context of *HE* 2.5 is a sign that Bede has copied all the names on the list from the text in front of him rather than simply excerpting certain individuals.

85 This delineation of the border is present in *HE* 2.5, and repeated in a similar form to describe the extent of Æthelberht's power in 1.25 and 2.3, as well as that of Æthelbald for 731 in 5.23.

86 *ASC* 827, *recte* 829.

87 Keynes' argument is the most obvious example of this; but it is also implicit in Eric John's case.

88 Keynes 1992, 113–15, gave a tour of some of the views propounded by earlier commentators.

89 For instance by Bruce-Mitford (1975, 689–717).

90 Keynes 1992, 115.

91 Keynes 1992, 110.

92 Wormald 2006, 131–2, additional note 1.

93 Examples of charters with this kind of language include Æthelbald's Ismere charter, S89. See also S155, a charter of Coenwulf, referring to Offa. As Yorke (1981, 181) pointed out, the parallel term *decus Britanniae* was also used of Offa in one of Alcuin's letters. Other similar examples include Asser's description of Alfred as 'omnium Brittanniae insulae Christianorum rector', in his dedicatory prologue to the king.

94 Not that this term was in the text of the *HE*, of course, but it was at least a phrase in political currency in the ninth century and which the Chronicler could have felt an apt one to describe generically these rulers' powers.

95 S427 is a charter of Athelstan of doubtful authenticity; but its reliability is not the issue here. What matters is that the word 'brytænwalda' was used as a translation of the Latin – and that the latter came first. Keynes' confusing statement (Keynes 1992, 111) that the draftsmen of this charter 'used it in a way that can only mean "wide ruler"', was probably no more than a simple slip.

96 As had been assumed, for instance, by John (1966, 8).

97 Asser, *Life of King Alfred*, Prologue, Stevenson 1959.

98 For instance, Keynes 1992, 109.

99 Indeed, the very inclusion of Northumbrians seems opposed to his view that the hegemony represented rule over 'cunctis australibus eorum prouinciis, quae Humbrae fluuio et contiguis ei terminis sequestrantur a borealibus (all the southern kingdoms, which are divided from the north by the river Humber and the surrounding territory)'. Other contradictions with information elsewhere in the *HE* have already been commented on above. The best summary remains Plummer 1896, 2.86.

100 See the discussion recorded at the end of Dumville 1997, 372–3, and also Kirby 2000a, 18–19.

101 *HE* 5.23: 'Et hae omnes prouinciae ceteraeque australes ad confinium usque Humbrae fluminis cum suis quaeque regibus Merciorum regi Aedilbaldo subiectae sunt (All these kingdoms and the other southern kingdoms which reach right up to the Humber, together with their various kings, are subject to Æthelbald, king of Mercia)'.

102 The Ismere charter is S89. Other charters of Æthelbald with a similar usage include: S94, S101 and S103. See also Wormald 2006, 125, n. 32.

103 This same charter, as seen above, called Æthelbald '*rex Britanniæ*'.

104 *Life of Gregory the Great*, 18, Colgrave 1985, mentions a certain priest Trimma from a monastery of the *Sudranglorum* in the time of Æthelred, *regis illorum*.

105 Keynes (1992, 121, n. 57) implied that the language of S89 could have been inspired by the *HE*, since this was completed before that particular diploma was written. But the influence is much more likely to have operated in the other direction: that is, Mercian protocols affecting Bede rather than Bede being the basis of charter language to describe the power of Mercian kings.

106 *HE* 5.23.

107 For instance, the description of the power of Rædwald of the East Angles, or of the peoples controlled by the Northumbrian monarchs.

108 In Yorke's words, Bede was 'projecting back the Humber as a major political boundary between northern and southern peoples into the sixth and early seventh centuries' (Yorke 2009, 84). Keynes (1992, 109) actually hinted in the same direction, although, confusingly, he also argued that the inconsistency of Bede's description of the scope of the overlordship with the power actually wielded by the listed hegemons was a sign that Bede had invented the list. See also Kirby 2000a, 18–19.

109 Bede's own refinements of the descriptions of the frontiers of authority of individual kings in the list shows that he himself recognized the limitations of the phrase as a general historical summary.

110 Once again, the apparent contradictions between Bede's gloss and the scope of actual power of the individuals on the list, as evidenced mainly by content elsewhere in the *HE*, is a further sign that the catalogue was not his own creation. If the list had been his invention then we should expect that the description of the hegemons' power, which was his insertion, would have been more consistent with the power of the individuals he had chosen.

111 The following summarizes the more detailed account of Bede's process in *HE* 2.5 presented in Shaw 2018.

112 'Anno ab incarnatione dominica DCXVI, qui est annus uicesimus primus ex quo Augustinus cum sociis ad praedicandum genti Anglorum missus est, Aedilberct rex Cantuariorum post regnum temporale, quod L et sex annis gloriosissime tenuerat, aeterna caelestis regni gaudia subiit (In the year of our Lord 616, the twenty-first year after Augustine and his companions had been sent to preach to the English nation, King Æthelberht of Kent, after ruling

his temporal kingdom most gloriously for fifty-six years, entered upon the eternal joys of the heavenly kingdom)'.

113 'Defunctus uero est rex Aedilberct die XXIIII mensis Februarii post XX et unum annos acceptae fidei, atque in porticu sancti Martini intro ecclesiam beatorum apostolorum Petri et Pauli sepultus, ubi et Berctae regina condita est (King Æthelberht died on 24 February, twenty-one years after he had accepted the faith, and was buried in the chapel of St Martin, within the church of the Apostles SS Peter and Paul, where his queen, Bertha, also lies)'.

114 'Qui inter cetera bona quae genti suae consulendo conferebat, etiam decreta illi iudiciorum iuxta exempla Romanorum cum consilio sapientium constituit; quae conscripta Anglorum sermone hactenus habentur et obseruantur ab ea. In quibus primitus posuit, qualiter id emendare deberet, qui aliquid rerum uel ecclesiae uel episcopi uel reliquorum ordinum furto auferret, uolens scilicet tuitionem eis, quos et quorum doctrinam susceperat, praestare (Among other benefits that he conferred upon the people under his care, he established with the advice of his counsellors a code of laws following the examples of the Romans. These are written in English and are still kept and observed by the people. Among these he set down first of all what restitution must be made by anyone who steals anything belonging to the church or the bishop or any other clergy; these laws were designed to give protection to those whose coming and whose teaching he had welcomed)'.

115 'Erat autem idem Aedilberct filius Irminrici, cuius pater Octa, cuius pater Oeric cognomento Oisc, a quo reges Cantuariorum solent Oiscingas cognominare, cuius pater Hengist, qui cum filio suo Oisc inuitatus a Uurtigerno Brittaniam primus intrauit, ut supra retulimus (Now Æthelberht was the son of Eormenric, whose father was Octa, whose father was Oeric whose surname was Oisc, whence the kings of Kent are known as Oiscingas. Oisc's father was Hengist, who with his son Oisc first entered Britain at the invitation of Vortigern, as related above)'.

116 *HE* 4.1.

117 These are included in the *HE* for Æthelberht (ruled fifty-six years: *HE* 2.5); Eorcenberht (twenty-four years – and some months (?): 3.8); Ecgberht (nine years: 4.5 and 4.26); Hlothere (eleven years and seven months: 4.5; simplified to twelve years: 4.26); Eadric (one year and a half: 4.26). Bede also gives the length of reign for Wihtred (thirty-four and a half years: 5.23), but this information is unlikely to have reached him at the same stage as the other dates; it may even have been Bede's own calculation.

118 This regnal list was probably provided to Bede by Albinus, via Nothelm, in the process set out in the *HE*'s preface.

119 Regnal years were frequently found in king lists and Bede makes direct reference to 'cunctis ... regum tempora computantibus (all those who compute the dates of kings)', in *HE* 3.1. Northumbrian king lists are likely to have been one of the key foundations for most of Bede's calculations of the years for Northumbrian monarchs – even up to Ida, whose accession in 547 and twelve years of reign are recorded in the annals in 5.24. On the latter point, see, for instance, Hunter Blair 1959, 141; and more generally on king lists: Hunter Blair 1950; Dumville 1976; Dumville 1977; and Thornton 2001.

120 *HE* 2.3: 'defunctus est septima kalendas Iunias (he died on 26 May)'. Bede did not know the year of Augustine's death, although the evidence exists to reconstruct when it must have been: Shaw 2016a.

121 In both cases copies of the texts of the epitaphs are most reasonably understood as having been supplied to Bede by Albinus via Nothelm. It is not impossible that Bede recorded them himself on a visit to Canterbury, but we have no evidence for such a visit, whereas this type of source would be entirely in line with Bede's description in the *HE* Preface of the material that Albinus collected and sent to Bede with Nothelm on the latter's first visit with resources for the *History*.

122 '[A]nnus uicesimus primus ex quo Augustinus cum sociis ad praedicandum genti Anglorum missus est'.

123 '[P]ost XX et unum annos acceptae fidei'.

124 The difference between Bede's calculation of the incarnational date of Æthelberht's death, 616, and the implication of the dating of the king's baptism twenty-one years before that – implicitly, 596 – that is, before Bede believed Augustine arrived (given as 597 in the *recapitulatio* in 5.24), probably explains why he adjusted the claim slightly at the start of the chapter, to relate the 'twenty-one years' to the departure of the mission from Rome which was in 596, as Bede knew from the Gregorian letters. Such an allusion also served Bede's purposes of subtly connecting this chapter in the reader's mind with 1.23. In repeating the figure later in the chapter, in its more correct context, however, Bede returned to the original meaning, and perhaps even wording.

125 Again, this would almost certainly have been supplied by Albinus.

126 *HE* 1.15: 'Erant [Hengist et Horsa] autem filii Uictgisli, cuius pater Uitta, cuius pater Uecta, cuius pater Uoden'.

127 The provenance of that source relating to the kings of Kent is likely to have been Canterbury and Albinus.

128 Indeed, as others have suggested, the lawcode and the genealogy may even have been in the same manuscript (Wallace-Hadrill 1988, 61). See also, Wormald 1977, 134.

129 As Wallace-Hadrill (1988, 58) presumed.

130 Whether the original was in Latin or Old English is probably now unknowable.

131 The following represents the bare minimum of information deducible as being in Bede's source.

132 As Wormald noted, Bede's knowledge of different forms for Cælin's name is a further point in favour of his use of a source: 'I am struck by his [Bede's] ability to give Anglian (or Kentish) as well as West Saxon forms of Ceawlin's name, implying that his status *was* somehow acknowledged by others than West Saxons' (Wormald 2006, 132, additional note 2 (emphasis in original)).

133 For all of the rulers other than Oswiu, Bede also gives the name of the people from which they came. It is possible that Bede's source provided him with this information. If so, then several of the designations Bede includes almost certainly represent his alterations from earlier terms in the text: this is likely for 'South Saxons', for Ælle, and 'West Saxons', for Cælin (Kirby 2000a, 19), and the anachronistic *Nordanhymbri*, for Edwin and Oswald.

134 The first four names on the list may suggest that this Northumbrian text represented the extension of a pre-existing southern original, although the 'document' is too short to propose a proper redactional history.

135 Incidentally, this is another argument for believing Bede included the entirety of the list. Had the source originally listed kings beyond Oswiu, reaching into Bede's own day, it would have ended with Mercian names, and presumably, therefore, have been more likely to have been maintained and derived from that kingdom rather than Northumbria. Bede had very meagre sources of information for Mercia, however, and it is difficult to imagine that he could have accessed archival material from that kingdom, including such a list. In contrast, Bede's access to a seventh-century source recording Northumbrian hegemony – possibly even preserved in his own monastery – is much more likely.

136 Wood 2008a; 2008b; and 2010.

137 *HE* 3.24. The Mercian nobility's 658 rebellion against Oswiu and their installation of Wulfhere as Mercian king must have damaged Oswiu's hegemony, but perhaps not sufficiently to make 658 a firm *terminus ante quem* for the production of the text. As seen above, the anachronistic delineation of the geographical borders of the hegemony given in *HE* 2.5 is no guide to the date of Bede's source, since this description represents no more than Bede's assumption, based on circumstances in his own times, read back into the past.

138 The following description summarizes the case for Bede's use of a hidage document, resembling the 'Tribal Hidage', set out in more detail in Shaw 2016b, 425–34.

139 Shaw 2016b, 412–25.

140 Such a term is, hopefully, general enough to cover the range of possibilities from taxation to a more traditionally 'barbaric' interpretation. There is neither the space nor the need to enter into the debate about the precise uses of such documents here.

141 There are nine in this group: 1.25 – Thanet (600 hides); 2.9 – Anglesey (960 hides) and the Isle of Man (over 300 hides); 3.4 – Iona (five hides); 3.24 – Southern Mercia (5,000 hides) and Northern Mercia (7,000 hides); 4.13 – Sussex (7,000 hides); 4.16[14] – Isle of Wight (7,000 hides); and 4.19[17] – Ely (600 hides).

142 Shaw 2016b, 425–9. On the Tribal Hidage see, for instance, Dumville 1989.

143 As John (1966, 13) noted: the power to take tribute is the 'most obvious attribute of this hegemony'. A similar point had been made by Corbett (1900, 207–8).

144 In 2.5 and 2.9.

145 In 2.5.

146 Shaw 2016b, 432–3. The inclusion of Southern Mercia, a subdivision apparently made by that king, is particularly telling: *HE* 3.24.

147 Although, once more, Bede's access to such a source is most simply explained if it were Ecgfrith who had deposited the text in the Wearmouth-Jarrow archives.

148 *HE* 2.5: 'necnon et Meuanias Brettonum insulas … Anglorum subiecit imperio'.

149 The use of the word *imperium* in both 2.5 and 2.9 is another indication in the same direction. For Bede's use of this term see Fanning 1991, 7–22.

150 One other point: in 2.5, Bede says Edwin *subiecit imperio* the Mevanian islands (and *imperio subiugauit* in 2.9). Colgrave translated this as 'brought under [English] rule' (or 'power' in 2.9), but something like 'made tributary' would work just as well.

151 Dumville 1997, 354.

Abbreviations

ASC *Anglo-Saxon Chronicle*.

HE Bede, *Historia Ecclesiastica*.

Charters are referred to by Sawyer number [S] from the updated electronic version produced by Simon Keynes and Susan Kelly at esawyer.org.uk.

Bibliography

Brooks, N. 1984. *The Early History of the Church of Canterbury*, London: Leicester University Press.

Bruce-Mitford, R. 1975. *The Sutton Hoo Ship Burial, I, Excavations, Background, the Ship, Dating and Inventory*, London: British Museum.

Campbell, J. 1986a. 'Bede I', in J. Campbell (ed.), *Essays in Anglo-Saxon History*, 1–27, London: Hambledon Press.

Campbell, J. 1986b. 'Bede II', in J. Campbell (ed.), *Essays in Anglo-Saxon History*, 29–48, London: Hambledon Press.

Colgrave, B. (ed. and trans.) 1927. *The Life of Bishop Wilfrid by Eddius Stephanus*, Cambridge: Cambridge University Press.

Colgrave, B. (ed. and trans.) 1985. *The Earliest Life of Gregory the Great by an Anonymous Monk of Whitby*, Cambridge: Cambridge University Press.

Colgrave, B. and Mynors, R. (ed. and trans.) 1991. *Bede's Ecclesiastical History of the English People*, Oxford: Oxford University Press.

Corbett, W. 1900. 'The Tribal Hidage', *Trans. of the Royal Hist. Soc.*, **14**, 187–230.

DeGregorio, S. (ed.) 2006. *Innovation and Tradition in the Writings of the Venerable Bede*, Morgantown: West Virginia University Press.

DeGregorio, S. 2010a. 'Monasticism and Reform in Book IV of Bede's "Ecclesiastical History of the English People"', *Jnl Ecclesiastical Hist.*, **61.4**, 673–87.

DeGregorio, S. (ed.) 2010b. *The Cambridge Companion to Bede*, Cambridge: Cambridge University Press.

Dumville, D. 1975–76. 'Nennius and the *Historia Brittonum*', *Studia Celtica*, **10–1**, 78–95.

Dumville, D. 1976. 'The Anglian Collection of Royal Genealogies and Regnal Lists', *Anglo-Saxon England*, **5**, 23–50.

Dumville, D. 1977. 'Kingship, Genealogies and Regnal Lists', in P. Sawyer and I. Wood (eds.), *Early Medieval Kingship*, 72–104, Leeds: University of Leeds.

Dumville, D. 1989. 'The Tribal Hidage: an Introduction to its Texts and their History', in S. Bassett (ed.), *The Origins of Anglo-Saxon Kingdoms*, 225–30, Leicester: Leicester University Press.

Dumville, D. 1997. 'The Terminology of Overkingship in Early Anglo-Saxon England', in J. Hines (ed.), *The Anglo-Saxons from the Migration Period to the Eighth Century: An Ethnographic Perspective*, 345–73, Woodbridge: Boydell Press.

Fanning, S. 1991. 'Bede, *Imperium*, and the Bretwaldas', *Speculum*, **66**, 1–26.

Foot, S. 1996. 'The Making of *Angelcynn*: English Identity before the Norman Conquest', *Trans. of the Royal Hist. Soc.*, **6.6**, 25–49.

Furry, T. 2013. *Allegorizing History: the Venerable Bede, Figural Exegesis and Historical Theory*, Eugene, Oregon: Pickwick Publications.

Goffart, W. 1988. *The Narrators of Barbarian History (AD 550–800): Jordanes, Gregory of Tours, Bede and Paul the Deacon*, Princeton: Princeton University Press.

Harrison, K. 1976. *The Framework of Anglo-Saxon History to A.D. 900*, Cambridge: Cambridge University Press.

Higham, N. 1995. *An English Empire: Bede and the Early Anglo-Saxon Kings*, Manchester: Manchester University Press.

Higham, N. 2006. *(Re-)Reading Bede: the* Ecclesiastical History *in Context*, Abingdon: Routledge.

Hunter Blair, P. 1950. 'The *Moore Memoranda* on Northumbrian History', in C. Fox and B. Dickens (eds.), *The Early Cultures of North-West Europe*, 245–57, Cambridge: Cambridge University Press.

Hunter Blair, P. 1959. 'Bernicians and their Northern Frontier', in N. Chadwick (ed.), *Celt and Saxon: Studies in the Early British Border*, 137–62, Cambridge: Cambridge University Press.

Hunter Blair, P. 1977. *An Introduction to Anglo-Saxon England*, Cambridge: Cambridge University Press.

John, E. 1966. '"Orbis Britanniae" and the Anglo-Saxon Kings', in E. John (ed.), *Orbis Britanniae and Other Studies*, 1–63, Bristol: Leicester University Press.

Jones, C. 1947. *Saints' Lives and Chronicles*, Ithaca: Cornell University Press.

Kendall, C. (trans.) 2008. *Bede: On Genesis*, Liverpool: Liverpool University Press.

Keynes, S. 1992. 'Rædwald the Bretwalda', in C. Kendall and P. Wells (eds.), *Voyage to the Other World: the Legacy of Sutton Hoo*, 103–23, Minneapolis: University of Minnesota Press.

Kirby, D. 2000a. *The Earliest English Kings*, London: Routledge.

Kirby, D. 2000b. 'Bede's Native Sources for the *Historia ecclesiastica*', in D. Pelteret (ed.), *Anglo-Saxon History: Basic Readings*, 55-81, New York and London: Garland Publishing.

Lapidge, M. (ed.) and Chiesa, P. (trans.) 2008–10. *Beda, Storia degli inglesi*, 2 vols, Rome: Fondazione Lorenzo Valla.

Lebecq, S., Perrin, M. and Szerwiniack, O. (eds.) 2002. *The Venerable Bede: Tradition and Posterity*, Lille: Université Charles de Gaulle.

Major, T. 2010. 'Literary Developments of the Table of Nations and the Tower of Babel in Anglo-Saxon England', unpublished PhD thesis, University of Toronto.

Major, T. 2013. 'The Number Seventy-Two: Biblical and Hellenistic Beginnings to the Early Middle Ages', *Sacris Erudiri*, **52**, 7–46.

Markus, R. 1975. *Bede and the Tradition of Ecclesiastical Historiography*, Jarrow: St Paul's Church.

Mayr-Harting, H. 1991. *The Coming of Christianity to Anglo-Saxon England*, Penn: Pennsylvania State University Press.

Mayr-Harting, H. 1994. 'Bede's Patristic Thinking as an Historian', in A. Scharer and G. Scheibelreiter (eds.), *Historiographie im frühen Mittelalter*, 367–74, Vienna and Munich: Oldenbourg.

Page, R. 1965–66. 'Anglo-Saxon Episcopal lists', Parts 1–2 and 3, *Nottingham Mediaeval Stud.*, **9** and **10**, 71–95 and 2–24.

Plummer, C. (ed.) 1896. *Bedae Opera Historica*, 2 vols, Oxford: Clarendon.

Shaw, R. 2016a. 'When did Augustine of Canterbury die?', *Jnl Ecclesiastical Hist.*, **67.3**, 473–91.

Shaw, R. 2016b. 'Bede's sources for his references to "hides" in the *Ecclesiastical History* and the *History of the Abbots*', *Hist. Research*, **89.245**, 412–34.

Shaw, R. 2018. *Methodology and Sources in Bede's Narrative of the Gregorian Mission to Kent*, Abingdon and New York: Routledge.

Stevenson, W. (ed.) 1959. *Asser's Life of King Alfred*, Oxford: Oxford University Press.

Thacker, A. 1983. 'Bede's Ideal of Reform', in P. Wormald (ed.), *Ideal and Reality in Frankish and Anglo-Saxon Society: Studies Presented to J. M. Wallace-Hadrill*, 130–53, Oxford: Blackwell.

Thornton, D. 2001. 'Regnal Lists', in M. Lapidge, with J. Blair, S. Keynes and D. Scragg (eds.), *The Blackwell Encyclopaedia of Anglo-Saxon England*, 388–9, Oxford: Blackwell.

Vollrath-Reichelt, H. 1971. *Königsgedanke und Königtum bei den Angelsachsen bis zur Mitte des 9. Jahrhunderts*, Cologne-Graz: Böhlau.

Wallace-Hadrill, J. 1988. *Bede's Ecclesiastical History of the English People: a Historical Commentary*, Oxford: Oxford University Press.

Wood, I. 2008a. 'Monasteries and the Geography of Power in the Age of Bede', *Northern Hist.*, **45.1**, 1–25.

Wood, I. 2008b. *The Origins of Jarrow: the Monastery, the Slake and Ecgfrith's Minster*, Jarrow: Bede's World.

Wood, I. 2010. 'The Foundation of Bede's Wearmouth-Jarrow', in S. DeGregorio (ed.), *Cambridge Companion*, 84–96.

Woolf, A. 2000. 'Community, Identity and Kingship in Early England', in W. Frazer and A. Tyrrell (eds.), *Social Identity in Early Medieval Britain*, 91–110, Continuum: Leicester.

Wormald, P. 1977. '*Lex Scripta* and *Verbum Regis*: Legislation and Germanic Kingship, from Euric to Cnut', in P. Sawyer and I. Wood (eds.), *Early Medieval Kingship*, 105–38, Leeds: University of Leeds.

Wormald, P. 2006. 'Bede, the *Bretwaldas* and the origins of the *Gens Anglorum*', in S. Baxter (ed.), *The Times of Bede: Studies in Early English Christian Society and its Historian*, 106–34, Oxford: Blackwell.

Yorke, B. 1981. 'The Vocabulary of Anglo-Saxon Overlordship', *ASSAH*, **2**, 171–200.

Yorke, B. 2009. 'The *Bretwaldas* and the Origins of Overlordship in Anglo-Saxon England', in S. Baxter, C. Karkov, J. Nelson and D. Pelteret (eds.), *Early Medieval Studies in Memory of Patrick Wormald*, 81–95, Farnham: Ashgate.

The Anglo-Saxon Settlement at Catholme, Staffordshire: a reassessment of the chronological evidence and possible reinterpretation

John Hines

Abstract

Catholme, on the northern side of the River Trent in Staffordshire, is the site of one of the best known large-scale Anglo-Saxon rural settlement excavations. In light of the prevalence of examples of settlement relocation in the course of the Anglo-Saxon period, the longevity of this site, apparently having been in continuous occupation for up to five centuries, was remarkable. The plan of buildings and enclosure features within the excavated area, however, does not reveal any particularly long stratigraphical sequences. A series of radiocarbon dates was obtained from samples from Anglo-Saxon contexts at Catholme in the late 1970s and early 1980s, most of them with error-margins (1 σ) of ±70/80 years. These have been subjected to fresh chronological modelling using the OxCal programme. The distribution of the dates supports a new and quite revisionary model for the development of the site, postulating that it was more mobile in location within the excavated area than the stratigraphical relationships could show. Combined with evidence from the Early Anglo-Saxon burials at the nearby cemetery of Wychnor at one end of the site-history, and the Domesday records for this and neighbouring vills at the other, Catholme may in fact be a settlement that graphically illustrates the systemic decline in social status of the free ceorl *class across the Anglo-Saxon period.*

Catholme in Anglo-Saxon settlement archaeology

The study of Anglo-Saxon settlement sites can draw upon relatively few examples that provide information retrieved through large-scale, open-area excavation; even fewer are sites where the evidence appears to represent settlement development across the greater part of the Anglo-Saxon period rather than within a more restricted time-frame of some two to three centuries at most. In these respects, the site excavated by the Trent Valley Archaeological Research Committee at Catholme in Staffordshire between summer 1973 and January 1980 has long been recognized as exceptional, and maybe even atypical. The first interim report in *Current Archaeology* used calibrated radiocarbon dates to propose that the site's occupation spanned from the late fifth to the early tenth centuries AD.[1] In the next major reflection published on the site this was adjusted to the early sixth to early tenth centuries, with reference to what was understood at that stage to be 'the earliest acceptable date' for Anglo-Saxon furnished burials within the area.[2]

In the 1980s, however, there was a growing consciousness that the major excavated early Anglo-Saxon settlement sites – especially West Stow (Suffolk) and Mucking (Essex) – appeared to have been abandoned in the late seventh or early eighth century, and this began to be explored as potentially a regular phenomenon. Continuity of settlement use from the fifth and sixth centuries of the Early Anglo-Saxon period to the tenth and eleventh centuries of the Late Anglo-Saxon period appeared to be virtually non-existent, and the concept of a widespread 'Mid-Saxon Shuffle' was introduced and its possible explanations explored.[3] The empirical basis for this normative model remains undiminished more than thirty years on, even if its pace and timing may seem to vary.[4] At Flixborough (North Lincolnshire) and Brandon (Suffolk), for instance, we now have well-documented sites whose history can only really be traced from the seventh or early eighth centuries onwards, and not to the end of the Anglo-Saxon period,[5] while Carlton Colville (Suffolk) flourished from the fifth to the seventh centuries and then appears to have been relocated before the start of the eighth century.[6] In an extensive study area between Cassington and Yarnton on the northern gravel terrace of the Thames in Oxfordshire, it is possible to discuss settlement evidence representing almost the entirety of the Anglo-Saxon period, from at least the late fifth century onwards, but this also involves radical phases of reorganization at two thresholds, assigned to *c.* AD 700 and *c.* AD 900.[7]

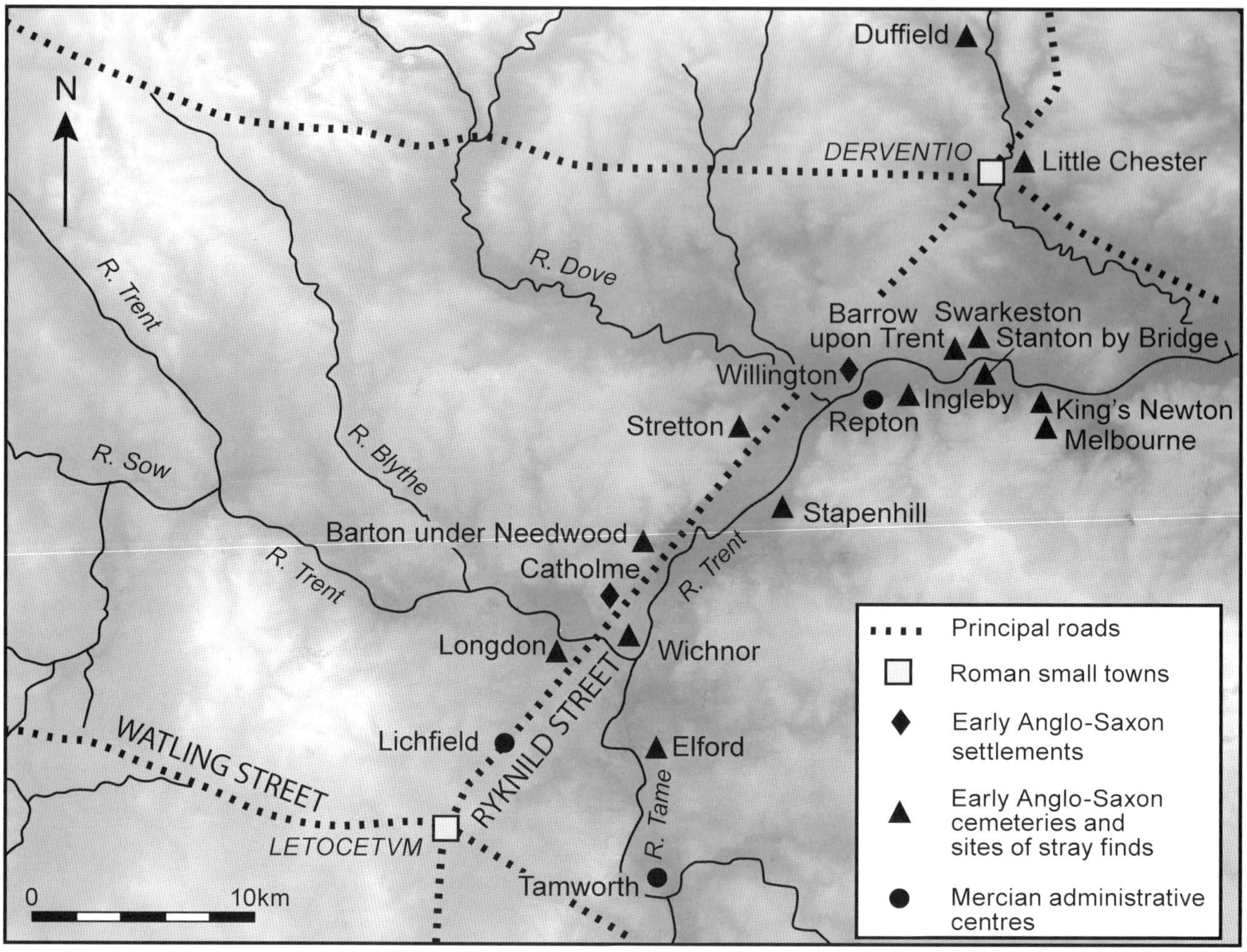

Fig. 1 The location of Catholme in the Middle Trent region, with principal routeways and Roman-period sites, other Early Anglo-Saxon sites and centres of the Mercian kingdom.

The apparent longevity of continuous settlement at Catholme is not the only significant aspect of its chronology. From the outset this site has been evaluated in the context both of the transition from sub-Romano-British to Anglo-Saxon cultural and political identity in the fifth to seventh centuries, and of the transition from Anglo-Saxon Mercia to the Danelaw in the second half of the ninth century. The site lies close to the confluence of the Tame and the Trent, and to the Roman road known as Ryknild Street, at the south-western end of a Middle Trent region extending northwards and eastwards to the Derby area on the Derwent, within which a number of Early Anglo-Saxon cemeteries represent what can be understood as the earliest core of what would become the powerful Mercian kingdom (Fig. 1).[8] Catholme also lies in the middle of a triangle formed by the principal Mercian royal and ecclesiastical centres of Lichfield, Tamworth and Repton. If the boundary between English Mercia and the Danelaw did follow the line of Watling Street,[9] Catholme was a few kilometres within the Danish side of it.

Catholme also has the distinction of being one of the first rural settlement sites of Anglo-Saxon England to have been interpreted as exhibiting a regular, planned layout from its inception. This theory developed from Losco-Bradley's initial emphasis on the extent to which the settlement originated as several well-defined groups of buildings separated by boundary ditches to the identification of parallel ditches running W–E across the site some 40–50 m apart as marking the layout of Phase 1.[10] The features concerned in the latter case, however, are very short stretches of ditch, and of demonstrably different functions: D11 and D12 to the north apparently delimit trackway T2, while D18 and D24 (the latter inexplicably shown truncated in the 1984 phase plan) were interpreted in later analysis as non-contemporary phases of the farmstead enclosure in the central zone (Zone VII), and D55 to the south is also part of a cornered enclosure ditch. The phasing proposed at the stage of post-excavation analysis represented by the 1984 presentation of the evidence did not make it into the full site publication.[11]

Andrew Reynolds included Catholme in his important study of boundaries and settlements in later sixth- to eleventh-century England, citing the enclosed Zone VII in the middle of the excavated site, with its dimensions of *c.* 60 m W–E and 45 m S–N, as an example of an enclosure 'module' for which such dimensions were characteristic.

Although close dating was not essential to his principal thesis, it was nonetheless consistent with the evolving picture he proposed that an early seventh-century origin for this feature could be suggested – a date derived in fact from the younger end of the 2-sigma probability range of the earliest radiocarbon dates from the site.[12] Reynolds' study also included an important observation, credited to John Blair, that trackway T4 leading into Zone VII from the west appears to be perfectly aligned with Catholme Lane and a field boundary mapped on an 1812 Enclosure plan.[13] Hamerow had in fact noted that Catholme was apparently exceptional in having 'some half-dozen farmsteads which appear to have been laid out along trackways as early as the sixth century'.[14]

The range in styles of building – sunken-feature buildings (SFBs), and post-pit and post-in-trench buildings – has also always attracted attention, with early recognition both of the fact that there are examples of post-in-trench buildings as successors to individual post-pit buildings, as well as of the presence of buildings which apparently combine both forms of wall structure.[15] Although the ranges of palaeobotanical and -zoological evidence and other find material were very sparse, the diversity of building types and their clustering in farmstead zones suggest practical/functional differentiation, both for arable farming and where iron smelting and forging slag had accumulated,[16] while the relationship between some of the trackways and the river points convincingly to the management of stock movement for watering.[17]

The chronology of Catholme

It is therefore beyond question that it is important to achieve the most reliable and precise chronological resolution possible for the Catholme settlement – not only the relative chronology of the site's phasing but also the 'absolute' chronology of the calendrical dates which can be assigned to its features and development. The two archaeological methods upon which the dating of Catholme has to depend are stratigraphy and radiocarbon dating. Diagnostic artefactual material for dating is effectively non-existent. The pottery is remarkably indistinct in terms of its form and decoration.[18] The substantial proportion of sherds of a granodiorite-tempered fabric associated with the Mountsorrel/Charnwood Forest area of Leicestershire is consistent with a high level of deposition pre-dating the later seventh century.[19] The Anglo-Saxon pottery from the site differs in its grades of abrasion and oxidization from the residual Roman-period pottery found in the fills of SFBs at the site, as one would expect.[20] As Kinsley notes, the Anglo-Saxon pottery is found in the fills of features right across the site.[21] Surprisingly not commented on, although plotted, is the very clear preponderance of Anglo-Saxon pottery in the topsoil from the higher southern end of the excavated area – hardly a distribution to be explained by colluvial movement in the way that the quantities of this pottery also found down the river terrace can be.[22]

The longest sequences of stratigraphical relationships are found in the central Zone VII, reinforcing its apparently dominant place within what is known of the settlement (Fig. 2). This zone is approached from the west by trackway T4, which leads into an enclosure defined primarily by boundary ditches; the ditches either side of the trackway itself extend a short way within the boundary ditch on the western side, but there is no recorded intercutting between these ditch lines. The southern boundary ditch was apparently moved southwards on two occasions (D21 > D24 > D25); D25 seems to have been superseded by a fence line, F35, probably along with F40, the post-holes of F35 apparently having been cut into the fill of D25. On the northern boundary, ditch D20 has two clear re-cuts shown on the major site plan; whether or not the short stretches of ditch and fence lying parallel a few metres further north (D18; F15 and F16) represent another expansion of the enclosed zone towards the north, the opposite edge of a trackway along the northern side, or some other structures, cannot be determined.

Building AS36, potentially a forge associated with a major accumulation of predominantly smithing slag, appears to have been deliberately constructed over the original northern boundary ditch D20, and can be shown to have had at least two phases of construction itself. The terminal of a third re-cut and thus a fourth phase of ditch D20 in fact respects the western gable end of building AS36. Several further buildings within this zone have more than one phase. The most prominent building within the whole complex is AS43, an L-shaped structure of two phases which overlaps or cuts both of the earliest southern boundary ditches (D21 and D24) and must also succeed a smaller rectangular post-pit building of two phases just within ditch D21 (building AS42). There are other building sequences within the zone. A few metres to the north-west of AS42 and AS43, AS40 and AS41 represent three phases of structure, although AS40 was distinctly small; in the north-western corner, building AS35 certainly has two phases and possibly three. In the centre, building AS38 may have up to four phases, while regularly spaced post-holes define an adjacent enclosure fence, F24, of uncertain extent and stratigraphical relationship with the buildings in this location. Other necessarily successive pairs of structures in the same locations within Zone VII are AS44/AS45 and AS46/47.

The sequences of four demonstrable phases identifiable in the features of Zone VII – five phases if we add the two phases of AS36 to the three preceding phases of D20 – represent the longest stratigraphical sequences anywhere on the site. There are, of course, several further relationships within other zones of the site involving features which cannot have been contemporary. In terms of sequential buildings, SFB AS1 is cut by post-pit building AS2 (Zone I); close by, post-pit building AS3 must be sequential with post-in-trench building AS4 (attributed to Zone II), and typology would suggest AS4 to be the later of the two although there is no observable stratigraphical

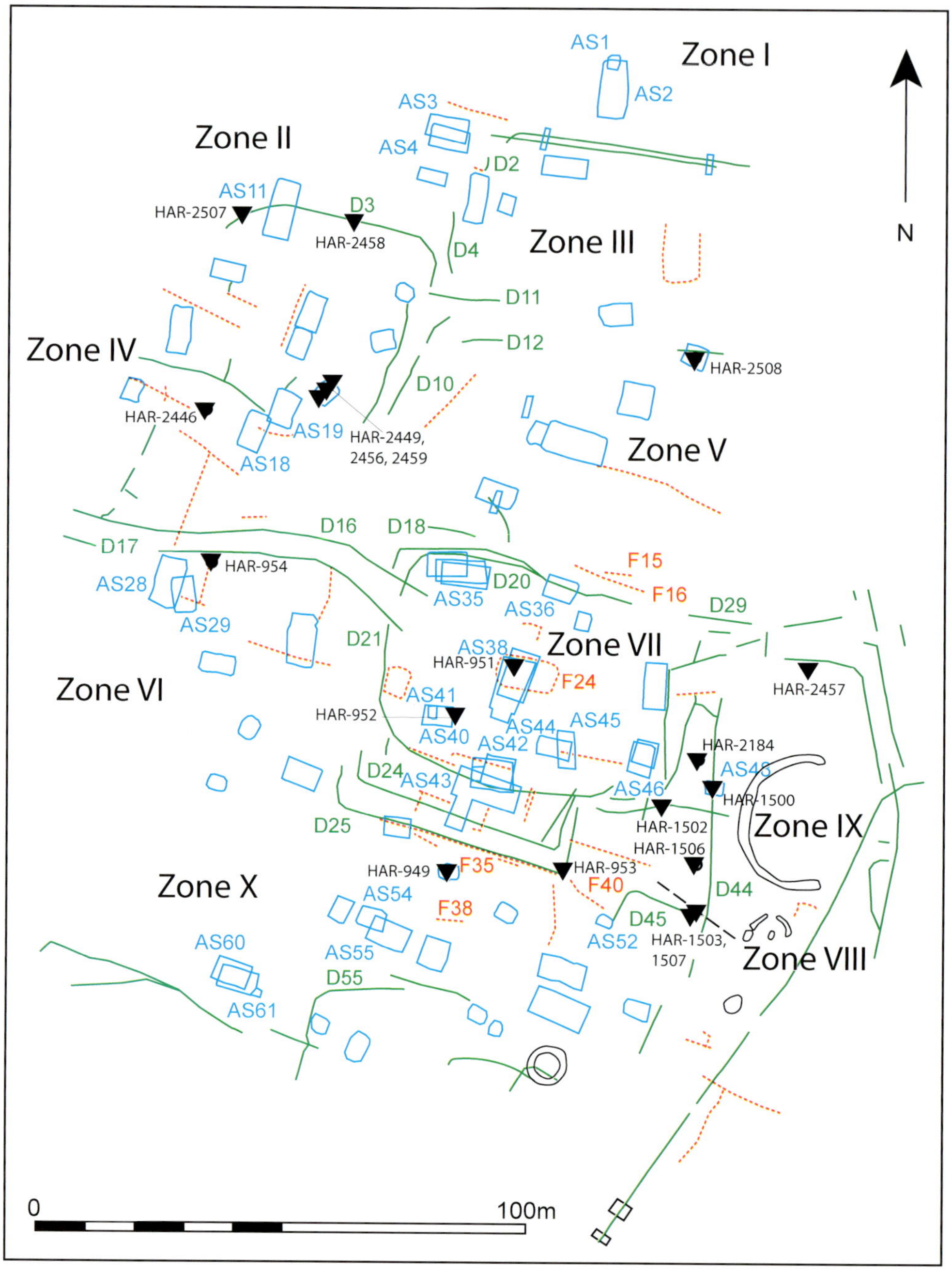

Fig. 2 Catholme: site plan (after Losco-Bradley and Kinsley 2002), showing the zoning applied to the settlement and the distribution of the radiocarbon-dated samples. Features referred to in the text are labelled.

relationship here to confirm this. AS28 and AS29, AS54 and AS55, and AS60 and AS61, are pairs of post-pit buildings with overlapping footprints in Zones VI and X respectively, but in each case there is no direct stratigraphical evidence to determine which is the earlier of the pair. It is not the objective here to note all of the stratigraphical relationships recorded on the site, although one further observation of interest is that instances of buildings and other structures apparently deliberately sited over the lines of preceding ditches are markedly the most frequent form of such relationships. Between Zones II and IV, AS11 is a post-pit building which cuts ditch D3; AS18 and AS19 are a pair of probably sequential buildings apparently deliberately located over the end of ditch D4 in Zone IV; AS28 cuts D17 (Zone VI); AS49 cuts D25 (between zones VII and X); AS52, an SFB, cuts D45, and AS62, another SFB, ditch D55 (both Zone X); AS48, a further SFB, cuts three phases of ditch D44, possibly the eastern boundary of Zone VII (discussed further below). As in the case of fence F35 and ditch D25 at the southern limit of Zone VII, noted above, there are a number of cases where fences, represented by lines of post-holes, succeed ditches as boundary markers or barriers.

All of the reports published on the site have recognized that the excavations have offered relatively little in the way of vertical stratigraphical sequences. In light of the evidence just summarized, that might appear to be a 'glass half empty rather than glass half full' position to adopt, but it is understandable in light of the longevity of the site as inferred from the radiocarbon dates: certainly

Table 1 The radiocarbon dates obtained from samples from stratified contexts within the Anglo-Saxon settlement at Catholme, Staffordshire, in descending age-order (after Losco-Bradley and Kinsley 2002, table 3.4).

HAR-2459	*1880*	*70*	*Zone IV*	*SFB AS20 fill. Treated as outlier.*
HAR-949	1580	80	Zone X	SFB AS50b fill.
HAR-2508	1500	60	Zone III–V	Fire-pit 3590 bottom.
HAR-954	1480	80	Zone VI	Charcoal pit 3445.
HAR-953	1450	70	Zone VII	Ditch D25 fill.
HAR-951	1440	80	Zone VII	Post-in-trench packing AS38b.
HAR-1503	1390	60	Zone VIII	Fire-pit 3501. See also HAR-1507.
HAR-1507	1340	80	Zone VIII	Fire-pit 3501. See also HAR-1503.
HAR-2184	1290	80	Zone VII	Fire-pit 3518.
HAR-2457	1290	80	Zone IX	Charcoal pit 3638.
HAR-2456	1280	70	Zone IV	SFB AS20 fill, immediately above occupation layer. See HAR-2449.
HAR-2458	1210	70	Zone IV	Ditch D3 initial fill. See HAR-2507.
HAR-2446	1180	70	Zone IV	Pit 3571 bottom.
HAR-952	1180	70	Zone VII	Post-pipe AS41a.
HAR-1502	1130	80	Zone VIII	Ditch D27 bottom fill.
HAR-2507	1100	80	Zone IV	Feature 3552, cutting ditch D3, bottom fill. See HAR-2458.
HAR-1500	1060	70	Zone VIII	SFB AS48 fill.
HAR-2449	1050	90	Zone IV	SFB AS20 fill, post-occupation. See HAR-2456.
HAR-1506	1010	70	Zone VIII	Pit fill

not less than three centuries and possibly more than four centuries. If a five-phase sequence were to represent the entirety of this span, each phase would need to have a mean duration of at least sixty years and possibly more than eighty, which, in terms of the features observed, is scarcely credible. To put the implications of this in the simplest but most significant terms, to postulate that the 'central' Zone VII was laid out when the settlement was founded (by or in the early seventh century) and survived – extended and rebuilt – through to the settlement abandonment (attributed to the early tenth century) is intrinsically implausible.

The radiocarbon dates and the scope for chronological modelling

A total of nineteen radiocarbon dates were obtained from stratified samples of charcoal associated with features within the Anglo-Saxon settlement, dated at the Carbon 14/Tritium Measurement Laboratory, Harwell (Table 1).[23] As already noted, interpretation of these data in terms of site chronology has in the past been rather simply – although not misguidedly – carried out by visual assessment of a diagram laying out the 2-sigma ranges of probability in age-order.[24] The availability of the free calibration and Bayesian modelling OxCal software now makes a more structured and ambitious evaluation of the data possible.[25]

The age determinations of the samples are at a relatively low level of precision, the majority having ranges of ± 70 or ± 80 years BP at 1 sigma. For the sake of clarity it has been judged best to cite calibrated dates (in normal type) and highest posterior density estimates (in italics), within the following discussion, to 1 sigma (68% probability), and rounded out to five-year intervals. However, Table 2 gives both 1- and 2-sigma ranges (68% and 95% probability respectively) for all such datings presented, showing the same results as returned to single-year intervals.

The interim report of 1977 referred to a first tranche of ten dates (HAR-949 to HAR-954, HAR-1500, and HAR-1502 to HAR-1507); nine further dates (HAR-2184, HAR-2446, HAR-2449, HAR-2456 to HAR-2459, and HAR-2507 to HAR-2508) were included within Losco-Bradley and Wheeler's 1984 discussion. Of the latter, it was recognized that HAR-2459, from the fill of SFB AS20 (Zone IV), was so much earlier than the other dated samples that it had to be considered intrusive, residual material, and treated as an outlier. There are a number of direct stratigraphical relationships between the dated samples. Two further samples from the fill of AS20 have a possible sequential relationship, HAR-2456 being from 'immediately above the occupation layer' and HAR-2449 from the 'post-occupation' fill. HAR-2458 is from the 'initial fill' of ditch D3 while HAR-2507 is from the bottom of an elongated feature suggested to have been a further ditch cutting the fill of D3. In the case of both of these sequenced dates, the *a priori* later sample is indeed younger in age than that from the earlier context.

Two samples of 'small branches' were dated from a single fire-pit, 3501 (HAR-1503 and HAR-1507), and the ages of the two samples prove to be statistically consistent ($T = 0.2$; $T(5\%) = 3.8$; $\nu = 1$). Consequently, their radiocarbon ages can be combined mathematically into a more precise age of 1372 ± 49 BP.

The first model to test, then, is one which postulates that the radiocarbon dates from Catholme represent a uniform and unbroken phase of activity which we may call the occupation of the site. The exceptionally early sample

Table 2 Highest posterior density estimates at both 95% probability (first column) and 68% probability (second column) for the models reported in the text, returned to single-year intervals.

a *Catholme occupation* as a single phase, with HAR-2459 treated as an outlier, but no stratigraphical relationships included.		
Start Catholme occupation	*cal* AD *403–611*	*cal* AD *489–586*
End Catholme occupation	*cal* AD *868–1130*	*cal* AD *932–1046*
b *Catholme occupation* as a single phase, with HAR-2459 treated as an outlier, and stratigraphical relationships included (Fig. 3).		
Start Catholme occupation	*cal* AD *386–617*	*cal* AD *475–587*
End Catholme occupation	*cal* AD *846–1140*	*cal* AD *938–1056*
Span	*257–704 years*	*381–571 years*
c *Sequence Catholme* of two phases: *Zone VII* (3 dates) succeeded by *Zone IV* (5 dates, with stratigraphical relationships included).		
Start Zone VII	*cal* AD *231–735*	*cal* AD *481–649*
Transition Zone VII/Zone IV	*cal* AD *674–880*	*cal* AD *710–834*
End Zone IV	*cal* AD *776–1140*	*cal* AD *837–1018*
d *Sequence Catholme* of two phases: *Zone VII (with fire-pits)* (5 dates) succeeded by *Zone IV* (5 dates, with stratigraphical relationships included) (Fig. 4).		
Start Zone VII (with fire-pits)	*cal* AD *415–771*	*cal* AD *550–654*
Transition Zone VII (with fire-pits)/Zone IV	*cal* AD *665–861*	*cal* AD *688–800*
End Zone IV	*cal* AD *772–1153*	*cal* AD *809–1016*
e *Sequence Catholme* of two phases: *Zone VII (with fire-pits)* (5 dates) succeeded by *Zones IV, VIII and IX* (9 dates, with stratigraphical relationships included) (Fig. 5).		
Start Zone VII (with fire-pits)	*cal* AD *405–686*	*cal* AD *546–651*
Transition Zone VII (with fire-pits)/Zones IV, VIII and IX	*cal* AD *668–874*	*cal* AD *696–821*
End Zones IV, VIII and IX	*cal* AD *817–1150*	*cal* AD *919–1044*

HAR-2459 has poor agreement with this model (A: 34.7), which confirms that it can be treated as an outlier and excluded from further models. With none of the stratigraphical relationships structured into the model, the single-phase model of the remaining eighteen radiocarbon dates shows good overall agreement (A_{model} 103.2), assigning *Start Catholme occupation* to *cal* AD *485–590 (68% probability)* and *End Catholme occupation* to *cal* AD *930–1050 (68% probability)* (Table 2, a; model not shown). Incorporating all of the stratigraphical relationships identified above within the single uniform phase produces an overall result that is little different: while the index of agreement is equally good (A_{model} 109.5), the parameters are spread out marginally more. *Start Catholme occupation* is estimated to have been within the range of *cal* AD *475–590 (68% probability)* and *End Catholme occupation* to have been within the range of *cal* AD *935–1060 (68% probability)* (Table 2, b; Fig. 3). The estimated *Span* of *Catholme occupation* is *380–575 years (68% probability)*. Clearly these estimates are not markedly out of line with the previous interpretations of the radiocarbon data. Altogether, though, we may note that this modelling suggests a rather longer span of occupation for the settlement at Catholme, between *Start* and *End* dates that are respectively earlier and later than non-mathematical interpretation of the data had increasingly been inclined to suggest.

These results consequently render the discrepancy between the limited length of observable stratigraphical sequences within the site and the absolute duration of occupation there all the more substantial. Something else that is immediately apparent from the tabulation of the radiocarbon age-determinations in age order, however, is that there is quite a clear grouping by Zone. Most of the samples associated with Zone VII are in the upper half of the Table 1 and are older than those associated with Zone IV.

We may therefore consider a simple re-interpretative model: that the occupation of Zones VII and IV forms a straightforward two-phase sequence, with IV superseding VII. Zone VII is directly dated by three samples: one from what is in fact understood to be the final, southernmost boundary ditch (HAR-953, D25); one from a post-pit of the earlier phase of the two-phase building AS41, which itself overlies a structure AS40 (HAR-952); and one from post-packing within a wall-trench of the second phase of a possibly four-phase building, AS38(b) (HAR-951). The samples from Zone IV include two sequences noted above: the two phases of the fill of SFB AS20 (HAR-2456 and HAR-2449), and the intercutting features D3 and the elongated pit or truncated ditch 3552 (HAR-2458 and HAR-2507), together with a deposit from the bottom of pit 3571.

A two-phase model including all of the data above has good overall agreement (A_{model} 87.8), with highest posterior density estimates for *Start Zone VII* of *cal* AD *480–650 (68% probability)*, for *Transition Zone VII/Zone IV* of *cal* AD *710–835 (68% probability)*, and for *End Zone IV* of *cal* AD *835–1020 (68% probability)* (Table 2, c; model not shown). Since, however, we are using these data and this method of quantitative evaluation as a means of exploratory interpretation of the site, we can also note the case for adding the dates of two fire-pits just to the east of Zone VII to the samples taken as representative of that phase of occupation. One of these is fire-pit 3518 (HAR-2184), which lies

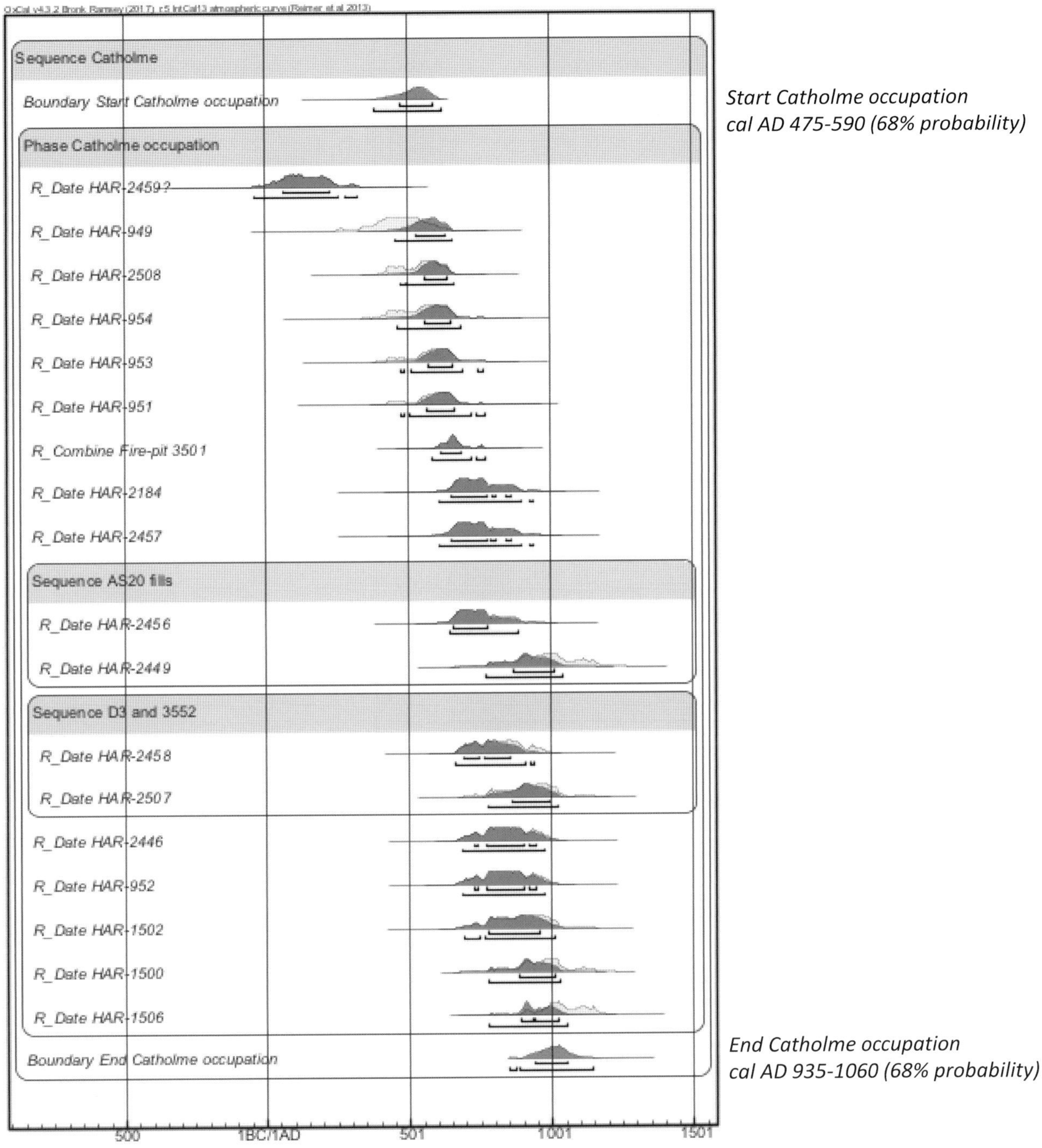

Fig. 3 Probability distributions for dates from the Catholme settlement (see Table 1) as a single uniform phase of occupation, incorporating the stratigraphical relationships between samples noted in the text.

just east of ditch D42, suggested to be the primary boundary ditch of Zone VII on this side, and just west of ditch D44, a multi-phase ditch (three phases can be discerned in the detailed site plan) which is discussed in the report as possibly the eastern side of a trackway adjoining D42, although also used to define the boundary between a Zone VIII on the south-eastern corner of Zone VII and Zone IX, the largely untouched area around a probable Bronze Age barrow. Around 30 m south of this, and also just west of the line of ditch D44, is double-dated fire-pit 3501 (HAR-1503 and HAR-1507; cf. above). *A priori* we can see that the ages of these samples are consistent with those from structural features within Zone VII. We can infer that with a prevailing westerly wind, it would be rational to site fire-pits on the eastern side of an area of housing.

Experimentally including these dates with the other three from Zone VII as a phase preceding Zone IV – thus now with five dates for each modelled phase – again has good agreement (A_{model} 93), with *Start Zone VII (with fire-pits)* narrowed to the range *cal* AD 550–655 (68%

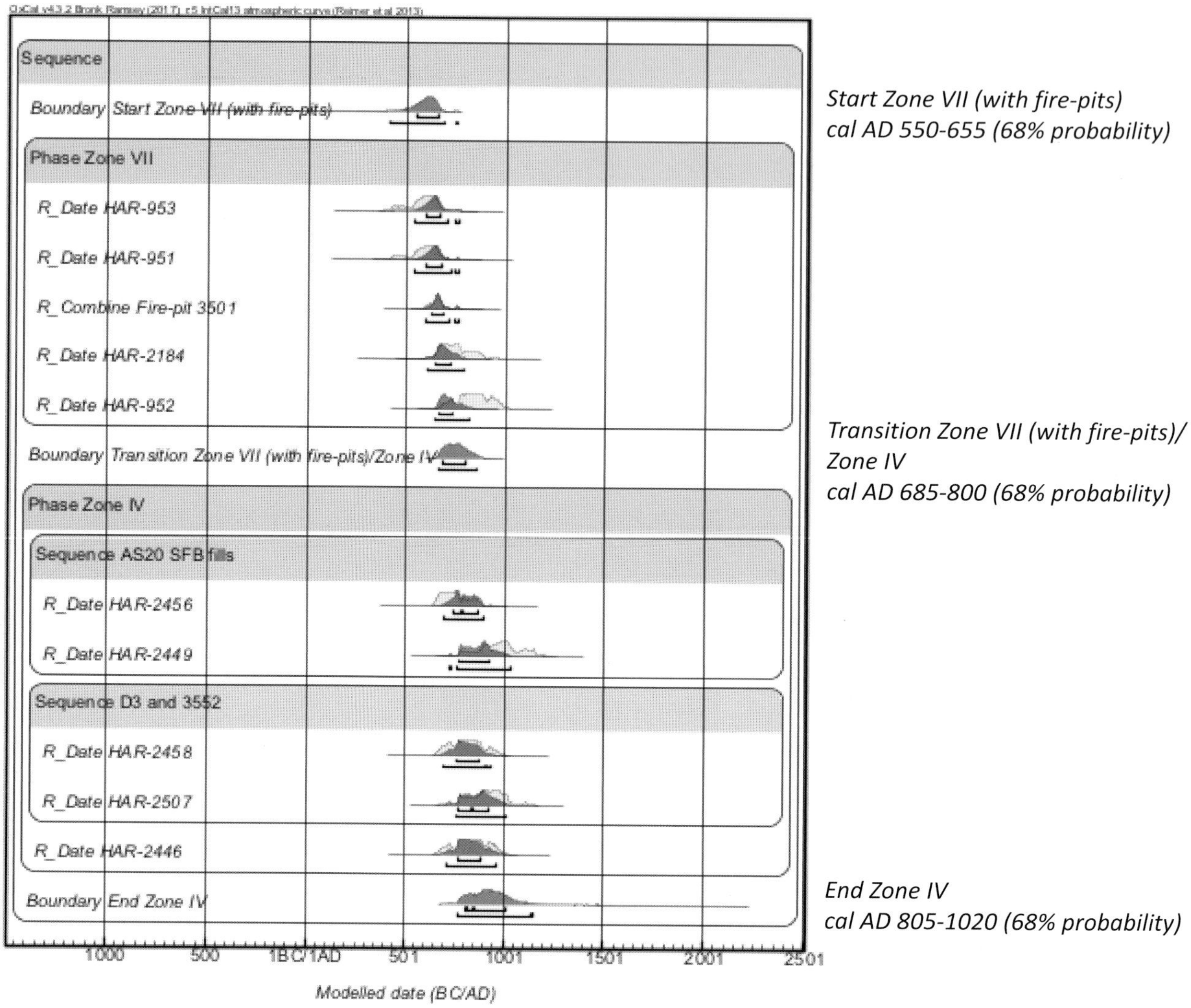

Fig. 4 Probability distributions for dates from Zones VII and IV of the Catholme settlement as a sequence of two phases of occupation, incorporating the stratigraphical relationships between samples noted in the text and assigning two fire-pits to the earlier phase by association with Zone VII.

probability), Transition Zone VII (with fire-pits)/Zone IV now a little earlier and tighter at *cal AD 685–800 (68% probability)*, but *End Zone IV* a little less precise in the range of *cal AD 805–1020 (68% probability)* (Fig. 4; Table 2,d).

We may therefore consider the proposition that the settlement site at Catholme developed in a phased manner, with Zone VII in the middle of the excavated area representing a (relatively) early stage in the settlement and Zone IV to the north-west a later, rather than contemporary, area of occupation. There are then, of course, further radiocarbon dates to consider. The earliest dated sample from the site, HAR-951, is from an SFB immediately south of the major building group AS42/AS43 of Zone VII, but outside all three phases of boundary ditch that define Zone VII. The next is from the bottom of another fire-pit, 3590, which sits within (and seems to be contemporary with) a post-built structure (AS22) some 50 m north of Zone VII.[26] Along with the dates from Zone VII, these might suggest an early focus of the settlement along the river terrace edge, on the eastern side of the area of excavation. A third sample dated earlier than anything directly associable with Zone VII, however, is from charcoal-filled pit 3445, just south of trackway T4 leading into Zone VII on the western side of the area of excavation, in what is designated Zone VI.

With the fire-pit 3501 experimentally attributed to the phase represented by the structural features of Zone VII (see above), the remaining younger radiocarbon samples dates are from Zones VIII and IX, east of Zone VII: from a charcoal-filled pit, 3638, cut by trackway-edge ditch D39 on the northern edge of Zone IX (HAR-2457), and from the fills at the bottom of ditch D27 (HAR-1502), above the occupation level of SFB AS48 (HAR-1500), and in pit 3500 (HAR-1506), all associable with Zone VIII. SFB AS48 is one of the structures that appear to have been deliberately located over, and cut into the fills of, the successive phases of ditch D44, which itself was discussed in relation to the fire-pits assigned to Zone VII just above.

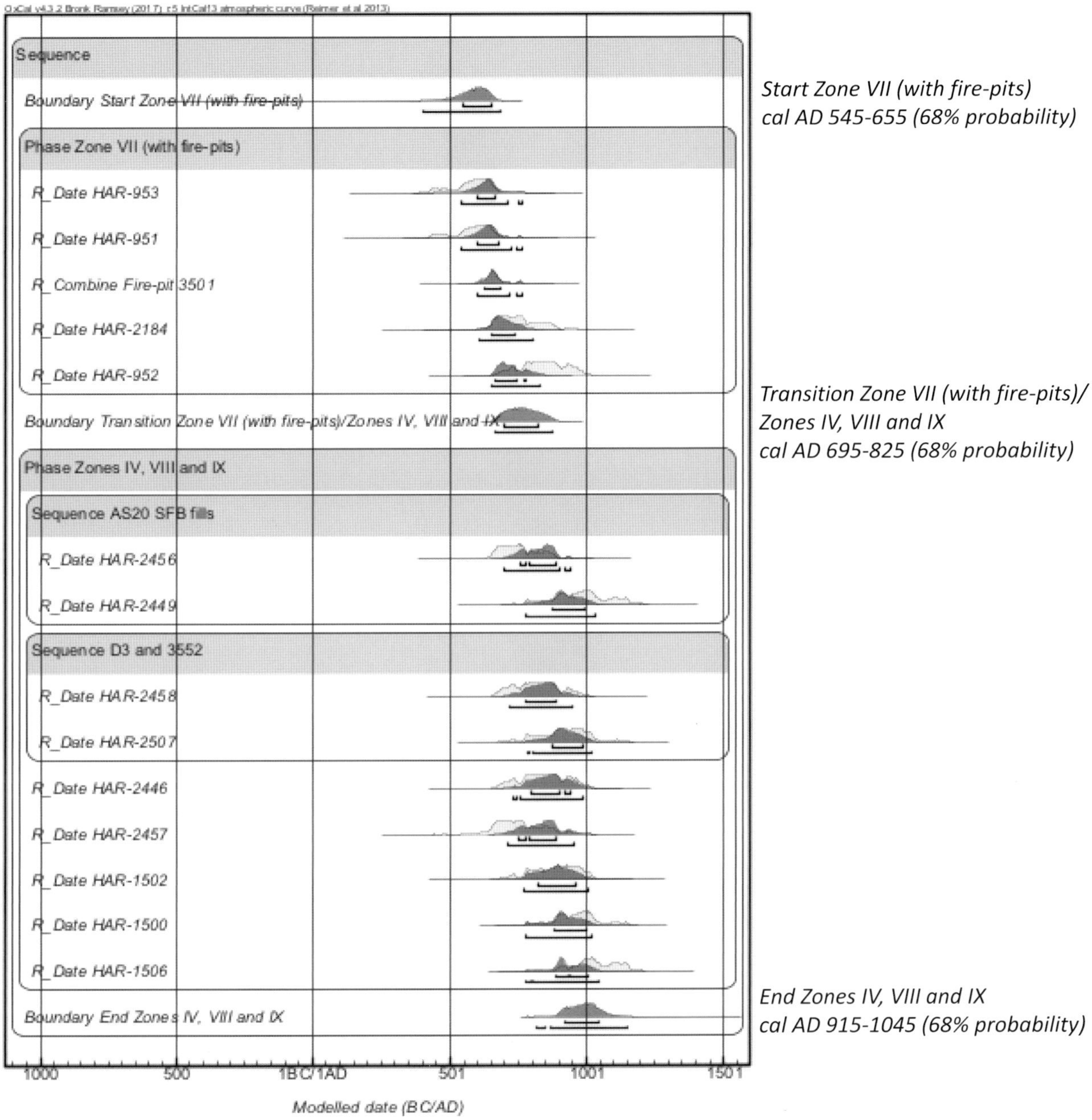

Fig. 5 Probability distributions for dates from Zone VII and Zones IV, VIII and IX of the Catholme settlement as a sequence of two phases of occupation, incorporating the stratigraphical relationships between samples noted in the text and assigning two fire-pits to the earlier phase by association with Zone VII.

We may therefore build our exploratory interpretative model yet further by postulating that the features dated within Zones VIII and IX are themselves contemporary with Zone IV in the sense of representing a successor phase to Zone VII. With this model, overall agreement remains good (A_{model} 90). The additional dates in the later phase nudge the highest posterior density estimate for *Start Zone VII (with fire-pits)* marginally earlier to *cal AD 545–655 (68% probability)*, while *End Zones IV, VIII and IX* is more precisely estimated at *cal AD 915–1045 (68% probability)*. The median range for *Transition Zone VII (with fire-pits)/Zones IV, VIII and IX* continues to sit over the eighth century at *cal AD 695–825 (68% probability)* (Fig. 5; Table 2, e). Helena Hamerow has noted that the date of sample HAR-1500 from the fill of SHB AS48 (*cal AD 777–1023* at *68% probability* in the model in Figure 5) is suspiciously late for such a structure on an Anglo-Saxon rural settlement site,[27] but if the sample derives from later re-use of an old SFB hollow, it can still be associated with Zones VIII and IX.

This is really as far as it is useful to go with chronological modelling of the site at Catholme. It is possible to build all of the chronological structure shown in Figure 5 into a model which also includes the outstanding early dates noted above within an overall *Catholme occupation* phase, but this does not add any precision to our

Fig. 6 Schematic plans of the Catholme settlement showing the distribution of features assignable to the two sequential phases modelled in Figure 5 and discussed in the text.

modelling for the *Start* and *End* of *Catholme occupation*: on the contrary, the latest dated sample we have, HAR-1506 from Zone VIII, then has poor individual agreement at A: 52.4 (model not shown). It should be emphasized again that all of the above is an exercise in the exploration and evaluation of data that endeavours to address an explicit archaeological problem: namely that the stratigraphical observations are hard to reconcile with the duration of activity implied by the radiocarbon dating. The good indices of agreement in the models produced by explicit reasoning show that a phased model is consistent with both the radiocarbon data and the actual features of the site. The results do not prove any particular model to be historically correct beyond further scope of refinement, or beyond the possibility of refutation or correction by further data should such ever become available. Nevertheless, on the present evidence we may conclude that:

1 The Anglo-Saxon settlement at Catholme may first have developed along the river terrace edge, close to a line of prehistoric barrows.
2 Zone VII must have been established early within the life-span of the settlement, although it need not have been the primary focus of occupation.
3 The enclosed Zone IV to the north-west, and occupation activities in Zones VIII and IX to the east of Zone VII, may have been successors to Zone VII, the transition taking place sometime between the late seventh and the early ninth centuries.

Even these rather tentantive conclusions do not amount to a comprehensive chronological model of the site (Fig. 6). Zones V and III, immediately north of Zone VII, look like a couple of slightly smaller farmstead zones, stratigraphically less developed than Zone VII. Despite the presence of one early radiocarbon date from a feature within Zone V, and another from a feature within Zone VI west of Zone VII, we can offer no confident views on the place of these zones within the phased chronological structure proposed for the overall site.

Catholme in context: an archaeological and historical interpretation

We now appear to be faced with a rather less stable and organized structure to the settlement at Catholme than has hitherto appeared to be the case. The inference of Catholme's 'exceptional … long-lived stability'[28] was entirely understandable, based upon the manifest zoning of the excavated site into clusters of buildings within a series of trackways, ditches and fences, and zones which all seemed to respect the areas of their neighbours. What could have happened is that an early pattern of trackways and boundaries, whatever their purpose, was established here, and that it continued to provide the blocks of land used for shifting areas of occupation, rather than having necessarily been maintained as a fully occupied and organized, zoned settlement structure throughout the history of the settlement.

Our estimated starting date for the settlement at Catholme now lies, by mathematical estimation, between the late fifth and late sixth centuries. Zone VII might not have come into being before the mid-sixth century. We should not, however, either overlook or underestimate the importance of the fact that the earliest dated of the relatively few samples associated with structures in this zone is from the fill of what is inferred to have been the third and final phase of southern boundary ditch of this zone.

In forthcoming publications, John Blair applies to Catholme the four short-perch square unit of grid-planned settlement layout, which he has deduced to have been in widespread use across Anglo-Saxon rural settlement sites.[29] The results show that the layout of Catholme conforms to this module (albeit within a grid aligned NNE–WNW rather than truly N–S), including both the earliest measurable boundary-ditches of the Zone VII farmstead unit and the size and position of successive post-pit buildings AS18 and AS19 of Zone IV. Even with the evidence for a more familiar style of occupation shifting around the site, as explored in this study, it is truly remarkable that the origins of any such layout were no later than the mid-sixth century. The early settlement focus of Zone VII appears to have been deliberately aligned with the still clear prehistoric feature with a ring ditch, presumably a Bronze Age barrow;[30] it is noticeable that the outer diameter of that ditch, which from the large-scale site plan I measure at 27.25 m,[31] also fits rather snugly into this grid at close to six short perches of 4.575 m (= 27.45 m). This observation does not undermine the proposition (in the way that absurd associations can sometimes be proposed along ley lines); rather, if valid, it would suggest that an especially suitable ancient feature was incorporated in the plan in a truly fundamental way. The multi-phase 'hall' building AS38 in the centre of the earliest enclosure of Zone VII (defined by ditches D20 to the north and D21 to the south) lies immediately WNW of the barrow; the important subsequent sequence of buildings AS42–43 is due west of the barrow. The case for grid-planning is something to be noted for further and future evaluation; in the present context, the implications need be no more than that a system of mensuration and alignments was introduced when Zone VII was laid out in or even before the sixth century which continued to be respected over several centuries of further evolution of the site.

Just 500 m south-west of the excavated area of the settlement is an Early Anglo-Saxon cemetery known as Wychnor, from which grave goods were recovered around the turn of the nineteenth to twentieth centuries.[32] The most precisely classifiable, and thus datable, artefacts from this site include two brooches: a trefoil-headed small long brooch and a gilt copper-alloy florid cruciform brooch with applied silver foil. The former could be late fifth- or early sixth-century; the latter is assigned by Toby Martin to his quite widespread Type 4.7.1, the 'Duston' Type, which he would date within the second and third quarters of the sixth century.[33] There are also five shield bosses of Classes SB1 and SB3 in the typology of the national chronological framework.[34] These are characteristic of phases AS-MA and AS-MB, and therefore, as with the brooches, of a period coinciding closely with the estimated *Start* date-range of Catholme's settlement occupation.

It is possible that the Wychnor cemetery was the burial place of the occupants of a different settlement to the west of Catholme. The historical parish boundary between Barton-under-Needwood and Wichnor separates the settlement site from the cemetery, but this looks very like a subdivision of a previously unitary area, and is relatively unlikely to represent a territorial boundary as early as the Early Anglo-Saxon Period. The known Anglo-Saxon cemetery site of Barton-under-Needwood lay considerably further from the settlement site of Catholme along the line of Ryknild Street. It is therefore entirely realistic to suggest that those who were buried in the Wychnor cemetery had resided in the Catholme settlement. We must also bear in mind that the settlement undoubtedly extended further south – and in fact closer to the Wychnor cemetery – in an area that has not been excavated. It is therefore equally realistic to postulate that the burials with grave goods from the earliest phase of Anglo-Saxon occupation of this area and the earliest phases of the farmstead in Zone VII of the settlement represent the same relatively well-standing free household(s), at least one of which then survived, probably into the eighth and possibly even into the early ninth century.

Does the settlement transition at Catholme, reliably dated before the Viking period (which would not have affected this area until perhaps as late as the final quarter of the ninth century), thus embody a major shift in the character of settlement rather than just periodic relocation? The fence-lines, trackways and ditches in and around Zone IV render it rather less clearly unitary a settlement zone than Zone VII, but in broad terms, between ditch D3 to the north and trackway T4 to the south Zone IV is no smaller than Zone VII, and its buildings are not noticeably humbler. However, our new estimates for the *End* of occupation at Catholme would now suggest that this occupation continued into the middle or later tenth, if not even into the first half of the eleventh century. Consequently the absence of widely distributed, distinctive ceramic wares characteristic of many settlements of those dates, which was previously used as a *terminus ad quem* for the duration of the settlement,[35] may rather characterize a relative material poverty in the site's latest stages of use.

This dating also, then, approaches the mid-eleventh-century *Tempus Regis Edwardi* (*T.R.E.*), the reign of Edward the Confessor (1042–1065) in respect of which we have Domesday Book records of the distribution of population and its social structure. The Staffordshire Domesday description of the area in question has an entry for a small vill of Wichnor (*Wicenore*) lying between royal vills at Kings Bromley and Alrewas to the west and at Barton-under-Needwood to the north-east.[36] Opposite Wichnor on the eastern side of the Trent lay the manor of Catton in Derbyshire, neighbour to yet another royal vill at Walton-on-Trent. In 1086–7 Robert de Stafford was tenant-in-chief of Wichnor, with another Robert as his tenant of two hides; the population otherwise is recorded as the households of four villeins and two bordars. Four freemen described as thanes (*teini*) had held the property of the vill before 1066. Of the four carucates (ploughlands) one was held in demesne. The vill also had a mill worth eighteen pence, woodland and twenty acres of meadow, and was valued as worth fifteen shillings per annum. Robert, younger son of Roger de Tosny, was second only to the king in terms of the value of his holdings in Staffordshire.

Wichnor is one of the many small vills of Staffordshire recorded in 1086–7 and thus not a particularly impoverished area. However, the contrast with the king's manor of Barton-under-Needwood is striking. That holding is rated at three hides with appendages, and at eighteen carucates. Two carucates were held in desmesne, with two slaves. The population is otherwise recorded as the households of seventeen villeins and eight bordars with nine ploughs. As at Wichnor, the meadowland is assessed at twenty acres, but there is much more woodland and a mill worth six shillings. *T.R.E.* the holding was worth £6 but that had risen to £7.

Typically for the king's holdings in the Stafforshire Domesday, no information is offered on the population and social structure of the manor *T.R.E.* other than that it had been held by Ælfgar, Earl of Mercia and East Anglia. Ælfgar apparently died in 1064, but the Domesday survey effectively refuses to recognize his son and successor Edwin, who rebelled against King William and was killed in 1070. The holding of the vill of Wichnor by four free thanes is paralleled in several other Domesday records from the shire, especially those recorded under the name of Robert de Stafford as tenant-in-chief. A little further up the Trent from Wichnor Robert held Ridware, with three thanes *T.R.E.*; variously between three and six men of the same rank are also recorded at Ellastone, Syerscote, Wilbrighton, Brineton, Stretton (Penkridge) and Great Saredon. As at Wichnor, in all of these cases by 1087 just one tenant is recorded under Robert, except at Ellastone, the largest holding of six carucates with six thanes *T.R.E.*, who had been superseded by two named individuals.

The evidence is tantalizingly incomplete, in that we cannot know what happened to the household(s) of Catholme when settlement in the excavated area came to an end in the tenth or eleventh century; in particular, if they were incorporated into the communities assigned to the vill of Barton or to that of Wichnor. The fact that the boundary between Barton-under-Needwood and Wichnor parishes apparently follows the ancient Catholme Lane, which looped to the south of the excavated area, and the possible drift of settlement focus northwards from Zone VII to Zone IV, might suggest that the population was incorporated into that of Barton rather than becoming one of the small land-holding free thanes of mid-eleventh-century Wichnor – but sheer speculation is all that can be. Whatever had happened, the archaeological evidence from Catholme, together with the Domesday records for the two vills by whose border it sat, appear to trace in a near perfect manner the reduction of status of the weapon-bearing freeman of the Early Anglo-Saxon period, represented by the weapon graves of Wychnor and the dress accessories of their contemporary womenfolk, to the tied villeins of the Norman period. It may be the case, as Henry Loyn suggested some forty years ago, that the relatively high number of minor freemen evident in the Domesday records for the former Danelaw area, and not least in Staffordshire, represents a distinctly Anglo-Scandinavian population with a social structure still influenced by the settlement of considerable numbers of free Viking-period colonist-farmers.[37] In the case of Catholme, however, the key horizons of change seem rather to be the start of the Anglo-Saxon period, either late fifth century or early sixth; then the period in which the Mercian kingdom, its chief centres so close to Catholme, flourished in the eighth century; and finally some time between the middle decades of the tenth century and the eleventh century, when the settlement moved out of an area it had occupied for four or five centuries. Apart perhaps from the very origins of the settlement, this chronological framework points us firmly towards social and economic processes of change within Mercia, as both a dominant Anglo-Saxon kingdom and as a Late Anglo-Saxon earldom, as the explanatory factors of greatest relevance, not the external impulses of further invasions and colonization.

Acknowledgements

The opportunity to undertake a thorough re-appraisal of the dating evidence from Catholme, a site which had intrigued me since the early 1980s, arose with the Staffordshire Hoard project, and a commission to evaluate that find in its archaeological context (Hines forthcoming). I am especially appreciative of the help and informed comments received on the initial drafts of this article from Professors Helena Hamerow and John Blair.

Notes

1 Losco-Bradley 1977.
2 Losco-Bradley and Wheeler 1984, 103–11.
3 Arnold and Wardle 1981; Hamerow 1991; Arnold 1997, 54–66.
4 Hamerow 2002, 120–4.
5 Loveluck and Atkinson 2007; Tester, Anderson, Riddler and Carr 2014.
6 Lucy, Tipper and Dickens 2009.
7 Hey 2004.
8 Hines forthcoming.

9 Keynes and Lapidge 1983, 171–2.
10 Losco-Bradley 1977, 361; Losco-Bradley and Wheeler 1984, 106–7, fig. 5a.
11 Losco-Bradley and Kinsley 2002, esp. p. 117. Serious health problems regrettably meant that Stuart Losco-Bradley was unable to continue working on the post-excavation analysis and the published report of the site himself (*ibid.*, xi–xii and 6); changes in the interpretation of the site, however, appear to be attributable primarily to a normal and proper process of exploration of possibilities rather than to be unfortunate consequences of a rupture in the process of study and reflection.
12 Reynolds 2004, 111; Losco-Bradley and Kinsley 2002, 122–3, fig. 3.99.
13 Reynolds 2004, 132.
14 Hamerow 2002, 97 n.16; cf. Hamerow 2012, 91, where the date has been adjusted to 'probably in the seventh century'.
15 Hamerow 2012, 27
16 Losco-Bradley 1977, 361–3; Brown in Losco-Bradley and Kinsley 2002, 113–15.
17 Hamerow 2012, 89.
18 Vince in Losco-Bradley and Kinsley 2002, 102–8.
19 Williams and Vince 1997; Leahy 2007, 83–4.
20 Leary in Losco-Bradley and Kinsley 2002, 99–100.
21 Losco-Bradley and Kinsley 2002, 108–10.
22 *Ibid.*, fig. 3.93, right; cf. *ibid.*, fig. 1.6 for the site contours.
23 *Ibid.*, 120–3.
24 *Ibid.*, fig. 3.99.
25 https://c14.arch.ox.ac.uk/oxcal.html. The programme used for the calculations and models reported and discussed in this paper is OxCal 4.3, and the calibration curve applied the current standard IntCal13 in all cases.
26 Losco-Bradley and Kinsley 2002, 55, fig. 3.36.
27 Pers. comm., 4 October 2017. An unfortunate typographical slip has created a significant discrepancy in the information reported on this sample, which is described as from 'a patch of charcoal, 500 mm above the occupation layer' in Losco-Bradley and Kinsley 2002, 75, but from a 'patch 60 × 80mm 20 mm thick 50 mm above occupation level', *ibid.,* table 3.4 (p.121). The profiles of AS48 illustrated in fig. 3.64 on p.74 of the report imply that a layer 500 mm above the bottom of the cut feature would be at or extremely close to the surface from which the feature was recognized and excavated.
28 Hamerow in Losco-Bradley and Kinsley 2002, 123; cf. Rippon 2010, 56.
29 Blair 2013; Blair, forthcoming 2018, 158–61 and figs. 50–1; and Blair, Rippon and Smart, forthcoming, ch. 5. I acknowledge with gratitude John Blair's kindness in supplying me with a copy of his gridded plan of Catholme to contribute to the preparation of this article.
30 Losco-Bradley and Kinsley 2002, 15 and 119.
31 *Ibid.*, figs. Y and Z, south.
32 *Ibid.*, 23–7.
33 Martin 2015, 78–80 and 90–128.
34 Høilund Nielsen in Hines and Bayliss eds. 2013, 148–58.
35 Losco-Bradley and Wheeler 1984, 103.
36 Slade 1958; Desborough 1991.
37 Loyn 1994, 94–8; however, cf. Hadley 2006, 88–9.

Bibliography

Arnold, C. J. 1997. *An Archaeology of the Early Anglo-Saxon Kingdoms*, rev. ed., London: Routledge.

Arnold, C. J. and Wardle, P. 1981. 'Early Anglo-Saxon settlement patterns in southern England', *Medieval Arch.*, **25**, 145–9.

Blair, J. 2013. 'Grid-planning in Anglo-Saxon settlements: the short perch and the four-perch module', *ASSAH*, **18**, 18–61.

Blair, J. forthcoming 2018. *Building Anglo-Saxon England*, Princeton NJ: Princeton University Press.

Blair, J, Rippon, S. and Smart, C. forthcoming. *Planning in the Early Medieval Landscape*, Liverpool: Liverpool University Press.

Desborough, D. 1991. 'An introduction to the Staffordshire Domesday', in A. Williams (ed.-in-chief) and G. H. Martin (gen. ed.), *The Staffordshire Domesday*, 1–20, London: Alecto Historical Editions.

Hadley, D. M. 2006. *The Vikings in England: Settlement, Society and Culture*, Manchester: Manchester University Press.

Hamerow, H. 1991. 'Settlement mobility and the "Middle Saxon Shift": rural settlement and settlement patterns in Anglo-Saxon England', *Anglo-Saxon England*, **20**, 1–17.

Hamerow, H. 2002. *Early Medieval Settlements: The Archaeology of Rural Communities in North-West Europe 400–900*, Oxford: Oxford University Press.

Hamerow, H. 2012. *Rural Settlements and Society in Anglo-Saxon England*, Oxford: Oxford University Press.

Hey, G. 2004. *Yarnton Saxon and Medieval Settlement and Landscape*, Oxford: Oxford Archaeological Unit.

Hines, J. forthcoming. 'Matters of material and social significance: the Staffordshire Hoard in its archaeological context', in C. Fern, L. Webster and T. M. Dickinson (eds.), *The Staffordshire Hoard: An Anglo-Saxon Treasure*, London: Society of Antiquaries of London and English Heritage.

Høilund Nielsen, K. 2013. 'Shield bosses', in J. Hines and A. Bayliss (eds.), *Anglo-Saxon Graves and Grave Goods of the 6th and 7th centuries AD: A Chronological Framework*, 148–62, Society for Medieval Archaeology: London.

Keynes, S. and Lapidge, M. (ed. and trans.) 1983. *Alfred the Great: Asser's Life of King Alfred and other Contemporary Sources*, Harmondsworth: Penguin.

Leahy, K. 2007. *'Interrupting the Pots': The Excavation of Cleatham Anglo-Saxon Cemetery*, CBA Research Report, 155, York: CBA.

Losco-Bradley, S. 1977. 'Catholme', *Current Arch.*, **59**, 358–64.

Losco-Bradley, S. and Kinsley, G. 2002. *Catholme: An Anglo-Saxon Settlement on the Trent Gravels in Staffordshire*, Nottingham: Dept of Archaeology, University of Nottingham.

Losco-Bradley, S. and Wheeler, H. 1984. 'Anglo-Saxon settlement in the Trent Valley: some aspects', in M. L. Faull (ed.), *Studies in Late Anglo-Saxon Settlement*, 101–14, Oxford: Oxford University Department for External Studies.

Loveluck, C. and Atkinson, D. 2007. *The Early Medieval Settlement Remains from Flixborough, Lincolnshire: The Occupation Sequence, c. AD 600–1000*, Excavations at Flixborough 1, Oxford: Oxbow.

Loyn, H. 1994. *The Vikings in Britain*, 2nd edit., Oxford: Blackwell.

Lucy, S., Tipper, J. and Dickens, A. 2009. *The Anglo-Saxon Settlement and Cemetery at Bloodmoor Hill, Carlton Colville*, East Anglian Archaeology, 131, Bury St Edmunds.

Martin, T. F. 2015. *The Cruciform Brooch and Anglo-Saxon England*, Woodbridge: Boydell.

Reynolds, A. 2004. 'Boundaries and settlements in later sixth to eleventh century England', in D. Griffiths, A. Reynolds and S. Semple (eds.), *Boundaries in Early Medieval Britain, ASSAH*, **12**, 98–136.

Rippon, S. J. 2010. 'Landscape change during the "long eighth century" in southern England', in N. J. Higham and M. J. Ryan (eds.), *Landscape Archaeology of Anglo-Saxon England*, 39–64, Woodbridge: Boydell.

Slade, E. F. 1958. 'Domesday survey', in L. Margaret Midgley (ed.), *Victoria Country History: Staffordshire*, Vol. 4, 1–60, Oxford: OUP for the University of London Institute of Historical Research.

Tester, A., Anderson, S., Riddler, I. and Carr, R. 2014. *Staunch Meadow, Brandon, Suffolk: A High Status Middle Saxon Settlement on the Fen Edge*, East Anglian Archaeology, 151, Bury St Edmunds.

Williams, D. and Vince, A. 1997. 'The characterisation and interpretation of Early to Middle Saxon granitic tempered pottery in England', *Medieval Arch.*, **41**, 214–20.

Objects from a distant place: transformation and use of Insular mounts from Viking-Age burials in Trøndelag, Central Norway

Aina Margrethe Heen Pettersen

Abstract

The most common Celtic and Anglo-Saxon objects found in Norway are various types of highly decorated copper-alloy or silver mounts, often found as fragments of the original piece. This article presents an overview of Insular mounts found in Trøndelag, Central Norway and discusses how this material was altered and transformed when brought over the North Sea from Britain and Ireland and placed into new Norse settings. By analyzing the objects' functions and contextual information, we can see how this material was adapted for use in female Norse dress in various ways: as third brooches, individual brooches, paired brooches, pendants or belt fittings/decorations. As distinctive elements of the Norse costume, it is argued that Insular mounts were actively used to visualize the household's involvement in successful overseas expeditions and the status accrued by a family member's return. This may be viewed as evidence of a new form of social identity which emerged in the first part of the Viking Age, where the wearing of such pieces created a visual distinction between those families and others within their community, highlighting the value of these items for creating and negotiating identity.

Introduction

The occurrence of a large quantity of Insular imports in Viking-Age Scandinavia is usually regarded as archaeological evidence for the extensive and historically-attested Scandinavian interaction with Britain and Ireland (the 'Insular area' referred to in this paper). The overwhelming majority of this material has been found in Norway, with over 400 pieces known so far.[1] The most common Insular imports are various types of highly decorated copper-alloy or silver mounts, most of which appear to be either reworked pieces of horse harness or derived from religious equipment such as reliquary shrines, books and altar furniture. These items are found over a large area of Norway, as far north as Tromsø.

This paper seeks to present an overview of the Insular mounts found in Trøndelag in Central Norway, and to consider how this material was transformed, used and invested with new meanings as the objects changed hands and came to be used and displayed in new cultural contexts. The material from the Trøndelag region is significant in both quality and quantity, but has, with notable exceptions, received limited academic attention. A review of the functions, contextual information and diverse life-stages (biographies) of these objects may therefore give new insight into how Insular mounts were incorporated, used and valued in the Scandinavian homelands.

The Trøndelag region

Trøndelag as a region is dominated by the Trondheimsfjord, an area rich in agricultural land and in a sheltered location, with excellent communications by both water and land. The fjord itself would have made the coastline easily accessible for communities based in the inner parts of Trøndelag, while several large valleys connect the fjord with central Sweden. The presence of numerous monumental burial mounds, high-status graves, cult and court sites within the region, all suggest that the Trondheimsfjord was an area of complex economic and social development in the Viking period, with well-established contacts both westward and to the east.

Snorre Sturlason's *Heimskringla*, a collection of sagas about the kings of Norway, refers to a number of strong and powerful chieftain centres in Trøndelag, especially from areas within the Trondheimsfjord. The family of the Jarl of Lade, situated close to the modern city of Trondheim was, according to the saga of Harald Fairhair, among the most powerful in Norway during the early part of the Viking Age.[2] Trondheim, or *Nidaros*, to use its early name, was a royal foundation of the late Viking Age, on the site of a trading centre that had grown at the mouth of the river Nid.[3] Also of great significance is the fact that the martyred king and later patron saint of Norway, St Olaf, lost his life in AD 1030 at the battle of Stiklestad near Verdal.

Insular material and contact

Given the importance and wide-ranging contacts of this region, it may be no coincidence that communities in Trøndelag appear to have had strong links with the British Isles during the Viking Age. An updated catalogue of Insular material shows that there are eighty-seven such objects at seventy-three sites from the region, most of which lie close to the Trondheimsfjord.[4] Imported items include both religious and secular objects of great rarity, value and beauty (see Table 1). Only one item (a ring-headed pin of possible Insular origin) derives from a settlement context, while the remaining objects originate from probable or confirmed burials.

The population of Trøndelag incorporated and used the foreign imports in various ways. The desire to wear Insular dress ornaments and fasteners is, for example, reflected in a number of ring-headed pins and ring-brooches (annular and penannular). Dress fasteners in the form of bronze ring-headed pins represent a widespread male fashion and were used to fasten an outer garment, for example a cloak. The commonest ringed pin in Norway is the plain, ringed loop-headed type, with origins in pre-Viking Ireland, and ringed pins found in Norway are often regarded as Insular imports.[5] Of the ringed pins from Trøndelag, at least four examples are regarded as Insular imports due to their design and decoration. The origins of nearly twenty simple pins from the region are more problematic since their lack of decoration complicates the problem of distinguishing imports into Scandinavia from possible local copies.

Of the rarer ring brooches, only twenty-two imported Insular examples have been identified in Norway, four of which are found in women's burials in Trøndelag. Ann Zanette Glørstad has suggested that Norse women buried with such brooches may have been communicating their personal connection with overseas colonies through their jewellery. As such, these items would display the economic and political resources that could be drawn from the Insular networks.[6] In connection with this, it is worth noting that two of the ring brooches from Trøndelag – found at Nes, Bjugn and at Snåsa – represent the finest and best-preserved examples of this type from the whole of Norway. The prestige of owning and being buried with such items may well indicate that the women, or at least their families, had a particularly important role within the overseas networks.

Swords appear relatively frequently in better-equipped male burials in Viking-age Norway. A small number of these swords, classed as Petersen type L, have been imported from Anglo-Saxon England. In Norway, eighteen swords belonging to this group are known, five of which were found in Trøndelag.[7] In addition to their practical use, swords are likely to have been used as status symbols in all social environments, while the quality of both blade and guard were determined by the owners' social standing and economic capacity.[8] Certain types of swords and other high-status weapons in Norse graves are likely to have marked the buried person's place in society

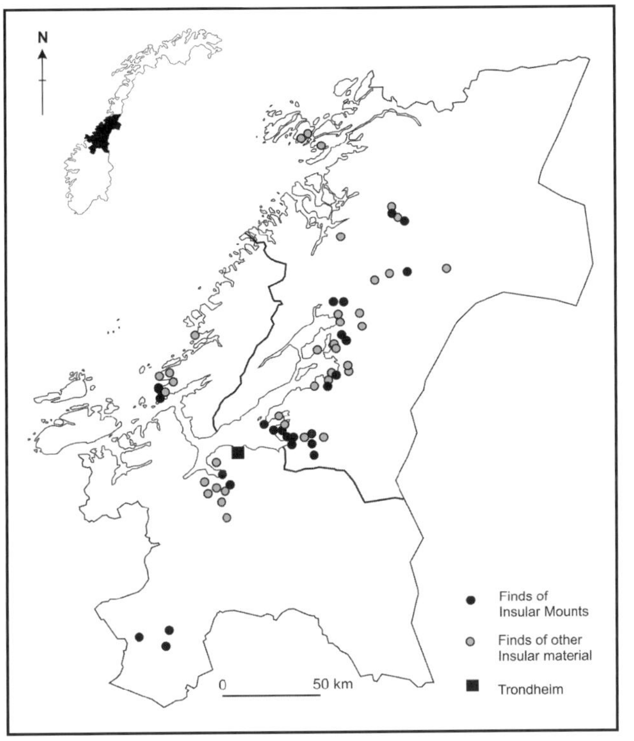

Fig. 1 Distribution of Insular finds in Trøndelag. Map by Aina Heen-Pettersen.

rather than purely reflecting an actual role as warriors or professional soldiers. Owing to their small number and distinctive design, it is thought these Anglo-Saxon swords were regarded as particularly strong symbols of power and status among the upper social levels of Norse society.[9]

From Trøndelag, twelve Viking-Age burials are also known which contain remains of balance scales, sometimes accompanied by weights. Their small size suggests the weighing of valuable commodities, which might have been principally silver, whether coins, ingots or hacksilver. Balance scales most commonly occur in men's graves, of both the ninth and tenth centuries. Several researchers have claimed that most of the scales found in Norway may be of Insular origin, based on their decoration and design, although Graham-Campbell has cautioned against this view.[10] Steuer has separated out one group of balances (Type 2), with collapsible beams, characteristic tinning and pans suspended on three strands, which he identifies as being of western origin.[11] Several of the well-preserved examples from Trøndelag display one or more of the characteristics of Steuer's Type 2, but a detailed study of this artefact group has not yet been carried out. The balances from Trøndelag are therefore considered here (in Table 1) as possible Insular imports, although this supposition must naturally be regarded with caution. Sometimes, combined with bronze boxes and lead weights, the scales from Norway have been interpreted generally as evidence of Norse trading activities. However, such weighing equipment may also have been used in a wide variety of forms of exchange, for example accurate loot-sharing, gift-giving, or collection of bails and taxes – all involving precious metals.[12]

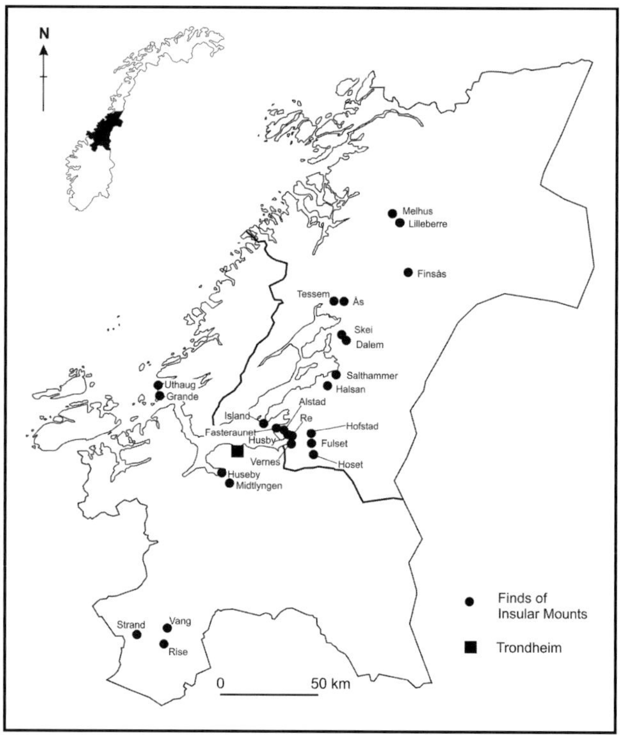

Fig. 2 Distribution of burials in Trøndelag containing Insular mounts. Map by Aina Heen-Pettersen.

Fig. 3 Anglo-Saxon bronze mount, stray find from Tessem, Steinkjer. Length 80 mm, © Bergen University, drawing by Per Rasmussen.

Other Insular imports were brought home for festive use as serving and drinking vessels on 'the high table'. This material includes eight drinking horns, six bronze vessels, five bronze ladles and three ornamented yew buckets. They occur mainly in women's burials, but such items have occasionally been found in the graves of men.[13] Sometimes two or more such items are found in the same burial, probably forming an exclusive set of serving equipment. These items are likely to have been highly valued pieces of household equipment in Norse communities, where feasting and formal entertainment played a major role in social and political strategies.

In addition to the groups described, there are also several individual Insular finds, including a complete reliquary shrine, two small buttons made of thin threads of silver, a bronze bridle, an Anglo-Saxon disc-brooch and a jet bead.

The insular mounts from Trøndelag – an overview

This article will focus on the largest group of Insular imports: decorated mount pieces of silver and bronze, most of which appear to stem from ecclesiastical objects or horse harness. Within the Trøndelag region, twenty-nine whole or partial mounts have been found, at twenty-seven locations spread across the region (Fig. 2). The latest example, a reworked harness mount, was found at Agdenes by a metal detectorist in the summer of 2016.[14] It is probably a Celtic piece of the eighth or early ninth century.[15] A noteworthy feature is the two facing creatures, possibly fish or dolphins, which flank the panel and end in paired, overlapping tails, which is an unusual feature. However, a parallel can be found on one of the Pictish stone crosses from Aberlemno in Scotland (Aberlemno 2). A secondary perforation which disturbs the original decoration can be seen at the base of the mount. Furthermore, the conservator also noted the existence of some rust, possible from a nail, at the back of the piece. This indicates a possible secondary use as a brooch.

In this paper, individual site names are given in the format of farm followed by township – for example Skei, Steinkjer. It should, however, be noted that a number of mounts from a man's cremation burial at Kolset, Stjørdal are not included since this find appears not to have been reworked, but retained its original function as horse harness. Also, two mounts from Solstad, Skaun and Tønnøl, Bjugn which were turned into weights, will not be further discussed in this paper.

All the Insular mounts from Trøndelag have traces of gilding, and, with the exception of two silver examples, all the pieces are made of copper alloy. The majority of the mounts are thought to be of Irish/Celtic origin.[16] Egil Bakka and Egon Wamers have, however, identified four pieces from Trøndelag which may be English products (Figs. 3 and 4). Three of these have been found in the region of Stjørdal, an area with a marked concentration of English-produced objects.[17] In this area, twelve burials with Insular material have been identified and half of these contained Anglo-Saxon metalwork, including two swords,

Table 1 Locations and overview of Insular finds from Trøndelag

Location	Artefact type	Sex	Burial type	Date	Accession year	Associated grave goods
Ryum, Vikna	Drinking horn (mount)	Female	Barrow	9th century	19th century	3 oval brooches (R652), 2 fragments of bronze
Ryum, Vikna	Balance scale (bowl)	Female	Barrow	AD 850–900	19th century	2 oval brooches (P42)
Rørvik, Vikna	Balance scale (bowl)	Uncertain	Uncertain	Viking Age	1876	-
Varø, Nærøy	Drinking horn (mount)	Uncertain	Stray find	Viking Age	1901	-
Bjørnes Nedre, Overhalla	Balance scale (fragment)	Male	Boat burial, barrow	AD 900–950	1874	Sword, spearhead, bead, lead weight, nails, wooden bowl, remains of textile and leather, iron fragments
Bjørnes Nedre, Overhalla	Balance scale (arm)	Uncertain	Boat burial, barrow	Viking Age	1905	-
Voll, Overhalla	Drinking horn, balance scale	Male	Stone cist, barrow	10th century	1873	Sword, 2 spears, axe, clover-shaped silver pin, comb, scissors, padlock, whetstone, iron punch, file, remains of textile and leather, several wooden vessels
Melhus, Overhalla	Bronze mount, reliquary	Female	Boat burial, barrow	*c.* AD 800		2 oval brooches (R643), large fibula (R649), 137 beads, whalebone plaque, whalebone weaving sword, spindle whorl
Lilleberre, Overhalla	Bronze mount	Female	Barrow	9th century	1886	2 oval brooches, glass beads, whalebone plaque, spindle whorl
Klingen, Namsos	Jet bead	Female	Wooden coffin, barrow	AD 900–950	1913	2 oval brooches (R652), 39 beads, spindle whorl, fragment of black glass
Unknown farm in Snåsa	Ring brooch	Female	Uncertain	10th century	19th century	3 oval brooches (R657)
Finsås, Steinkjer	Silver mount	Female	Stone cist	9th century	1946	2 oval brooches (R649), knife, sickle, nails
Heggestrøa, Steinkjer	Sword, type L	Male	Boat burial, barrow	9th century	1942	Spearhead, axe
Øksnes, Steinkjer	Bronze ladle	Male	Simple dug grave	10th century	1953	2 swords (type H), 3 beads, iron mount
Ås, Steinkjer	Bronze mount	Male	Barrow	AD 850–900	1921	Sword (type M), knife, whetstone, 2 nails
Tessem, Steinkjer	Bronze mount	Uncertain	Stray find	Viking Age	1946	-
Egge, Steinkjer	Bronze bowl	Female (?)	Cremation, barrow	Viking Age	1873	2 beads, whalebone plaque, frying pan, iron hook, nails, iron mount
Fossem., Steinkjer	Ring brooch	Female	Barrow	Viking Age	1954	Spindle whorl, whetstone, nails
Lø, Steinkjer	Balance scale, ringed pin	Male	Boat burial, barrow	AD 900–950	2003	2 shield bosses, sword (type H), spear, 7 arrowheads, knife, whetstone, 3 glass beads, flint, iron object
Lø, Steinkjer	Silver threaded button	Uncertain	Cremation in boat burial, barrow	AD 920–960 or later	2002	Knife, simple bronze mount
Lø, Steinkjer	Bronze bowl	Uncertain	Boat burial, barrow	AD 900–950	1969	Iron cauldron, chain of metal rings, scissors, 3 beads of carnelian, bridle, whetstone, nails, small silver mount, 3 fragments of silver thread
Bjerkem, Steinkjer	Ringed pin	Male	Barrow	Viking Age	1882	2 axes
Skei, Steinkjer	Bronze mount, bucket, bronze ladle, hanging bowl	Female	Stone cist, barrow	*c.* AD 800	1986	Oval brooch (Berdal 1a), whalebone plaque, bridle, wheel-shaped brooch, 7 beads, horse harness mounts
Dalem, Steinkjer	Bronze mount	Male	Barrow	Viking Age	1871	Sword

Location	Artefact type	Sex	Burial type	Date	Accession year	Associated grave goods
Smolan, Steinkjer	Ring brooch	Female	Cairn	9th century	1891	2 oval brooches (R647), 3 glass beads, iron fragments
Kolset, Stjørdal	Set of horse harness mounts	Male	Cremation	10th century	1931	Sword (type M), spearhead, bridle
Sundnes, Inderøy	Sword, type L	Male (?)	Barrow	Viking Age	1871	-
Haug, Verdal	Balance scale	Male	Boat burial, barrow	9th century	1969	Sword (type E , Ulfberth inscription), amber bead, spearhead, blacksmiths tongs, scissors, sickle, whetstone
Rosvold, Verdal	Sword, type L	Male (?)	Uncertain	Viking Age	1953	-
Storborg, Levanger	Balance scale	Female	Simple dug grave	9th century	1858	2 oval brooches (R647), 3 silver pendants, 2 gilded bronze pendants, 22 beads, iron fragment
Salthammer, Levanger	Bronze mount	Female	Simple dug grave	AD 850–900	1900	Oval brooch (R647)
Gjeite, Levanger	Bronze bowl, 2 drinking horn mounts	Female	Cremated boat burial, barrow	*c.* AD 800	1987	2 oval brooches (R652), fragments of a silver chain, 188 beads, comb, 2 knives, iron key/latch-lifter, fragments of iron and lead, whalebone plaque, animal bones, casket mounts, nails and hinges
Alstadhaug, Levanger	Bronze bowl	Male	Possible boat burial	10th century	1923	Spearhead
Halsan, Levanger	Yew bucket, 2 bronze mounts	Female	Barrow	Viking Age	1869	11 beads, 1 piece of glass, wooden bowl
Island, Frosta	Drinking horn mount, 2 bronze mounts	Uncertain	Barrow	9th century	1872	Iron rattle, iron fragment
Steinvik, Stjørdal	Sword, type L	Male (?)	Stray find	Viking Age	1900	-
Alstad, Stjørdal	Bronze mount	Female	Cairn	AD 800–850	1875	2 oval brooches (P37), 128 beads, whetstone, glass ring, bronze fragment
Fasteraunet, Stjørdal	Drinking horn mount, bronze mount	Female	Stone cist	AD 800–850	1911	2 oval brooches (P37), 158 beads, bronze ring, needle, 2 spindle whorls, 2 arrowheads, 2 iron rings, remains of textile and leather
Re, Stjørdal	Silver mount	Female	Uncertain	AD 800–850	1881	2 oval brooches (P37), 75 glass beads, bronze chain, knife, iron fragments, textile fragments
Vernes, Stjørdal	Bronze mount	Female	Boat burial, barrow	AD 850–900	1942	2 oval brooches (P42), 18 beads, spindle whorl
Moksnes, Stjørdal	Balance scale	Male	Boat burial, barrow	*c.* AD 900	1930	Sword, spearhead, axe, shield boss, knife, hammer, blacksmiths tongs, belt buckle, whetstone, scythe
Bjørken, Stjørdal	Sword, type L	Male	Cremation, barrow	AD 850–900	1892	Axe, arrow, whetstone
Hofstad, Stjørdal	Bronze mount	Uncertain	Stray find	Viking Age	1881	-
Kongshaug, Stjørdal	Bronze ladle	Female	Barrow	9th century	1934	Oval brooch (R647)
Fulset, Stjørdal	Disc brooch	Female	Uncertain	AD 900–950	1871	2 oval brooches (P51)
Hoset, Stjørdal	Bronze mount	Female	Cremation, barrow	AD 900–950	1964	2 oval brooches (P51), metal ring
Husby, Stjørdal	Bronze mount	Female	Boat burial	AD 800–850	1936	2 oval brooches (R657), slag, remains of textile and leather
Tårnes, Åfjord	Ringed pin	Uncertain	Stray find	Viking Age	1925	-
Tønnøl, Bjugn	Balance scale, lead weight with bronze mount	Male	Boat burial, barrow	10th century	1872	Shield boss, arm ring of silver, whetstone

Location	Artefact type	Sex	Burial type	Date	Accession year	Associated grave goods
Steinvik, Bjugn	2 bronze ladles, bronze cauldron, 2 handle plates of a yew bucket	Uncertain	Boat burial, barrow	Viking Age	1894	Fragmented oval brooch
Nes, Bjugn	Ring brooch	Female	Cairn	AD 800–850	1928	3 oval brooches (R647, R650), 3 beads, 2 spindle whorls, iron weaving sword, loom weight fragment, knife, iron mount
Uthaug, Ørland	Bronze mount	Female	Simple dug grave	AD 800–850	1953	2 oval brooches (R648), 22 beads, spindle whorl, whalebone weaving sword, sickle, key, iron mount, iron hook, dog skeleton
Grande, Ørland	Bronze mount	Female	Wooden cist, simple dug grave	*c.* AD 800	1956	2 oval brooches (R640), 2 bronze keys, 4 spindle whorls, whalebone plaque, 3 beads, comb, sickle, knife, nails, remains of textile
Viklem, Ørlandet	Ringed pin	-	From building	10th century	2013	-
Byneset, Trondheim	Silver threaded button	-	Stray find	-	2014	-
Huseby, Skaun	Bronze mount, drinking horn mount	Female	Simple dug grave	9th century	1908	2 oval brooches (R657), Frankish trefoil silver mounting, fragmented silver chain, 3 silver rings, 2 bronze keys, scissors, sickle, knife, iron fragments
Midtlyngen, Melhus	Bronze mount	Female (?)	Uncertain	Viking Age	19th century	Possibly found with some beads
Gravråk, Melhus	Balance scale	Male	Barrow	9th century	1864	Sword, knife, fork-shaped iron tool, scissors
Rimol, Melhus	Bronze object, uncertain function	-	Stray find	-	2014	-
Vollan, Melhus	Drinking horn mount	-	Stray find	-	2015	-
Vigdal, Skaun	Balance scale (arm)	Male (?)	Barrow	Viking Age	1872	Possibly found with a sword and a spearhead
Nerrian, Skaun	Bronze bridle	-	Stray find	Viking Age	1931	-
Solstad, Skaun	Weight with bronze mount	-	Stray find	Viking Age	1884	-
Eistenstad, Støren	Ringed pin	-	Stray find	Viking Age	19th century	-
Vang, Oppdal	Bronze mount	Male	Uncertain	9th century	1885	Sword (type K), 2 spearheads, bead, bridle
Vang, Oppdal	Bronze mount	Male	Cremation, barrow	AD 900–950	1981	Sword (type I, Ulbfberht inscription on the blade), spearhead, axe, shield boss, 9 beads, scissors, 2 knives, 2 sickles, 2 bridles
Vang, Oppdal	Bronze mount	Female	Cremation, barrow	AD 900–950	1990	Oval brooch (P51), 2 beads, knife, hook shaped key, iron mounts
Strand, Oppdal	Bronze mount	Uncertain	Uncertain	Viking Age	1934	-
Rise, Oppdal	Bronze mount	Female	Uncertain	AD 900–950	1834	Oval brooch (P51)

*Notes: R = typology types in Rygh 1885
P = typology types in Petersen 1928
Swords are defined after the typology types in Petersen 1919
Simple types of ringed pins of uncertain origin are not included in the list

Fig. 4 Anglo-Saxon bronze mount, from a woman's burial in Alstad in Stjørdal, ninth century. © Bergen University, drawing by Per Rasmussen.

three bronze/silver mounts and a disc-brooch.[18] A review of Insular objects from burials countrywide indicates that Stjørdal is among the areas with the highest number of artefacts of English origin in Norway. Only in Vestfold, near Oslo, and in adjacent areas have similar or higher concentrations of finds of English origin been identified.[19]

In the last twenty years, the distribution map of Insular imports in Scandinavia has changed significantly, mainly due to metal-detector finds which have increased the number of imported items considerably, especially in Denmark, which previously appeared to be lacking Insular finds. While only five finds of Insular metalwork were known from Denmark in 1985, today more than fifty such objects have been identified, including thirty-eight mounts or fittings. At least twenty-two of these show evidence of secondary working.[20] It seems clear, however, that Insular mounts in this part of Scandinavia circulated and were deposited differently to those in Norway. The Norwegian examples derive mostly from graves, usually with only one piece in each burial.[21] Other find contexts are rare, but there are occasional exceptions, for example at the trading town of Kaupang. Here, a number of mounts have been found at the settlement site as well as in nearby graves. The fragmented condition of the items from the settlement area indicates that many of these were probably the waste produced when larger objects were reworked.[22]

While the Norwegian examples were mostly sealed in graves, it seems that the majority of Insular mounts in Denmark had a more dynamic life circle. Here, the majority of the known pieces ended up as scrap-like metal in settlement contexts associated with the elite, after first being reworked and repaired.[23] Although deposited differently from the Norwegian examples, these newer finds provide evidence that the wearing and use of reworked decorative Insular metalwork extended far wider in Scandinavian areas than previously believed.[24]

Following the national pattern, nearly all of the Insular mounts found in Trøndelag originate from certain or relatively certain burial contexts. Only four examples are stray finds and these items, as with many other artefacts from the period without contextual information, are assumed to be from destroyed graves. It has long been established that the majority of Insular metalwork which was brought back to Norway ultimately found its way into female graves.[25] Based on the occurrence of jewellery or textile implements and of weapons, indicative of female and male burials respectively, it is apparent that the Insular mounts from Trøndelag mainly appear in women's burials, most of which are dated to the ninth century. Only four male burials from the region are known to have contained such items. The clear association of Insular mounts with women's burials is also apparent

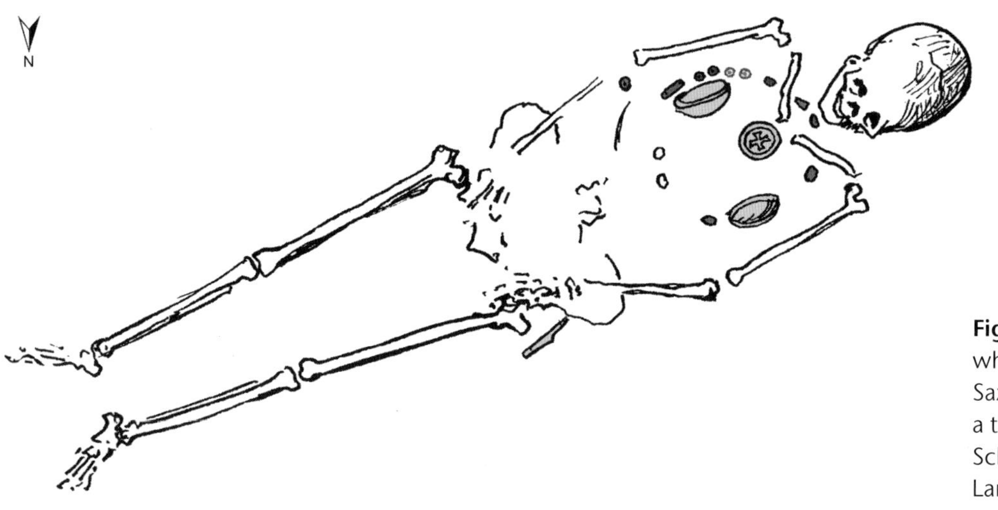

Fig. 5 Burial from Hedeby where a reworked Anglo-Saxon plate has served as a third brooch. © Stiftung Schleswig – Holsteinische Landesmuseen Schleswig.

in other parts of Norway. In south-eastern Norway, for example, reworked Insular mounts have been found in twenty-seven graves, only two of which are possible men's burials. Hanne Aannestad has suggested that if the pieces belonged to the men, they are likely to represent a gift given to the buried or a personal memento, rather than their own personal decoration or jewellery.[26] Oddmunn Farbregd has put forward a similar explanation in connection with the find of a reworked harness mount from a man's burial at Vang, Trøndelag.[27]

Insular imported goods were, in all probability, acquired through a variety of processes and modes of interaction, and it can be somewhat difficult to separate different forms of exchange in the archaeological record. Traditionally, Insular mounts are often interpreted as exotic gifts or souvenirs given to the wives and mothers of men returning from raids overseas.[28] A typical explanation was given by Johannes Bøe, who stated that: 'The custom of wearing souvenirs presented to them by the Vikings on the return from his westward expedition, has evidently been high fashion among the Norwegian women in the first half of the ninth century'.[29] This view is supported by two mounts from Gausel, Western Norway and St. Germain in Paris, which are likely to have belonged to the same Irish reliquary. While the Gausel mount derives from a richly furnished woman's burial, the St. Germain mount has no recorded provenance. Bakka has argued that these mounts are evidence of the breaking down of ecclesiastical items as redistribution of loot.[30] However, a number of Insular mounts have been found in graves from the contemporary trading settlements of Kaupang, Hedeby, Helgø and Birka, leading to the suggestion that some of this material represents merchandise and was sold second-hand.[31] Such exchange may also have taken place in the Insular area as indicated by certain finds such as the *Shanmullagh* hoard or stock of metalwork from the River Blackwater, near Armagh, Northern Ireland. The hoard contained a large amount of metalwork, including scrap metal, parts of hanging bowls and ecclesiastical objects, Hiberno-Scandinavian 'hack-silver', ring-headed pins and lead weights. The composition of this assemblage may indicate a systematic collection and 'export' of these metal objects, possibly carried out by a Scandinavian who met misfortune on the river.[32] Furthermore, attention has been drawn to the circulation of ecclesiastical objects in secular contexts within the British Isles, and the fact that monastic and secular craft production would have overlapped to a degree.[33] This may indicate that production of decorated metalwork was intended for a wider market than just the Church, leading to the possibility that Vikings also may have been customers for these goods and had the opportunity to acquire seemingly ecclesiastical objects by peaceful means.[34] Wamers, in contrast, has in several works stressed that it is unlikely that ecclesiastical artefacts found in Scandinavia represent merchandise.[35] He has proposed that some of this material from trading settlements may derive from a Norse custom of 'pillage-trading', where people who traded also took part in raids whenever this was more profitable. In later work Wamers has, however, pointed out that the second-hand trade in Insular ornament was probably more considerable than he had previously believed, but he considers the extent of any such trade to have been fairly minor. Other researchers have put forward an alternative explanation, suggesting that several ecclesiastical objects found in Norway may have been brought to Scandinavia by missionaries.[36] It is possible that any such early missionary missions were unsuccessful, resulting in the objects being confiscated and later used for decorative purposes.[37] Nonetheless, based on the ninth-century dates for the majority of graves containing mounts, it seems that these objects were most valued and appreciated during the first phase of contact and colonization of the British Isles.

Insular mounts and Norse female costume

The various life-stages of Insular mounts – e.g. place of origin, exchange, ownership and original function – may all have affected the way in which these artefacts were used and understood in Norse societies. As objects are recontextualised, their functions and meanings are renegotiated and changed to the current situation.[38] The following sections of the article aim to consider in more detail how Insular mounts were altered and transformed after they were removed from their original contexts, brought over the North Sea and placed into new Norse settings.

The majority of Insular mounts from both Trøndelag and the rest of Norway are almost exclusively found in women's graves, many of which contain oval brooches (the usual Scandinavian term for tortoise brooches). In Trøndelag, oval brooches are found in association with Insular mounts at nineteen locations. Oval brooches emerged at the very start of the eight century, and were fashionable throughout much of the Viking Age before they fell out of use towards the end of the tenth century.[39] They were worn as part of the traditional Viking-Age dress of a Scandinavian woman to fasten the shoulder straps of a tunic or dress worn over a shift, and are usually seen as jewellery reserved for the freeborn housemistress of some standing.[40] There exists also a rare example of a Norse burial from Carn a'Bharraich, Scotland where a woman was found with a pair of shrine hinges that had been reworked into matching dress fasteners, worn in the place of oval brooches.[41] Perhaps she had lost or broken her original brooches and had to find other ways to replace them, since the supply of such dress fasteners to the Insular areas is likely to have been limited.

In addition to the oval brooches, a third dress fastener was sometimes worn. Back in 1928 Petersen found that nearly half (143 of 322) of all Norwegian Viking-Age burials with oval brooches contained an additional dress-fastener, which he defines as a 'chest brooch'.[42] Although this is an old study, it is believed that that the ratio between burials containing only oval brooches and burials with an additional

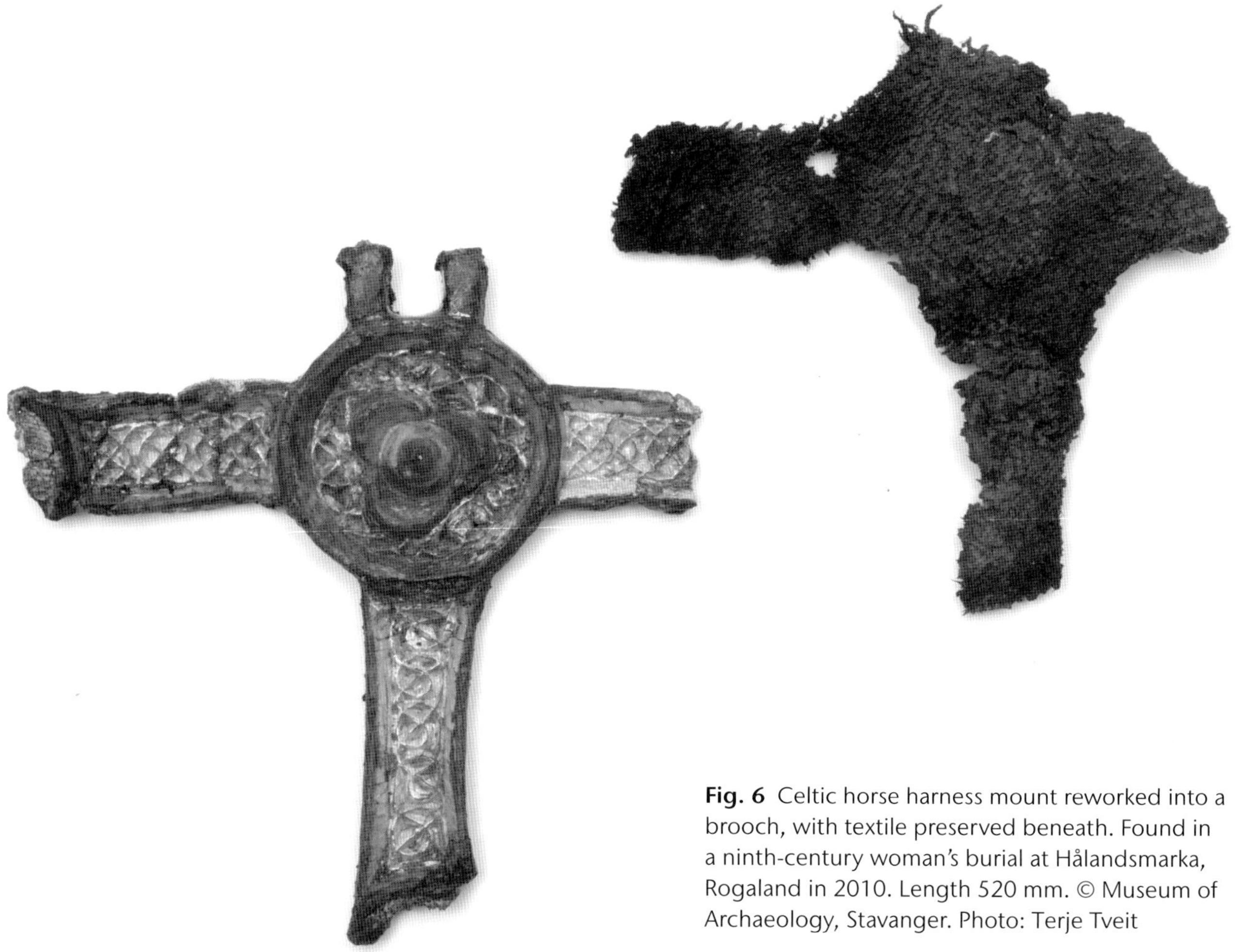

Fig. 6 Celtic horse harness mount reworked into a brooch, with textile preserved beneath. Found in a ninth-century woman's burial at Hålandsmarka, Rogaland in 2010. Length 520 mm. © Museum of Archaeology, Stavanger. Photo: Terje Tveit

third brooch is still relatively correct. The use of third dress fasteners is therefore likely to have been a relatively widespread fashion throughout much of the Viking Age.[43] These brooches exist in a variety of shapes and sizes and could hence have had different uses. The largest examples may have been most suitable for use on thicker and more robust textiles or outer garments, for example to fasten a cape or a cloak. In contrast, the smallest brooches may rather have been worn on thinner inner garments or dresses.[44]

At least nineteen of twenty-eight mount pieces from Trøndelag display clear signs of alteration, by the addition of one or more holes or pins/pin fittings. This alteration is likely to have happened after the items were brought to Norway.[45] Since a great many of the Insular mounts from Norway appear to have been converted into brooches and occur in burials with oval brooches, it was suggested as early as 1926 that the adapted mounts were mainly used as a *third brooch*.[46] This suggestion arose from a grave find at Vinjum, Rogaland (south-west Norway), where the position of a reworked square silver casting (the terminal of an Insular ring brooch) indicated such a use. Following the discovering at Vinjum, at least three further graves in Norway have been uncovered – at Kaupang, Skiringssal (two burials) and Laland, Klepp which support the interpretation of these mounts as third brooches. In these cases, the mounts were each found *in situ* and apparently undisturbed on the chests of the buried women, between two oval brooches. The two mounts from Kaupang appear to be reworked pieces of a horse harness and a book mount,[47] while the example from Laland, Klepp has been identified as a strap-end.[48] An additional example is known from the Viking-Age trading town at Hedeby near present-day Schleswig in Germany, where a reworked Anglo-Saxon circular plate seems to have served as a third brooch (see Fig. 5).[49] Also worth noting is a burial from Hålandsmarka in Rogaland, excavated in 2009, where a reworked harness mount was found in the 'head end' of the grave, slightly above the remains of a bead necklace.[50] The *in situ* position clearly indicates that the mount was used on the upper body of the individual, although it functioned as an individual brooch rather than a third dress fastener, since the burial lacked the usual oval brooches. Remains of textile preserved on the back of the piece also seem to confirm that the mount was once attached to the clothing of the individual (see Fig. 6).

Based on the find circumstances of the above cases, the interpretation of the mounts' use as third brooches has become well established and repeated in numerous papers and publications.[51] Are there any examples from Trøndelag which also fit this interpretation?

Fig. 7 Celtic mount reworked into a brooch, with textile preserved beneath. Found in a ninth-century woman's burial at Lilleberre, Overhalla in 1886.

Reviewing the Trøndelag evidence for Insular mounts in general, there are in fact only nine burials containing mount fragments for which there is any detailed information on the relative locations of the finds. Of these, three of the professionally investigated graves were cremation burials, which, naturally, provide no information regarding the mounts' use in relation to Norse costume.

In a female burial from Huseby, Stjørdal an Insular mount was found in 1936 accompanied by two oval brooches, remains of fur and textile, nutshells and some pieces of slag. In the museum catalogue the find circumstances are described: 'The piece (*Insular mount*) was, when discovered, covered by a layer of wool cloth, which could be seen to be partly folded onto the (mount's) underside'.[52] The locations of the artefacts within the grave are not described further. It is therefore uncertain whether the piece had originally been attached to the clothing of the buried woman.

In two cases from Fasteraunet, Stjørdal and Skei, Steinkjer, Insular mounts are indeed recorded as having been found at the 'head end' of the graves. In the Skei burial (excavated in 1986), the mount was found approximately 0.30m below the head of the woman, in the same area as some beads and an oval brooch. It had been reworked by the addition of a pin-fastener, and remains of two layers of different textiles, probably from a tunic or dress worn over a shift, were preserved on the back of the mount.[53] This part of the grave was, however, disturbed by a modern posthole and the original positions of the artefacts are again, therefore, uncertain. Two layers of different textiles were also preserved behind a reworked mount piece from Lilleberre, Overhalla, now stored at the British Museum (Fig. 7). Although the burial was excavated in 1886, the mount has only recently been 'discovered' hidden in a lump of organic material when the finds from this burial were re-examined in 2010.[54] Other finds from this burial included a pair of oval brooches, also with remains of two layers of textile preserved on the back. Finally, according to the museum catalogue concerning the finds from Fasteraunet, Stjørdal, the mount was found near the south (head) end of the grave, in the same area as a drinking vessel, two oval brooches and a bead necklace.[55] The mount lay on top of a piece of textile, but the description is not clear as to whether the mount was actually attached to the clothing of the buried woman or found beside her. However, fragments of textile on the reverse of the piece combined with the fact that it was found at the 'head end' of the grave, may indicate a use as a third brooch.

Charlotte Blindheim has questioned the theory regarding the use of Insular mounts as third brooches. She has highlighted that such items could have had a range of uses and hence been attractive objects for trade and exchange.[56] However, Blindheim does not suggest what such varied uses could have been, especially not in association with the Norse, female dress. Aannestad has recently researched reworked imported mounts from south-eastern Norway, including Kaupang. Although her detailed study of the objects indicates that they were mostly reworked into dress fasteners, she has also identified that ten out of the forty-four Insular mounts from this region have remains of rivets or rivet-holes for possible suspension loops, indicating their use as pendants rather than brooches. These mount pieces are likely to have been suspended from oval brooches or used as individual pendants hung around the neck by the use of simple threads or other organic material.[57] Examples from Trøndelag may also throw light on the varied uses Insular mounts may have been had in association with female costume. A review of the Insular mounts from this region has revealed several further unpublished burials where the mounts have been found at or beside the waist of the buried women, accompanied by keys and knives, indicating their use as belt decorations/fittings.[58] This is a use in female Norse dress which has not previously been recognized. This is particularly evident in three female burials from Finsås, Steinkjer and Uthaug/Grande, Ørlandet, which are discussed below. These burials were discovered during the period 1946 to 1953 by the archaeological museum in Trondheim, and therefore reports or other records exist from the excavations.

Finsås

The grave from Finsås, Steinkjer was discovered in 1946. The burial was orientated NW–SE and comprised a stone cist, 1.8 m long, 0.85 m wide and with a height of approximately 0.5 m. The cist contained the remains of a woman in her twenties, laid on her back with her head at the south-eastern end of the burial.[59] Her grave goods comprised two oval brooches, an Insular mount of silver, a knife and a sickle. Based on the type of oval brooches (R649), the grave is dated to the ninth century. The Insular mount has a square form, and measures 45 × 39 mm (Figs. 8 and 9). The mount is a corner fragment from a larger piece. It is decorated with a border of Style II stranded interlace,[60] each one with an inner line of raised dots. The surviving part of the central panel has three fields of decoration, two of which incorporate birds' heads, and interlace throughout. The piece has been reworked by the addition of three small holes, disturbing the original decoration. In two of these the remains of smaller iron nails are still preserved.

Fig. 8 Silver mount from Finsås, Snåsa. © NTNU, Vitenskapsmuseet. Photo: Per Fredriksen.

The excavation report states that the oval brooches were found 'in the usual place, high up on each side of the chest'.[61] The mount, however, was found 0.4 m below the oval brooches, on the pelvis of the buried woman, close to the knife. The location of the mount clearly indicates that the piece had been fastened to a belt. In addition, the remains of leather were preserved on the reverse, which supports the suggestion that the mount was used as a belt fitting or decoration. In connection with this, it may be worth noting that remains of leather were also found preserved on the back of a further mount piece from Huseby, Skaun. In this example, however, the *in situ* location of the mount is not known.

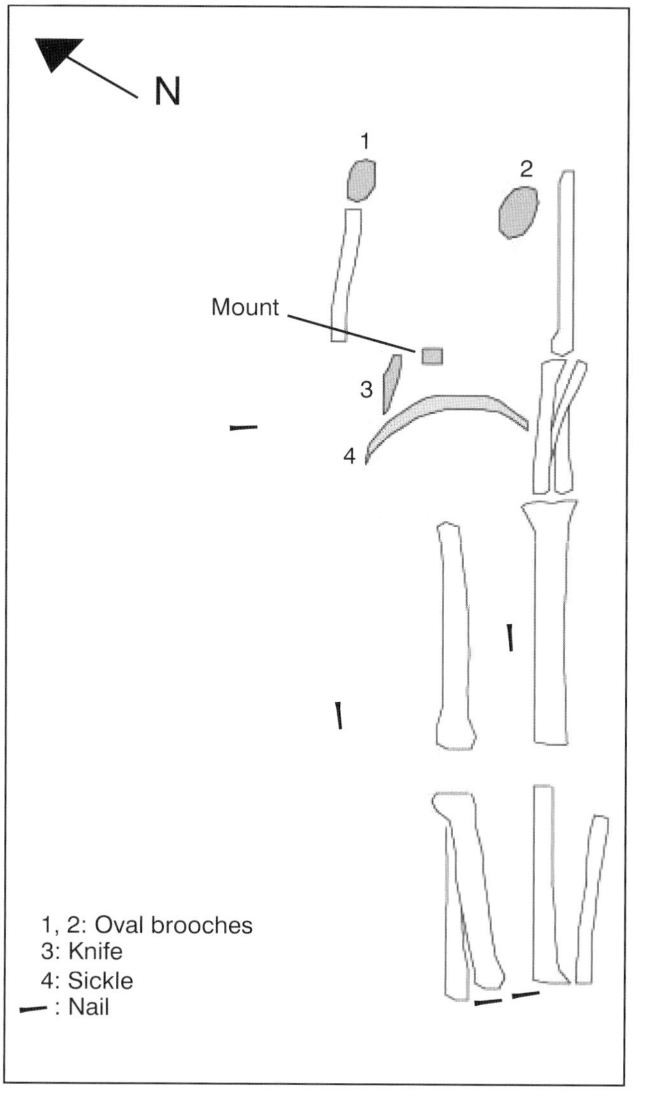

Fig. 9 Site drawing showing the position of the Finsås mount at the waist of the buried woman. Drawing based on grave plan in Petersen 1946.

Uthaug

Two other examples of female burial where Insular mounts had probably been attached to belts were excavated at the farms of Uthaug and Grande in the area of Ørlandet, by the mouth of the Trondheimfjord. The burial at Uthaug was discovered in 1953 during house building work. The grave was orientated S–N and can be dated to the first half of the ninth century. There exists no grave-plan of this burial, but the excavation report describes the location of the grave goods:

> The woman was buried with her jewellery, two chest brooches, and around her neck a necklace of glass and mother of pearl beads. Below the waist, on the right hand side lay a belt fitting of bronze (*the Insular mount*) and a small bronze tube, approximately 3cm long, which also belonged to the belt. Below the belt were several metal objects, which had probably been keys.[62]

Conservation of the metal objects later revealed that these artefacts comprised typical belt hangings including a knife, key and an iron hook. The *in situ* position of these finds indicates that they were likely to have been attached to the same belt as the Insular mount. The mount itself is a reworked harness mounting (Fig. 10). It consists of a bar with a centrally placed, lobed projection. At either end of the bar a secondary hole has been added, and in one of these the remains of an iron nail survives. The example from Uthaug is well matched by a mount found at Navan, Meath in Ireland, that forms part of an assemblage of harness mounts considered to represent grave goods of a Scandinavian burial.[63]

Grande

The second Insular mount from Ørlandet was discovered in 1956 at Grande, approximately 5 km south of Uthaug. The burial was orientated NW-SE and the woman (in her early thirties) had been placed on her back with her head at the north-west end of the grave. Remains of wood and nails around the edges of the grave indicate that this was

Fig. 10 Bronze mount from Uthaug, Ørlandet. © NTNU, Vitenskapsmuseet. Photo: Per Fredriksen.

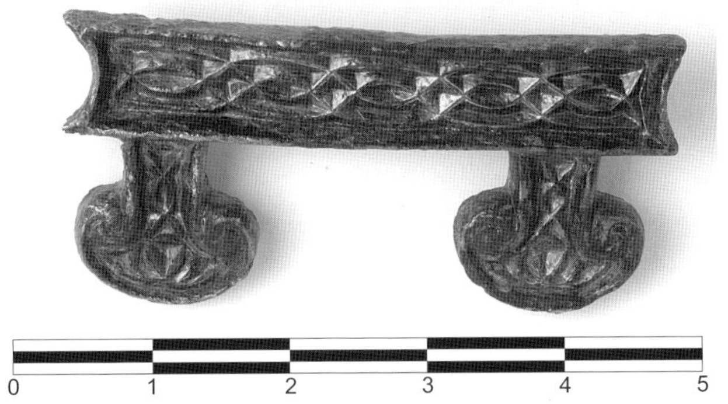

Fig. 11 Bronze mount from Grande, Ørlandet. © NTNU, Vitenskapsmuseet. Photo: Per Fredriksen.

a coffined burial. The grave goods comprised a bronze mount, two oval brooches, two bronze keys, a whale bone plaque, two knives, three beads, a comb, sickle and nails thought to originate from a small wooden box. The simple type of oval brooches (R640) suggests that the woman was buried at the very start of the ninth century or perhaps even slightly earlier.

The Insular mount lay together with the two bronze keys above waist height, under the buried woman's right arm. At approximately the same height as the mount and keys, but further left in the grave, two knives were also found.[64] The position of the mount, keys and knives indicates that theses artefacts had originally been attached to a (textile?) belt. This interpretation corresponds with information in the museum catalogue which states that: 'The keys and the Irish mount lay together at the belt area by the deceased's right hand side. The textile remains which were attached to the mount indicate that this piece was attached to the woman's belt'.[65] The gilded mount is decorated with interlacing ornaments in relief on a 45 mm long plate, which had originally been part of a horse harness (Fig. 11). On the back of the piece, near each end, two secondary pin fittings have been added. According to the excavation report, the remains of a rusty pin were preserved along the back of the piece, but the pin flaked off during the excavation work.

Overseas voyages and new markers of identity?

Within their communities, Insular mounts must have been viewed as exclusive and exotic forms of dress ornament, with a clear association with the Insular world. Whether used as brooches, belt-fittings or other types of accessory, these items would have been objects suitable for display, forming a prominent part of the clothing to which they were attached. Material culture constitutes an active element of social interaction, and several types of dress ornaments are often highlighted as artefacts utilized as particularly strong and important symbols of the wearer's status and social background.[66] In Randall Whites' view, 'personal ornaments, perhaps more than any other aspect of the archaeological record, are a point of access for archaeologists into the social world of the past'.[67] Personal artefacts have dramatic effects on the individual's property and performance characteristic, and thereby greatly influence communication.[68] Elements of a person's dress and appearance visualize and mark the wearer's role and place in society and therefore form components in displaying, creating and reformulating identities.[69] Hence, dress ornaments contribute to the 'identification, categorization and ranking' of various groups as signs of status and role.[70] It has been suggested that this may have been especially the case for exotic items, obtained from distant landscapes.[71] The apparent use of Insular mounts as various types of dress or belt ornaments indicates that these items should be considered as a part of a wider symbolic repertoire expressed through the wearer's visual appearance.

Even though mounts are the largest group of Insular objects found in the region, there are still good reasons to believe that these pieces must have been regarded as rare items. The artefacts are found spread over a larger geographical area, from Oppdal in the south to Overhalla in the northern part of Trøndelag, and are limited to a small proportion of the population in this region (see Fig. 1). The exclusiveness of the mounts is likely to have meant that they were items of great importance.

Although it is often stressed that Insular mounts are generally of trifling metal value, it seems that this would have been compensated for by their great artistic worth and rarity. In connection with this it is worth highlighting that the two silver mounts from Trøndelag appear to have been altered and used as costume decoration in the same way as the bronze pieces. This seems to confirm that the value of these items mainly lay in their decorative and exotic nature – or display value – rather than in the value of the metal. More or less every mount found in Norway has been extensively gilded, effectively masking the original bronze composition and consequently making the objects *appear* as pieces of precious metal. In addition, the mounts show a great variety in shape, decoration and size, and each item is unique. The great variation in appearance enhances the possibility that each item had a stronger and perhaps specific meaning to its audience compared with the more common Norse ornaments, e.g. oval brooches, which often appear more standardized. Regardless of whether the pieces were used as third brooches, belt decorations, pendants or other forms of dress ornaments, the gilt and highly decorated surfaces must have made the mounts difficult to ignore, forming a distinctive element of the wearer's appearance. One can imagine that the wearing of such pieces was an act loaded with meaning and significance for both wearer and gift-giver. They stood out as markers of travels into the unknown, and certain distinctive pieces may have become 'bespoke' jewellery, carrying the story of particular places, expeditions or people.[72]

Participating in early overseas voyages and expeditions must have represented a significant risk and the number of crewmembers losing their lives due to shipwrecks, accidents and violence must have been substantial. However, in a world where it was possible for individuals to draw upon campaign experience to navigate their way up the social hierarchy, the risks involved were often worth taking.[73] Portable wealth acquired on long journeys also provided an important means of boosting power and prestige for individuals upon their return to their communities.[74] The economic and ideological resources that could be drawn from the Insular networks must have been significant, providing a considerable source of income and status for those involved. For young men, especially younger sons with little chance to inherit land, it would provide an opportunity to acquire the means needed to provide a dowry, buy land and establish a household. They were joined by would-be chieftains, royal deputies, exiles and others seeking to gain wealth and reputation in the face of increasing competition within Scandinavia.[75] Individuals involved in the overseas voyages were not equal partners, and burials from Trøndelag containing Insular mounts or other Insular imports show how members from different levels of society organized, took part in, or were involved in other ways in the early overseas expeditions. Some of these graves (e.g Skei, Melhus and Gjeite) are examples of the richest female burials known from the region and show the continued importance of some pre-Viking centres. The archaeological evidence from these burials and their nearby surroundings indicates that these communities had the necessarily political organization, contacts and resources to organize overseas ventures during the early phase of the Viking Age.[76] The majority of the mounts, however, appear in moderate to well-equipped, but far from richly furnished, burials (see Table 1). The grave assemblages in these cases are characterized by a high proportion of oval brooches and beads, often found together with some tools and everyday equipment including keys, knives, sickles and spindle whorls. Several of these burials, including the case studies presented above, may well represent family members of non-elite or lower-elite freemen and farmers who became involved in the overseas adventures.

In addition to the economic prospects, taking part in the early overseas campaigns made it possible for individuals to gain honour, prestige and success. These values may have been materialized through the incorporation and transformation of foreign goods brought home from the journeys, including various mount pieces which were reworked into personal decoration and gifted to female members of the family.[77] Distinctive mount pieces may, therefore, have been strongly associated with the individual owner or household to which they belonged. Insular metalwork worn as an element of dress were clearly intended for public display, and would be an effective way to visualize a household's involvement in successful overseas expeditions and the status accrued by a family member's return. The incorporation of reworked Insular mounts may hence be viewed as evidence of a new form of social identity which emerged in the first part of the Viking Age, where the wearing of such pieces created a visual distinction between families involved in the overseas ventures and others within their community. Amongst these households, the wearing of Insular mounts can be said to have created a sense of group identity and unity by making reference to past shared experiences, while also acting as a visible statement of family members' personal achievement. As such, the integration and use of Insular mounts serve as an example to illustrate how the extensive overseas interaction resulted in the active construction and display of new or altered self-conscious identities, which found their own material expressions through the use of imported objects.[78]

Concluding thoughts

This paper has attempted to shed light on how Insular mounts were transformed and associated with new meanings as the objects changed hands, were (often) physically altered, and came to be used and displayed in new cultural contexts as various types of dress ornaments and identity markers in Norse communities. Such a transformation represents a radical resetting of the objects' use and meaning – or a sharp break in the artefacts' biographies.[79]

Several recent works have highlighted the multifarious ways in which Insular material was adopted within the Viking homelands, showing that diverse practices existed through Viking-Age Scandinavia in the way Insular items circulated, were used and eventually were deposited.[80] The group of imported mounts from Norway adds another dimension to this, showing how this material could be adapted for use in female dress in various ways as third brooches, individual brooches, paired brooches, pendants and belt fittings/decorations. Consequently, it may be more appropriate to view this group of artefacts as costume ornaments or elements of dress rather than third brooches, as this broader interpretation gives more scope for the investigation and understanding of these items in association with Norse female dress.

The visual aspect of these mounts must also have been significant. Not only were they of foreign origin and of high quality, they were also individually different, which gave them even greater display value. As distinctive elements of Norse costume, such exotic items were worn as important markers, signalling status and involvement in successful overseas expeditions. Participation in these long-distance voyages was materialized in distinctive foreign goods which were used to enhance their owners' standing in their local communities.[81] By owning objects from distant places, certain people created a visual distinction between themselves and others within their community. The incorporation of Insular mounts as elements of dress therefore indicates 'a strong desire to integrate foreign imports into society to make them part of one's own social and cultural identity'. These pieces, many of which originally formed part of prestigious church objects in Ireland and Britain, ended up in Viking society where their function was somewhat different, but perhaps no less important, than their original purpose.

Acknowledgements

I wish to express my sincere gratitude to Philip Nicholas Wood and Gail Drinkall for their valuable help in commenting on the text and language-editing the paper. I am also most grateful to Dr Jane Kershaw for her helpful advice on the identification of several Insular mount pieces and to Dr Volker Hilberg for providing me with the illustration of the Hedeby burial.

Notes

1 Wamers 1998.
2 Røskaft 2003, 105.
3 Solberg 2000, 320.
4 Heen-Pettersen 2014.
5 E.g. Jåtten 2006; Grønnesby and Ellingsen 2012.
6 Glørstad 2010, 124–6.
7 Heen-Pettersen 2014.
8 Martens 1994; Andersen 2004.
9 Andersen 2004, 99–100.
10 E.g. Petersen 1940; Jondell 1974; Graham-Campbell 1980, 88.
11 Steuer 1997.
12 Pedersen 2008, 159–61.
13 E.g. Heen-Pettersen 2014; Jåtten 2006.
14 The original fitting on the back and the low relief cast interlace in the central panel, holding settings for a now-missing stud in the centre, are typical of harness mounts. Furthermore, the rounded shapes at the top suggest that the piece originally interlocked with another mount, as part of a set.
15 Identified by Dr Jane Kershaw (personal communication).
16 Bakka 1963; 1965; Wamers 1985. The more recent pieces have been identified as probably Irish by Dr Jane Kershaw (personal communication).
17 Pettersen 2013, 72.
18 Heen-Pettersen 2014.
19 Pettersen 2013, 72.
20 Wamers 1985; Baastrup 2013.
21 Jåtten 2006; Pettersen 2013; Aannestad 2015.
22 Wamers 2011, 93.
23 Baastrup 2014, 358.
24 Wamers 2011, 96.
25 E.g. Bøe 1926; Wamers 1985; Geber 1991.
26 Aannestad 2015, 91.
27 Farbregd 1993, 70–6.
28 E.g. Lucas 1967; Wamers 1985; Jåtten 2006.
29 Bøe 1926, 15.
30 Bakka 1965, 39–40.
31 E.g. Blindheim 1978; 1999.
32 Bourke 2010.
33 Gaut 2001, 113–25; Blindheim 1999.
34 Blindheim 1999.
35 Wamers 1985; 1998.
36 Mikkelsen 2002; Nordeide 2011.
37 Mikkelsen 2002, 119–21; Nordeide 2011, 152.
38 As highlighted by many sholars, e.g. Kopytoff 1986; Gosden and Marshall 1999.
39 Gjessing 1934, 144–59.
40 Jørgensen 2008, 12.
41 McGuire 2009, 165.
42 Petersen 1928, 205–7.
43 Aannestad 2015, 118.
44 Krag 1994, 43; Aannestad 2015, 120.
45 Aannestad 2015, 112.
46 Bøe 1926, 15.
47 Blindheim 1999, 49.
48 Jåtten 2006, 40.
49 Hilberg 2009, 97–9.
50 Thingnæs 2010.
51 E.g. Sjøvold 1946; Petersen 1940; Bakka 1963; Wamers 1998, 2011; Graham-Campbell 2001; Crawford 1987; Geber 1991; Jåtten 2006; Stylegar 2010; Sørheim 2011; Melgaard 2013.
52 Author's translation, unpublished museum catalogue information from 1936.
53 Stenvik 2001, fig.11.
54 Berglund and Dahl 2014, 37.
55 Unpublished museum catalogue information from 1911.
56 Blindheim 1999, 48–50.
57 *Ibid.*, 125–7.
58 Heen-Pettersen 2015. Some of the results presented here stem from this paper.
59 Petersen 1946.
60 Salin 1904.
61 Author's translation, Petersen 1946, 2.
62 Author's translation, Digre 1953.
63 O'Floinn 1989, 117, fig. 113.
64 Møllenhus 1956.
65 Author's translation, unpublished museum catalogue information from 1956.
66 E.g. Gustin 2004; Glørstad 2012; Kershaw 2013.
67 White 1992, 39.
68 Schiffer 1999, 24.
69 Crane 2002; Harlow 2004.
70 Glørstad 2012, 33.
71 Hines 1994; Glørstad 2010.
72 Ashby 2015, 96.
73 See, for instance, Barrett 2008; Ashby 2015.
74 Helle 1991, 26.
75 Barrett 2008, 676–81.
76 Heen-Pettersen 2015.
77 Aannestad 2015, 243–5.
78 E.g. Gustin 2004; Glørstad 2012; Kershaw 2013; Aannestad 2015.
79 See also Aannestad 2015.
80 E.g. Glørstad 2010; Baastrup 2014; Aannestad 2015.
81 Ashby 2015; Aanestad 2015.
82 Baastrup 2014, 365.

Bibliography

Aannestad, H. L. 2015. 'Transformasjoner, omforming og bruk av importerte gjenstander i vikingtid', unpublished PhD thesis, Oslo University.

Andersen, E. 2004. 'Vikingtidens sverdtyper. Deres sosiale og symbolske betydning', unpuplished MA thesis, Oslo University.

Ashby, S. P. 2015. 'What really caused the Viking Age? The social content of raiding and exploration', *Arch. Dialogues*, 22, 89–106.

Baastrup, M. P. 2013. 'Continental and Insular imports in Viking Age Denmark, distribution and circulation', *Zeitschrift für Archäologie des Mittelalters*, 41, 85–205.

Baastrup, M. P. 2014. 'Continental and Insular imports in Viking Age Denmark – on transcultural competences, actor networks and high-cultural differentiation', in H. C. Gulløv (ed.), *Northern World – Landscape, Interactions and Dynamics. Research at the National Museum of Denmark. Proceedings of the Northern Worlds Conference, Copenhagen 28–30 November 2012*, 353–66, Copenhagen: University Press of Southern Denmark.

Bakka, E. 1963. 'Some English decorated metal objects found in Norwegian Viking graves', Årbok *for universitet i Bergen*, 1963:1, 1–66.

Bakka, E. 1965. 'Some decorated Anglo-Saxon and Irish metalwork found in Norwegian graves', in A. Small (ed.), *The Fourth Viking Congress*, 32–40, London: Oliver and Boyd.

Barrett, J. H. 2008. 'What caused the Viking Age?, *Antiquity*, 82, 671–85.

Berglund, B. and Dahl, K. 2014. 'Tur-retur: De britiske øyer – Namdalen', *Spor*, 2014, 36–41.

Blindheim, C. 1978. 'Vikinger – pirater eller handelsmenn? Noen refleksjoner over importmaterialet fra markedsplassen på Kaupang', *Det norske videnskabsakademiens årbok*, 1977, 15–40.

Blindheim, C. 1999. 'Smykker, beslag av fremmed opprinnelse', in C. Blindheim, B. Heyerdal-Larsen and A. S. Ingstad, *Kaupang-funnene, bind I1 del B og C. Gravplassene i Bikjholbergene/Lamøya. Undersøkelsene 1950–1957*, 47–59, Oslo: Universitetets kulturhistoriske museer.

Bourke, C. 2010. 'Antiquities from the River Blackwater IV, Early-Medieval non-ferrous metalwork', *Ulster Journal of Archaeology*, 69, 24–57.

Bøe, J. 1926. 'An ornamented Celtic bronze object found in a Norwegian grave', *Bergens Museums* Årbok, 1926, 2–36.

Crane, S. 2002. *The Performance of Self: Ritual, Clothing and Identity during the Hundred Years War*, Philadelphia: University of Pennsylvania Press.

Crawford, B. 1987. *Scotland in the Early Middle Ages 2: Scandinavian Scotland*, Leicester: Leicester University Press.

Digre, O. 1953. *Undersøkelse av en kvinnegrav fra vikingtiden på Uthaug, Ørlandet*, unpublished excavation report, Trondheim University.

Farbregd, O. 1993. *'Menn, kvinner, graver og status', in O. Farbregd (ed.), Vikingtids funn på Vang*, 67–80, Oppdal: Oppdal Historielag.

Gaut, B. 2001. 'Britain and Western Scandinavia in the Vendel period, *c.* 570 – *c.* 800. The evidence of artefacts', unpublished PhD thesis, York University.

Geber, Ø. 1991. 'Brede seil over Nordsjø går. Import til Vestlandet i vikingtid', unpublished MA thesis, Bergen University.

Gjessing, G. 1934. *Studier i norsk merovingertid*, A.W. Brøggers Boktrykkeri A/S.

Glørstad, Z. 2010. 'Ringspennen og kappen. Kulturelle møter, politiske symboler og sentraliseringsprosesser Norge *c.* 800–950', unpublished Phd thesis, Oslo University.

Glørstad, Z. 2012. 'Sign of the Times? The transfer and transformation of penannular brooches in Viking Age Norway', *Norwegian Arch. Review*, 45, 30–51.

Gosden, C. and Marshall Y. 1999. 'The cultural biography of objects', *World Arch.*, 31, 169–78.

Graham-Campbell, J. A. 1980. *Viking Artefacts: a Select Catalogue*, London: British Museum.

Graham-Campbell, J. 2001. 'National and regional identities: the 'Glittering Prizes', in M. Redknapp (ed.), *Pattern and Purposes in Insular Art: Proceedings of the Fourth International Conference on Insular Art held at the National Museum and Gallery, Cardiff 3–6 September 1998*, 27–38, Oxford: Oxbow Books.

Grønnesby, G. and Ellingsen, E. 2012. 'Kaupangen på Steinkjer', in G. Grønnesby (ed.), *Graver i veien. Arkeologiske undersøkelser E6 Steinkjer*, 30–47, Trondheim: Akademika Forlag.

Gustin, I. 2004. *Mellan gåva och marknad. Handel, tillit og materiell kultur under vikingatid*, Lund Studies in Medieval Arch., 34.

Harlow, M. 2004. 'Clothes make the man', in L. Brubaker and J. M. H. Smith (eds.), *Gender in the Early Medieval World: East and West, 300–900*, 44–69, Cambridge: Cambridge University Press.

Heen-Pettersen, A. M. 2014. 'Insular artefacts from Viking-Age burials from mid-Norway. A review of contact between Trøndelag and Britain and Ireland', *Internet Arch.*, 38, http://dx.doi.org/10.11141/ia.38.2.

Heen-Pettersen, A. M. 2015. 'Insulære beslag fra vikingtidsgraver i Trøndelag: En undersøkelse av gjenstandenes bruk og betydning', *Primitive Tider*, 17, 1–24.

Helle, K. 1991. 'Tiden frem til 1936', in R. Danielsen (ed.), *Grunntek: Norsk historie fra vikingtid til våre dager*, 13–106, Oslo: Universitetsforlaget.

Hilberg, V. 2009. 'Hedeby in Wulfstan's days: a Danish emporium of the Viking Age between East and West', in A. Englert and A. Trakadas (eds.), *Wulfstan's Voyage. The Baltic Sea Region in the Early Viking Age as seen from Shipboard*, 79–113, Roskilde: Special-Trykkeriet Viborg A/S.

Hines, J. 1994. 'The becoming of the English: identity, material culture and language in early Anglo-Saxon England', *ASSAH*, 7, 49–59.

Jørgensen, E. A. 2008. 'Ovale skålspenner fra Trøndelag – En arkeologisk analyse av opphav og betydning', unpuplished MA thesis, Trondheim University.

Jondell, E. 1974. 'Vikingetidens Balansvåger i *Norge*', unpublished MA thesis, Uppsala University.

Jåtten, T. 2006. 'Insulære gjenstander fra yngre jernalder funnet på Vestlandet. Betydning og funksjon i ny kontekst', unpublished MA thesis, Bergen University.

Kershaw, J. 2013. *Viking Identities, Scandinavian Jewellery in England*, Oxford: Oxford University Press.

Kopytoff, I. 1986. 'The cultural biography of things: commoditization as process', in A. Appadurai (ed.), *The Social Life of Things: Commodities in Cultural Perspective*, 64–91, Cambridge: Cambridge University Press.

Krag, A. H 1994. 'Dragtutviklingen fra 8–10 årh. e. Kr. I Sydskandinavien - med utgangspunkt i skålformede spænder, *LAG*, **5, 7-73.**

Lucas, A. T. 1967. 'The plundering and burning of churches in Ireland, 7th to 16th century', in E. Rynne (ed.), *North Munster Studies. Essays in Commemoration of Monsignor Michael Moloney*, 172–229, Limerick: Thomond Archaeological Society.

Martens, I. 1994. 'Norwegian Iron Age weapons, some questions concerning their production and distribution', in B. Ambrosiani and H. Clarke (eds.), *The Twelfth Viking Congress*, 180–2, Stockholm: Birka Studies.

McGuire, E. L. H. 2009. 'Manifestations of identity in burial: evidence from Viking-Age graves in the North Atlantic diaspora', unpublished PhD thesis, Glasgow University.

Melgaard, H. 2013. 'Insulær import i vikingtid: bruksgjenstander eller aristokratiske statussymbol?', unpublished MA thesis, Oslo University.

Mikkelsen, E. 2002. 'Handel, misjon og religionsmøter', *Viking*, **2002**, 91–136.

Møllenhus, K. 1956. *Innberetning om etterundersøkelse av en kvinnegrav (T17739) på Grande*, Ørland Sogn, unpublished archaeological excavation report, Trondheim University.

Nordeide, S. W. 2011. *The Viking Age as a Period of Religious Transformation. The Christianization of Norway from AD 560 – 1150/1200*, Turnhout: Brepols Publishers

O' Floinn, R. 1989. 'Secular metalwork in the eighth and ninth century', in S. Youngs (ed.), *The Work of Angels. Masterpieces of Celtic Metalwork, 6th–9th centuries AD*, 72–130, London: British Museum Publication Ltd.

Pedersen, U. 2008. 'Weights and balances', in D. Skre (ed.), *Means of Exchange. Dealing with Silver in the Viking Age*, Kaupang Excavation Project Publication Series, vol. 2, 119–95, Århus: Aarhus University Press.

Peterson, J. 1919. *De norske vikingesværd*, Christiania: Dybwad.

Petersen, J. 1928. *Vikingetidens smykker,* Christiania: Dreyers grafiske anstalt.

Petersen, J. 1940. *British Antiquities of the Viking Period found in Norway*, Viking Antiquities in Great Britain and Ireland, Part V, Oslo: Aschehough & Co.

Petersen, Th. 1946. *Beretning om gravundersøkelse på Finsås, Snåsa,* unpublished excavation report, Trondheim University.

Pettersen, A. M. H. 2013. 'Mellom De britiske øyer og Midt-Norge: En arkeologisk analyse av insulær kontakt og gjenstandsfunn fra vikingtidsgraver iTrøndelag', unpublished MA thesis, Trondheim University.

Røskaft, M. 2003. 'Maktens landskap. Sentralgårder i Trøndelag ved overgangen fra vikingtid til kristen middelalder, *c.* 800–1200', unpublished PhD thesis, Trondheim University.

Rygh, K. 1885. *Norske oldsager ordnede og forklarende*, Christiania: Cammermeyer.

Salin, B. 1904. *Die altgermanische Thierornamentik*, Stockholm: Beckmans Boktrykkeri.

Schiffer, M. 1999. *The Material Life of Human Beings*, London: Routledge

Sjøvold, T. 1946. 'Et vesteuropeisk bronsebeslag fra Troms', *Stavanger Museums* Årbok, **1946**, 86–91.

Solberg, B. 2000. *Jernalderen i Norge,* Oslo: Cappelen Akademiske Forlag.

Stenvik, L. F. 2001. *Skei – et maktsenter frem fra skyggen,* Vitark, 2.

Steuer, H. 1997. *Waagen and Gewichte aus dem Mittelalterlichen Schleswig,* Zeitschrift fur archaologie des Mittelalters, 10.

Stylegar, F.-A. 2010. 'Hvorfor er det færre kvinne – enn mannsgraver fra vikingtiden i Norge?', *Primitive tider*, **12**, 71–80.

Sørheim, H. 2011. 'Three prominent Norwegian ladies with British connections', *Acta Archaeologica*, **82**, 17–54.

Thingnæs, S. 2010. 'En kvinne utenom det vanlige?', *Fra haug ok heidni,* **2 - 2010, 3**–7.

Wamers, E. 1985. *Insularer Metallschmuck in wikingerzeitlichen Gräbern Nordeuropas. Untersuchungen zur skandinavischen Westexpansion,* Neumunster: Karl Wachholtz Verlag.

Wamers, E. 1998. 'Insular finds in Viking Age Scandinavia and the state formation of Norway', in H. B. Clarke, M. Mhaonaigh and R. O'Floinn (eds.), *Ireland and Scandinavia in the Early Viking Age,* 37–72, Dublin: Four Courts Press.

Wamers, E. 2011. 'Continental and Insular metalwork', in D. Skre (ed.), *Things from the Town. Artefacts and Inhabitants in Viking-Age Kaupang,* 65–98, Aarhus: Aarhus University Press.

White, R. 1992. 'Beyond art: toward an understanding of the origins of material representation in Europe', *Ann. Rev. of Anthropology*, **21**, 537–64.

Anglo-Saxon Studies in Archaeology and History 21, 2018

Two rural Anglo-Saxon sites in Suffolk: archaeological excavations at Church Road, Snape and Lime Avenue, Oulton

Antony R.R. Mustchin

with contributions by Nicholas J. Cooper, Julia E.M. Cussans, Andrew Peachey, Peter Thompson, John R. Summers and Julie Walker

illustrations by Kathren Henry and Thomas Light

Abstract

Archaeological investigations in Suffolk, at Church Road, Snape and Lime Avenue, Oulton, have revealed parts of rural Anglo-Saxon settlement landscapes, collectively spanning the fifth to twelfth centuries AD*. Both sites occupy elevated positions on deep, free-draining soils overlooking river valleys and within easy reach of the Suffolk coast. Encountered features included sunken-featured buildings and pits containing large quantities of burnt flint and charcoal, while a substantial, probably agricultural enclosure was also identified at Oulton. Pottery from both sites is of a domestic character, while animal bone and environmental assemblages suggest a mixed agrarian economy. Finds of interest include curated sherds of samian ware from Snape and a group of eleven late Anglo-Saxon or Viking-period weights from Oulton, four of which include embedded Carolingian and Roman coins. The sites are discussed with reference to regional research themes regarding settlement and economy, while the landscape context of the Church Road site is also explored with respect to the high-status Anglo-Saxon cemetery at Snape.*

Introduction

The form of rural Anglo-Saxon settlements and the functions of the buildings they contain are important topics of current archaeological research in the East of England.[1] So too is the need better to understand the infrastructure of these sites as a prelude to investigating trade and communication between rural settlements and urban centres, as well as broader cultural links. With reference to these themes, this paper presents the findings of recent archaeological excavations at the Suffolk sites of Church Road in Snape and Lime Avenue in Oulton.[2] It outlines the chronology and the structural evidence for both sites, before examining in detail evidence relating to the economy. Of particular interest in the latter section is a group of eleven late Anglo-Saxon or Viking-period weights from Oulton, four of which have Carolingian coins (×2) and Roman coins (×2) embedded in their upper surfaces.

The Sites

The sites in question (Table 1) were excavated by Archaeological Solutions Ltd between 2013 and 2015. They occupy similar geographical locations, close to Suffolk's North Sea coast (Fig. 1), and at the time of excavation, were both laid down to pasture. The topographical and geological setting of the sites is also similar; each occupies a locally elevated position overlooking a river valley (historically in the case of the Oulton site), and both are situated on free-draining sandy soils.[3] These soils overlie drift geology of aeolian and/or glaciofluvial drift and are well suited to cereal agriculture.[4] The sites also have good access to other resources, including extensive wetland habitats.

Archaeological background

Although the Church Road and Lime Avenue sites are located in landscapes favourable to settlement and with good archaeological potential, there is a dearth of Anglo-Saxon settlement evidence known from these locations. Until the excavation of the extensive Anglo-Saxon complex at Bloodmoor Hill, Carlton Colville,[5] the north-eastern corner of Suffolk, around Oulton, appeared more-or-less devoid of early, post-Roman settlement sites.[6] The Suffolk Historic Environment Record contains only three

Fig. 1 Site locations.

Table 1 Site summary

Site Name	SHER Code	NGR (point)	Area (hectares)
Church Road, Snape	SNP 103	TM 4014 5932	1.6
Lime Avenue, Oulton	OUL 037	TM 518 941	3.2 (excavated area)

SHER = Suffolk Historic Environment Record; NGR = National Grid Reference

Table 2 Chronological Phasing

Site	Period	Pottery Date Range	Radiocarbon Date Range (Combined)
Church Road, Snape	Early to middle Anglo-Saxon	Mid-5th to mid-9th centuries AD	344–575 cal AD
Lime Avenue, Oulton	Early to middle Anglo-Saxon	5th to 9th centuries AD	-
	Middle to late Anglo-Saxon	9th to mid-12th centuries AD	-

confirmed Anglo-Saxon entries within a 2-km radius of Lime Avenue, Oulton.[7] These are the documented rubbing of a middle Saxon *sceatta* (a coin type with widespread currency across eastern and southern England), the find-spots of two further middle Saxon coins (probably unrelated), and a late Saxon disc brooch, all from Lowestoft. Wade's map of Anglo-Saxon and medieval sites in East Anglia shows Burgh Castle – some 11 km to the north – as the being closest large site to Oulton.[8] The more recently excavated site at Bloodmoor Hill is located less than 4.5 km to the south, however.

Similarly, although the village of Snape is well known for its mixed-rite Anglo-Saxon cemetery, a Scheduled Ancient Monument,[9] the Church Road excavation comprises the first domestic evidence from the immediate vicinity. Other, partially investigated settlements exist at Hacheston, *c.* 9.2 km to the west of Snape, and Little Bealings, some 19.5 km to the south-west.[10]

The cemetery at Snape was initially excavated in 1827, with modern investigations of the site beginning in 1985.[11] Excavations in 1862 unearthed a richly furnished ship burial, the first to be identified archaeologically in England and the first European example to have its plan published.[12] The boat was of clinker-built and riveted construction, stylistically identical to that within Mound 1 at Sutton Hoo.[13] The resultant mound at Snape (Mound I) is thought to have been erected above an existing Bronze Age tumulus and contained the inhumation burial of a high-status individual.[14] The burial is identified as a male, based on the presence of two iron spearheads, while other grave goods included fragments of a glass claw beaker of mid-sixth-century style,[15] and a gold ring set with a Roman intaglio.[16] The ring, which has a Germanic setting of continental manufacture, is of early-sixth-century date and constitutes a clear indication of elevated, perhaps royal status.[17] The burial as a whole is thought to date to the early seventh century.

Modern investigations of the surrounding cemetery have identified cremations of fifth- to seventh-century date and inhumations dating between the sixth and seventh centuries.[18] Two of the inhumations (graves 4 and 47) had been laid to rest within dugout longboats, analysis of which suggests that they constituted light, single-person craft ideally suited to navigation on the neighbouring Alde, Deben and Stour/Orwell estuaries.[19] Other finds of significance from the cemetery include a lyre from grave 32 and a horse's head with tack, also from grave 47. The extraordinary survival of organic remains, including wool cloth, was also noted.[20]

The proximity of the Church Road site to the Snape Anglo-Saxon cemetery (explored further below), located within 1 km to the north-east (Fig. 1), certainly adds to the significance of the former. Although a lack of demographic data from the Church Road site prevents any detailed review of their precise relationship,[21] it is highly unlikely that the Church Road population did not make use of the cemetery.

Chronological phasing
with Peter Thompson

The archaeological excavations at Snape and Oulton both revealed multi-phase activity spanning the prehistoric to modern eras. In addition to the Anglo-Saxon settlement, the Church Road site at Snape contained significant early Iron Age and early Romano-British evidence, including a mid- to late-first-century-AD pottery kiln located within an area of ditched enclosures,[22] while the Oulton site included evidence of Romano-British agriculture (not closely datable) and a metalworking waste area tentatively dated to the Saxo-Norman/medieval period. There was no continuity of activity between the Romano-British and Anglo-Saxon periods at Snape, while the lack of closely datable Roman finds from Oulton prevented any investigation of settlement continuity at this site. The archive reports for each site present a full review of project findings, including all specialist data and analyses.[23]

Dating of Anglo-Saxon activity at Oulton was based on an assessment of the recovered pottery assemblage and stratigraphic sequence, whilst the similar phasing of features at Snape was complemented by a targeted programme of radiocarbon dating. Unfortunately, key contexts at Oulton lacked securely stratified carbonized remains of a quantity or quality deemed suitable for reliable scientific dating.

Activity at Oulton was split between two distinct subphases: the early to middle Anglo-Saxon period (fifth to ninth centuries AD) and the middle to late Anglo-Saxon period (ninth to mid-twelfth centuries AD; Table 2). Pottery

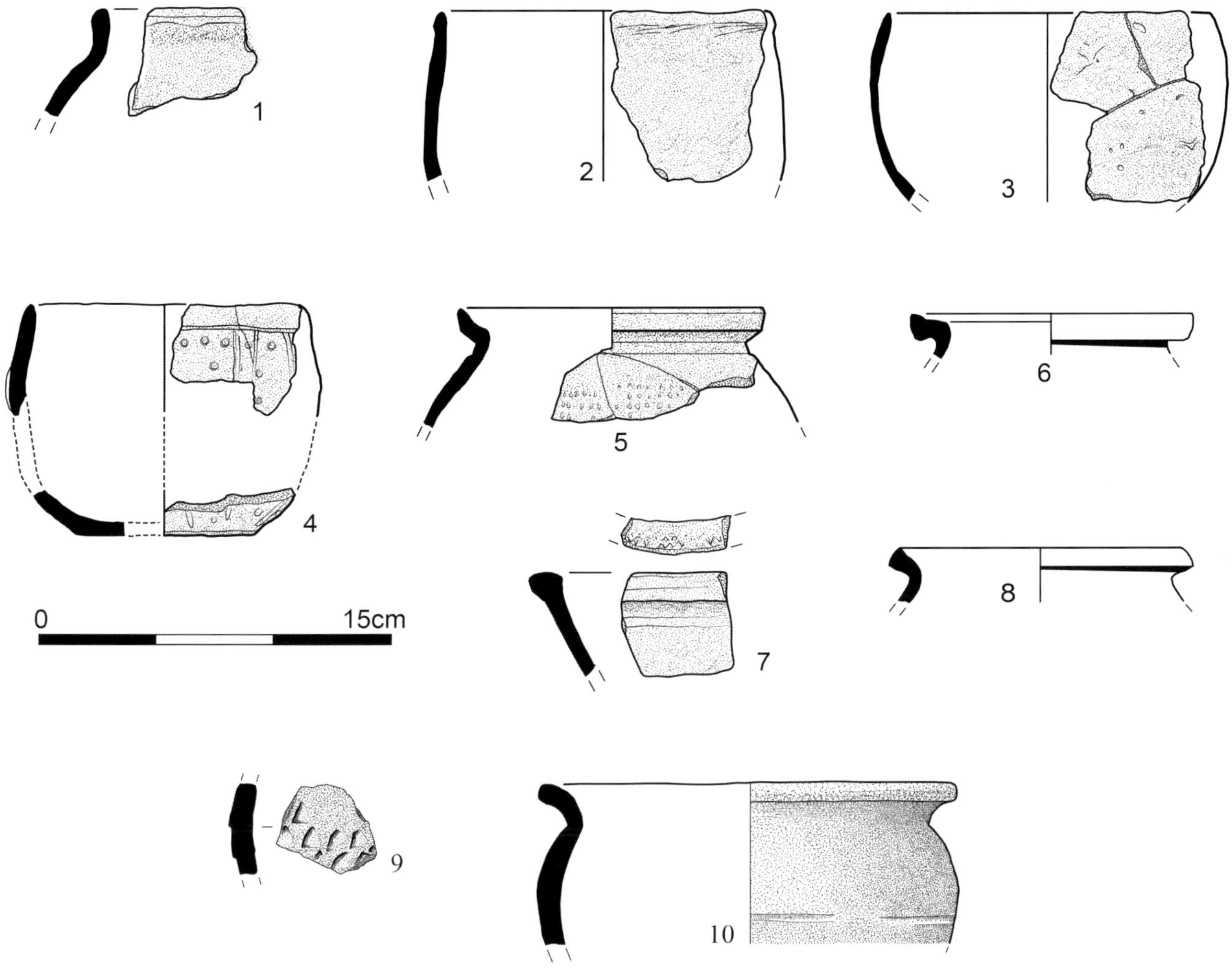

Fig. 2 Selected pottery illustrations (2.1–2.8 from Lime Avenue, Oulton; 2.9–2.10 from Church Road, Snape)

from the first phase of occupation falls into six handmade fabric groups (based on principal inclusions), with the most abundant fabrics – constituting 33.6% and 26.2% of the total assemblage by sherd count – displaying a predominance of organic and quartz-based temper (including sand). This contrasts somewhat with Snape, where 58.6% of the assemblage contained organics, with very little containing only sand or quartz. With one or two exceptions, the forms present can be characterized as shouldered (Fig. 2.1), straight-sided ovoid (Fig. 2.2) and globular or ellipsoid (Fig. 2.3). However, the presence of only partial profiles makes it difficult to differentiate between jars and bowls. In only one example could a rim be certainly matched to a base, due in part to its decoration (Fig. 2.4). However, the forms broadly match those from Bloodmoor Hill, with the exception of low-bulbous jars and biconical/sub-biconical profiles that appear to be absent at Oulton.[24] Incidences of burnishing and decoration are low in the assemblage, although three vessels display a total of four different stamps.[25] Overall, the earlier Anglo-Saxon pottery from Oulton comprises 390 sherds weighing 4661 g.

The later pottery group constitutes twenty-five sherds (305 g) of wheel-made Thetford ware. These pots were in use between the late ninth and mid-twelfth centuries, with the closest known kilns at Norwich, probably of late tenth to mid-twelfth century date.[26] The Oulton sherds include four cooking pot rims, one with a band of rouletting across the shoulder, and a bowl with rouletting across the rim (Fig. 2.5–2.8).

Anglo-Saxon pottery from Church Road, Snape – dating exclusively to the earlier part of this period (mid-fifth to mid-ninth centuries AD; Table 2) – is chiefly present in fine to medium quartz sand fabrics, frequently with varying amounts of burnt organics and occasionally other inclusions (e.g. grog and calcareous material). Two sherds contain coarse silver mica, while two contain possible granitic material. Forms present mainly comprise either weak, baggy or round-shouldered jars with upright or slightly everted rims, or open bowls with fairly upright rims. Curving body sherds from the assemblage also indicate the presence of rounded or globular forms, but only one carinated sherd is present. Just over half of the rims present are simple, fairly upright forms. An exception to the above is a round-shouldered jar with a flaring rim. Two slightly rounded or sagging bases and one flat rounded base were also identified. Only a single stamped sherd is

Table 3 Radiocarbon determinations for Church Road, Snape (calibrated using the University of Oxford Radiocarbon Accelerator Unit calibration program, OxCal4; conventional ages and calibrated age ranges were calculated by Dr Elaine Dunbar (SUERC)).

Feature/ Structure	Context	Sample Type	Genus/Species	Lab. No. (SUERC-)	Date BP	Calibrated Date/ Date Ranges*
SFB S1 Sunken Feature F2575	L2576A	Charred grain	*Triticum aestivum/ compactum* type	51160 (GU32884)	1560 ±35	415–575 cal AD
	L2576D	Charred grain	*Hordeum* sp.	50949 (GU32885)	1594 ±29	403–540 cal AD
SFB S3 Sunken Feature F2406	L2407B	Charred grain	*Triticum aestivum/ compactum* type	50946 (GU32881)	1631 ±29	474–535 cal AD
	L2407D	Charred grain	*Hordeum* sp.	50947 (GU32882)	1597 ±29	401–540 cal AD
Burnt Flint Pit F2058	L2060C	Charcoal	*Quercus* sp.	50945 (GU32880)	1564 ±26	421–554 cal AD
Burnt Flint Pit F2365	L2366	Charcoal	*Corylus* sp.	50948 (GU32883)	1597 ±26	406–538 cal AD

BP = before present (AD 1950); * = at 95.4% confidence

present (Fig. 2.9), while two sherds display incised horizontal grooves, and a third displays horizontal and vertical incised lines (Fig. 2.10). The surfaces are mostly smoothed and in some cases polished, but only five are burnished. A single rusticated sherd is also present; the form, fabric and surface treatment of this sherd are typical of the region, with similar vessels known from sites including West Stow,[27] dating between the fifth and seventh centuries AD.[28]

Radiocarbon Dating Determinations

with John R. Summers

The radiocarbon dating of Anglo-Saxon features at Church Road, Snape formed part of a broader scientific dating programme.[29] Six samples from four Anglo-Saxon features were submitted to the Scottish Universities Environmental Research Centre (SUERC; University of Glasgow; Table 3). Carbonized cereal grains and charcoal for dating were recovered via a targeted programme of bulk environmental sampling and subsequent flotation.[30] The submitted oak charcoal (*Quercus* sp.) from Burnt Flint Pit F2058 was a fragment of roundwood with its terminal growth ring preserved. The age at death of this material was likely to be closely associated with the use/firing of the pit and, as such, represented a prime candidate for dating. The sample of charcoal from Pit F2365 was a fragment of hazel (*Corylus* sp.), a fast-growing species widely coppiced for fuel wood in Anglo-Saxon England.[31]

The results of the radiocarbon-dating programme are presented in Table 3 and Figure 3.

The Early to Middle Anglo-Saxon settlements

The two early to middle Anglo-Saxon settlements shared a broad commonality of form and location. As previously mentioned, both occupied locally elevated positions (between 10 m and 20 m above ordnance datum) on deep, free-draining sandy soils overlooking river valleys. The location of these sites on easily worked soils is typical of the Anglo-Saxon period in Suffolk;[32] the light, fertile soils of

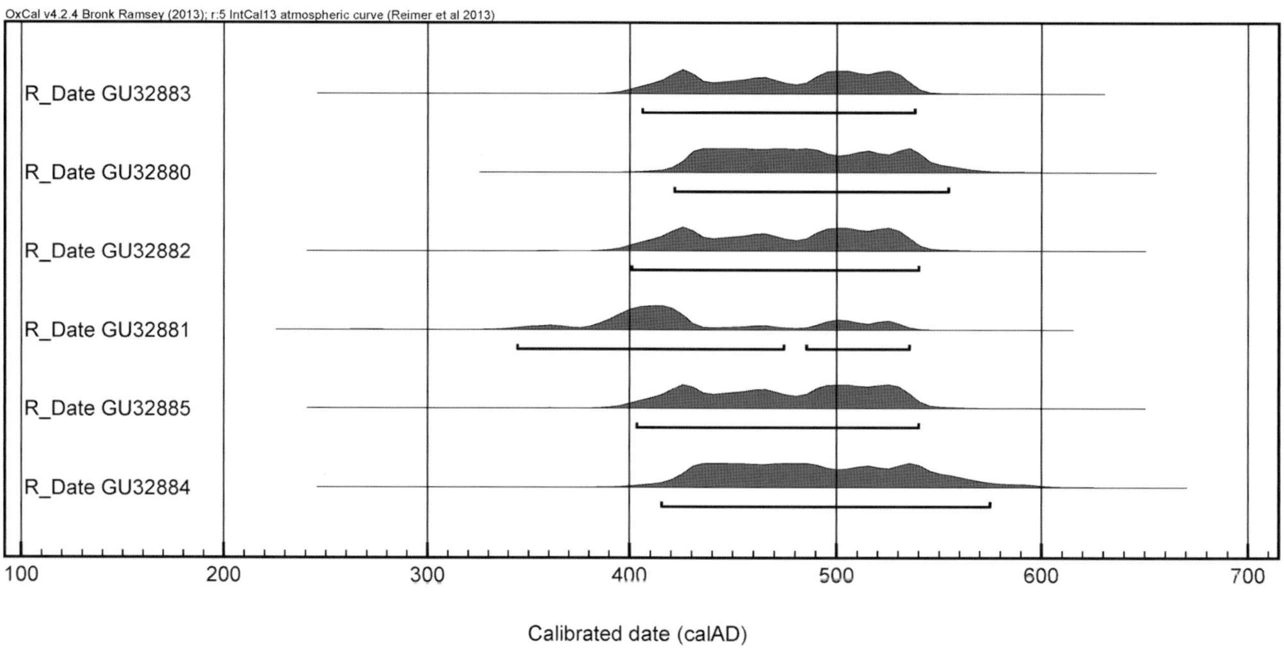

Fig. 3 Radiocarbon probability distributions for Church Road, Snape

Fig. 4 Plan of excavated area at Lime Avenue, Oulton

river valleys were the main focus of clearance, settlement and cultivation at this time, with the rivers themselves forming major arteries of communication and commerce.[33] In contrast, Suffolk's central claylands are devoid of early Anglo-Saxon settlement evidence, with the exploitation of these heavier soils only beginning around AD 650–850.[34]

Both sites were characterized by sunken-featured buildings, or *Grubenhäuser* (hereafter 'SFB's), numbering five at Oulton and three at Snape, while pits containing large quantities of burnt flint and charcoal were also ubiquitous (Figs. 4–5). Possible refuse pits were present in both cases, although true 'refuse pits' are uncommon within settlements of this date,[35] and none of the recorded pits contained a significant quantity of cultural material. At Snape, a single earth-fast structure of uncertain function existed alongside the SFBs, while several ditches, some of which appeared to form early elements of a later Anglo-Saxon enclosure (see below), were encountered at Oulton.

The Structural Evidence

The sunken-featured buildings at each site provided the only clear evidence of activity associated with early- to middle-Anglo-Saxon structures (Figs. 6–10). The earth-fast structure encountered at Snape (Fig. 11) – although similar in size and plan to other Suffolk examples, including the 'halls' at West Stow and 'hall'-type structures at Flixton Quarry – lacked internal deposits and only produced a sparse assemblage of contemporary pottery.[36] This dearth of evidence, although possibly for taphonomic reasons, might suggest that the structure was subsidiary/ancillary to the nearby SFBs, perhaps fulfilling a storage function. Alternatively, the sterile nature of this structure may have resulted from the regular cleaning out of floor deposits during its lifetime.[37] However, Tipper notes that the majority of early Anglo-Saxon settlements excavated in recent decades contain both SFBs and 'posthole buildings',[38] perhaps suggesting some difference in the function(s) of these distinct structural forms.

The recording of SFBs at Oulton and Snape followed conventions used in the publications for West Stow,[39] Pennyland,[40] Hartigans,[41] and, more recently, Dernford Farm.[42] Summary descriptions of the SFBs are presented in Tables 4 and 5.

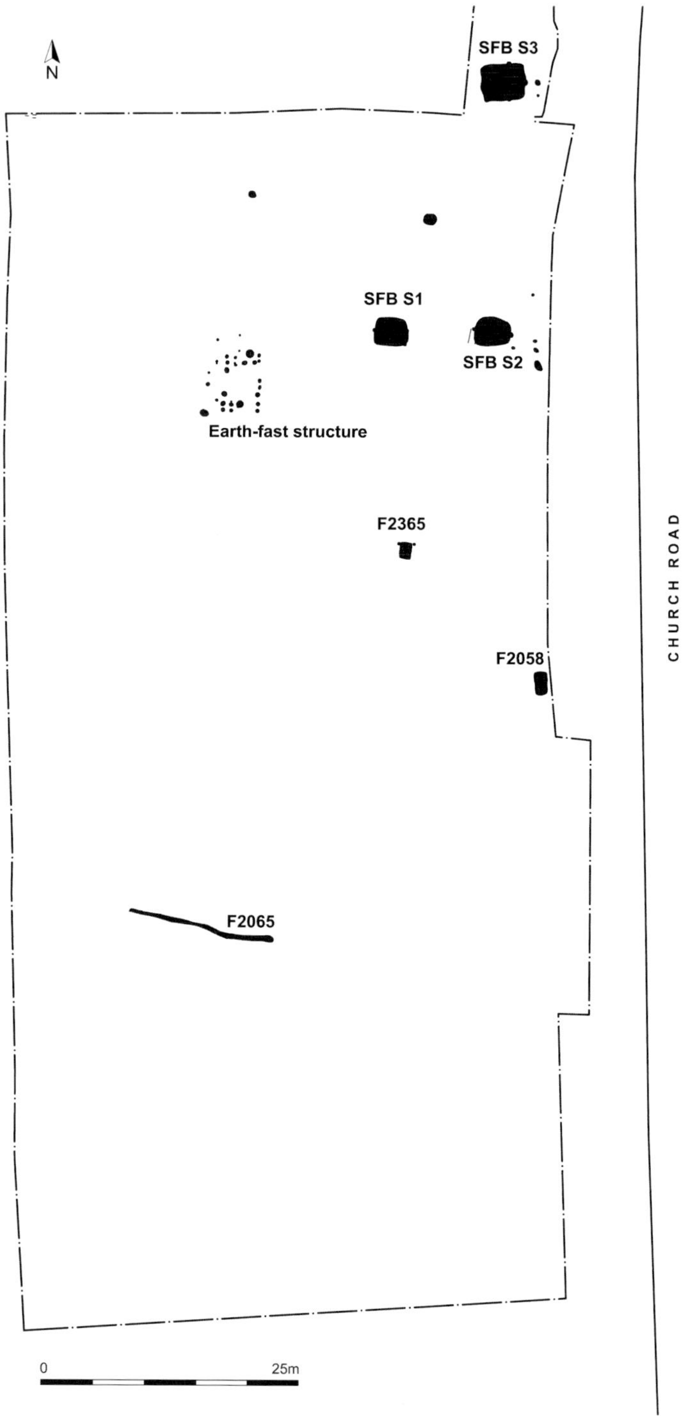

Fig. 5 Plan of excavated area at Church Road, Snape

In general, SFBs are characterized by substantial sunken features – with average measurements of 3 × 4 m in plan and 0.3 – 0.5 m deep[43] – most often in association with structural postholes, though an absence of postholes has been noted in some cases.[44] The size of SFB O4 at Oulton, measuring 4.7 m in length and 14.99 m² in plan (Table 5; Fig. 9), might suggest a seventh-century date for this building, as Hamerow has noted that later examples tend to be larger.[45] SFB typologies have previously been described by von Guyan and Ahrens.[46] Three of the Oulton SFBs (O1, O2 and O4) and all of the Snape examples displayed evidence of central postholes at their gable ends (Figs. 6–9). These are thought to have housed upright posts which in turn supported ridgepoles and associated roofing timbers. This structural format is defined by Ahrens as a *Giebelpfostenhaus* or 'gable-post house'.[47] SFBs O1, S1 and S3 also displayed evidence of corner posts (Figs. 6–8), most probably tied into horizontal, gable-end crossbeams.[48] Two-post SFBs,[49] of which O2, O4, S1 and S2 may have been examples, are common, whilst six-post formats, with post settings similar to SFBs O1 and S3, are largely confined to south-east England and East Anglia.[50] Both forms were present at West Stow and the Norfolk site of Spong Hill.[51]

The stratigraphic relationships of posthole and sunken feature fills in most of the encountered SFBs indicate that structural timbers had either rotted *in situ* or been removed prior to abandonment and backfilling. In four cases the basal fills of the sunken features sealed the underlying posthole fills, while in SFB O1 the basal fill (L2034) had formed around extant timbers; most of these had been removed or had rotted prior to the deposition of the uppermost fill, however. In only two cases – SFBs S2 and O5 – had all sunken feature fills formed around *in situ* posts, suggesting that timbers had been left to rot rather than being removed for reuse elsewhere.[52] The possibility of post-abandonment recycling of above-ground structural elements cannot be discounted, however.

Suspended wooden floors are structural features sometimes attributed to SFBs.[53] These are thought to have overlain sunken features, possibly preserving the latter as storage space or as sub-floor voids, designed to promote ventilation and prolong the useful lifespan of structural timbers.[54] SFB 15 at West Stow included evidence of a collapsed wooden floor, although such occurrences are extremely rare.[55] Although direct evidence for the original presence or absence of suspended floors was lacking at Snape and Oulton, the bases of the sunken features did not appear trampled. This is notable given the sandy nature of the underlying geology at both sites. The SFBs also lacked evidence of prepared floors in their bases. This is in contrast to other examples, where 'furniture', including hearths, has attested to activity within sunken features, e.g. SFB 2037 at Marham in Norfolk.[56] At Yeavering in Northumberland the base of one such feature (Building D3) was found to contain clay floors and 'occupation' deposits sealed by burnt layers and demolition material.[57]

SFB S3 at Snape presented the clearest evidence to suggest the original presence of a suspended wooden floor. Two opposing beam slots were cut into the northern and southern edges of the sunken feature and are thought to have housed a large horizontal crossbeam (Fig. 7). The slots had been cut to the level of a well-defined 'sill', preserved to varying degrees around all four sides of the sunken feature, which may have acted as a bedding platform for additional crossbeams, which in turn supported a floor. Similar sills have been identified on a number

Table 4 Summary of the Snape SFBs.

SFB No.	Summary				
S1	Type	?Two-post			
	Dimensions	a: 3.30 m	b: 3.15 m	c: 2.57 m	d: 0.15 m
	Area	8.48 m^2			
	Form	Two postholes (F2577 and F2579) located centrally on east and west sides; additional postholes (F2581 and F2583) present at the south-eastern and south-western corners			
	Orientation	East to west			
S2	Type	Two-post			
	Dimensions	a: 3.50 m	b: 3.60 m	c: 2.58 m	d: 0.30 m
	Area	9.03 m^2			
	Form	Two postholes (F2233 and F2251) located centrally on east and west sides			
	Orientation	East to west			
S3	Type	Six-post			
	Dimensions	a: 4.30 m	b: 3.90 m	c: 3.45 m	d: 0.51 m
	Area	14.84 m^2			
	Form	Two postholes (F2415 and F2417) located centrally on east and west sides; corner posts at the north-west (F2447, F2449 and F2453), south-west (F2419), north-east (F2413 and F2451) and south-east (F2455) corners; beam slots (F2411 and F2470) cut into the north and south sides; peripheral postholes (F2398 and F2400) forming a ?porch at the south-east corner; linear arrangement of stakeholes (F2458, F2460, F2462, F2464 and F2466) running east to west across the base			
	Orientation	East to west			

Key to dimensions: a = maximum overall length; b = distance between gable post centres; c = mean width; d = depth below stripped archaeological surface

Table 5 Summary of the Oulton SFBs.

SFB No.	Summary				
O1	Type	?Six-post			
	Dimensions	a. 4.32 m	b. 4.05 m	c. 3.00 m	d. 0.31 m
	Area	12.96 m^2			
	Form	Two postholes located centrally at the eastern and western gable ends (F2150 and F2152). Additional postholes at the north-west and south-west corners (F2129 and F2141); no corresponding postholes at the north-east and south-east corners. One posthole located centrally on the northern side (F2127).			
	Orientation	East to west			
O2	Type	?Two-post			
	Dimensions	a. 4.36 m	b. 2.10 m	c. 4.26 m	d. 0.60 m
	Area	18.57m^2			
	Form	Two postholes (F2662 and F2688) were located within the base of the sunken feature, set in from its northern and southern edges. A third posthole (F2660) was located close to the feature's western edge, at the break of slope; no corresponding eastern posthole was present.			
	Orientation	?			
O3	Type	?			
	Dimensions	a. 3.36 m	b. N/A	c. 2.14 m	d. 0.52 m
	Area	7.19 m^2			
	Form	?			
	Orientation	North-east to south-west			
O4	Type	?Two-post			
	Dimensions	a. 4.70 m	b. N/A	c. 3.19	d. 0.34 m
	Area	14.99 m^2			
	Form	One posthole (F2752) located centrally at the north-eastern gable end of the sunken feature. No corresponding posthole to the south-west.			
	Orientation	North-east to south-west			
O5	Type	?			
	Dimensions	a. 3.56 m	b. N/A	c. 3.52m	d. 0.24m
	Area	12.52 m^2			
	Form	Three postholes (F2536, F2538 and F2540) located in the north-western quadrant of the sunken feature			
	Orientation	East to west			

Key to dimensions: a = maximum overall length; b = distance between gable post centres; c = mean width; d = depth below stripped archaeological surface

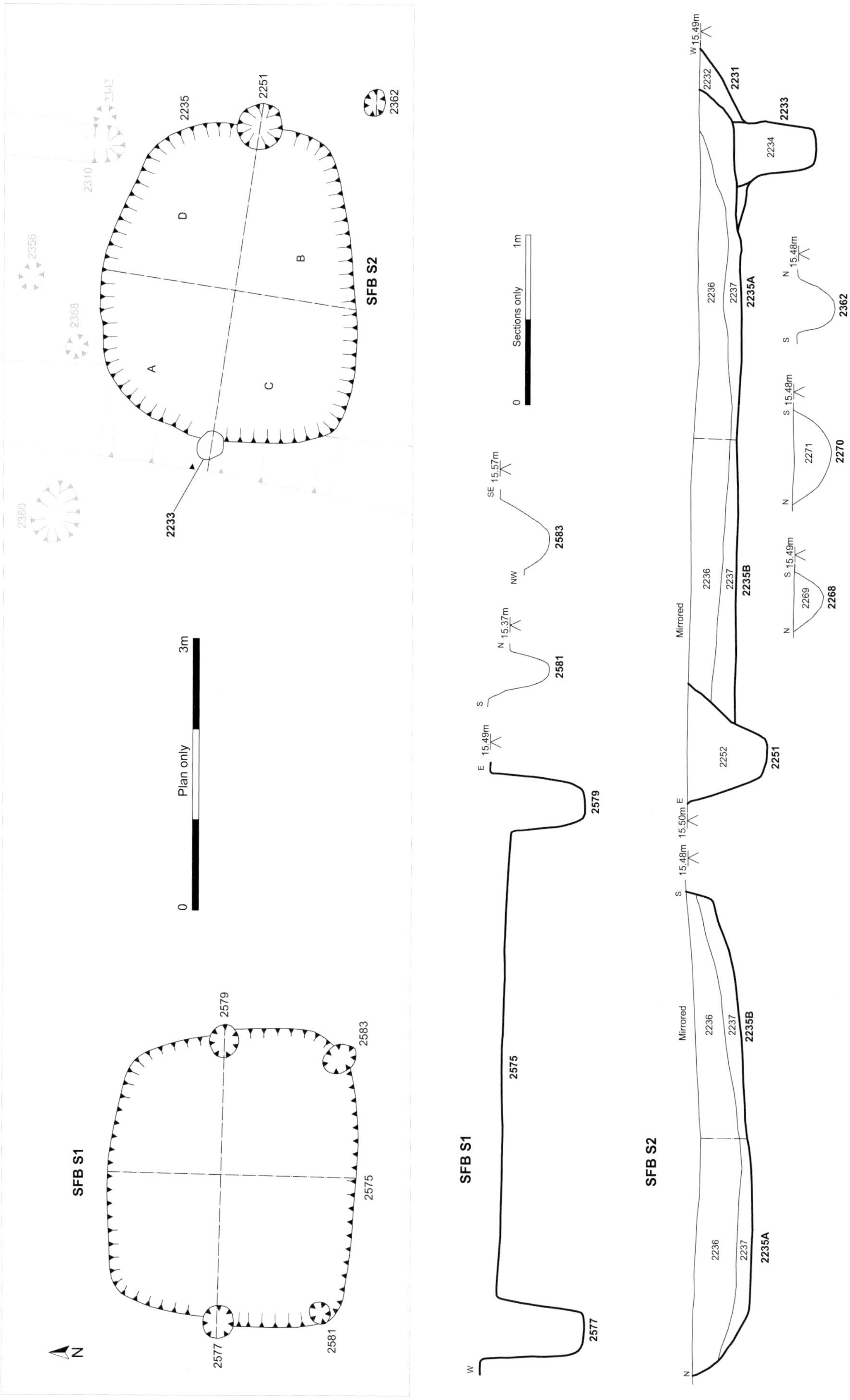

Fig. 6 Plans and sections of Sunken-Featured Buildings S1 and S2 at Church Road, Snape

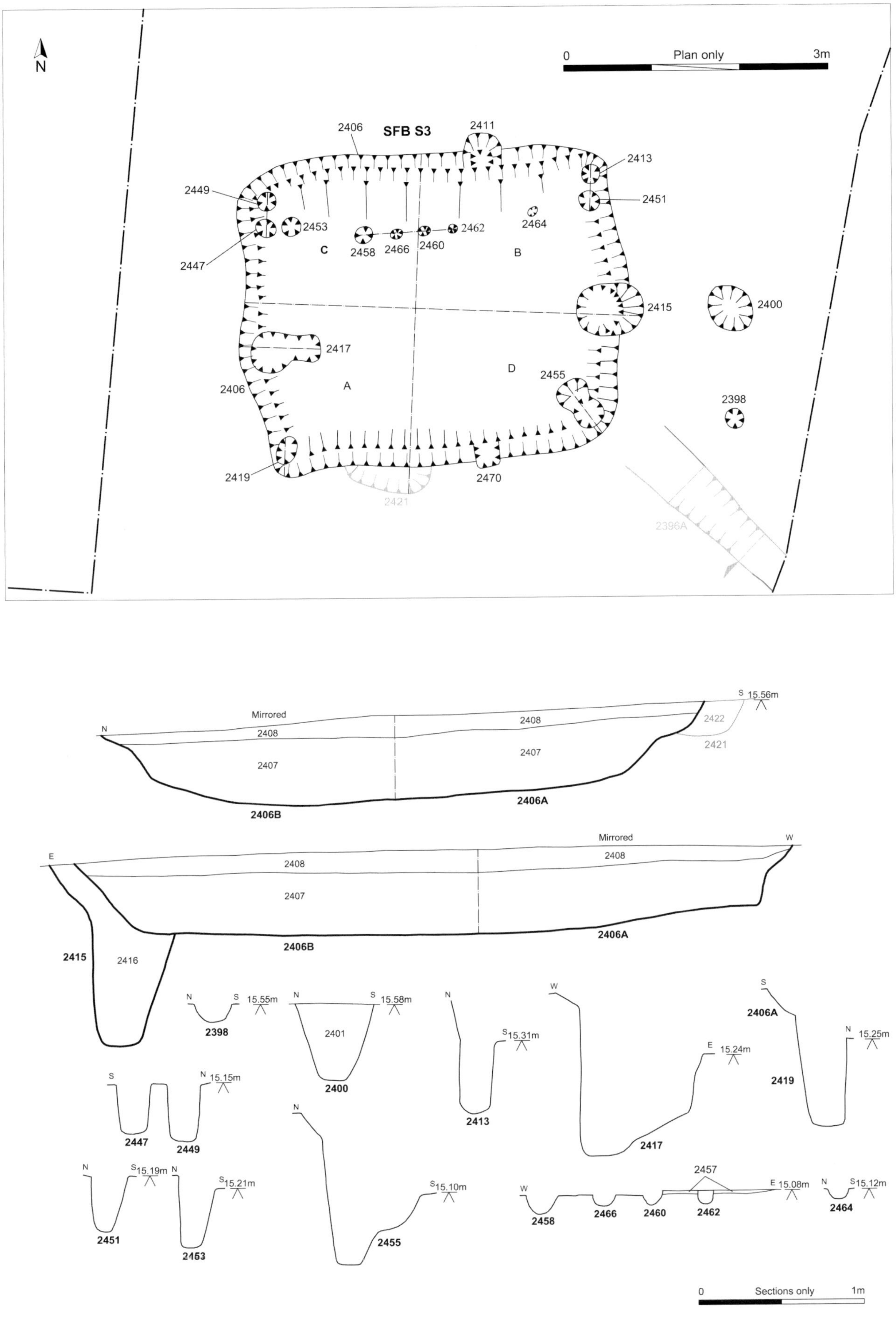

Fig. 7 Plan and sections of Sunken-Featured Building S3 at Church Road, Snape

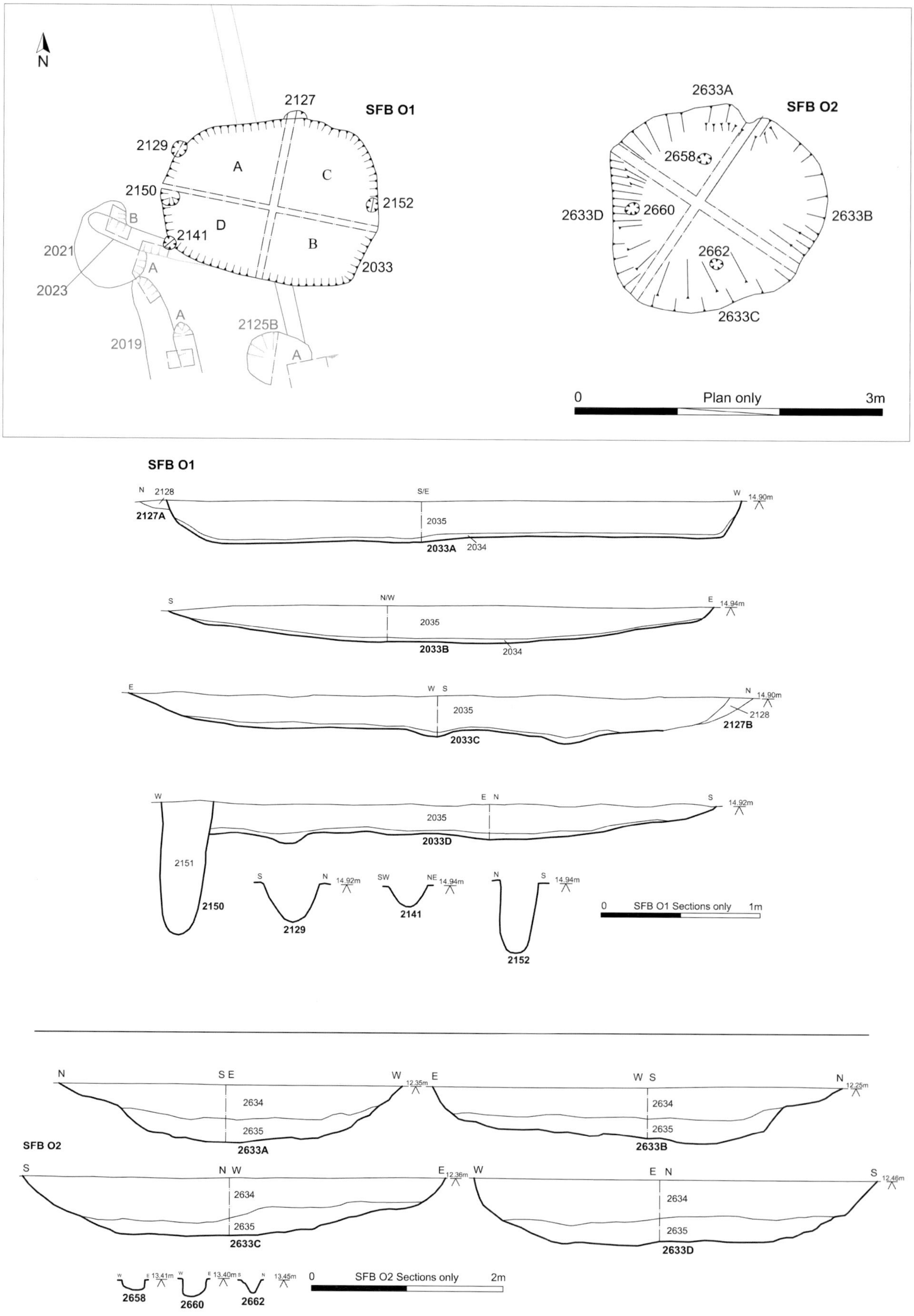

Fig. 8 Plans and sections of Sunken-Featured Buildings O1 and O2 at Lime Avenue, Oulton

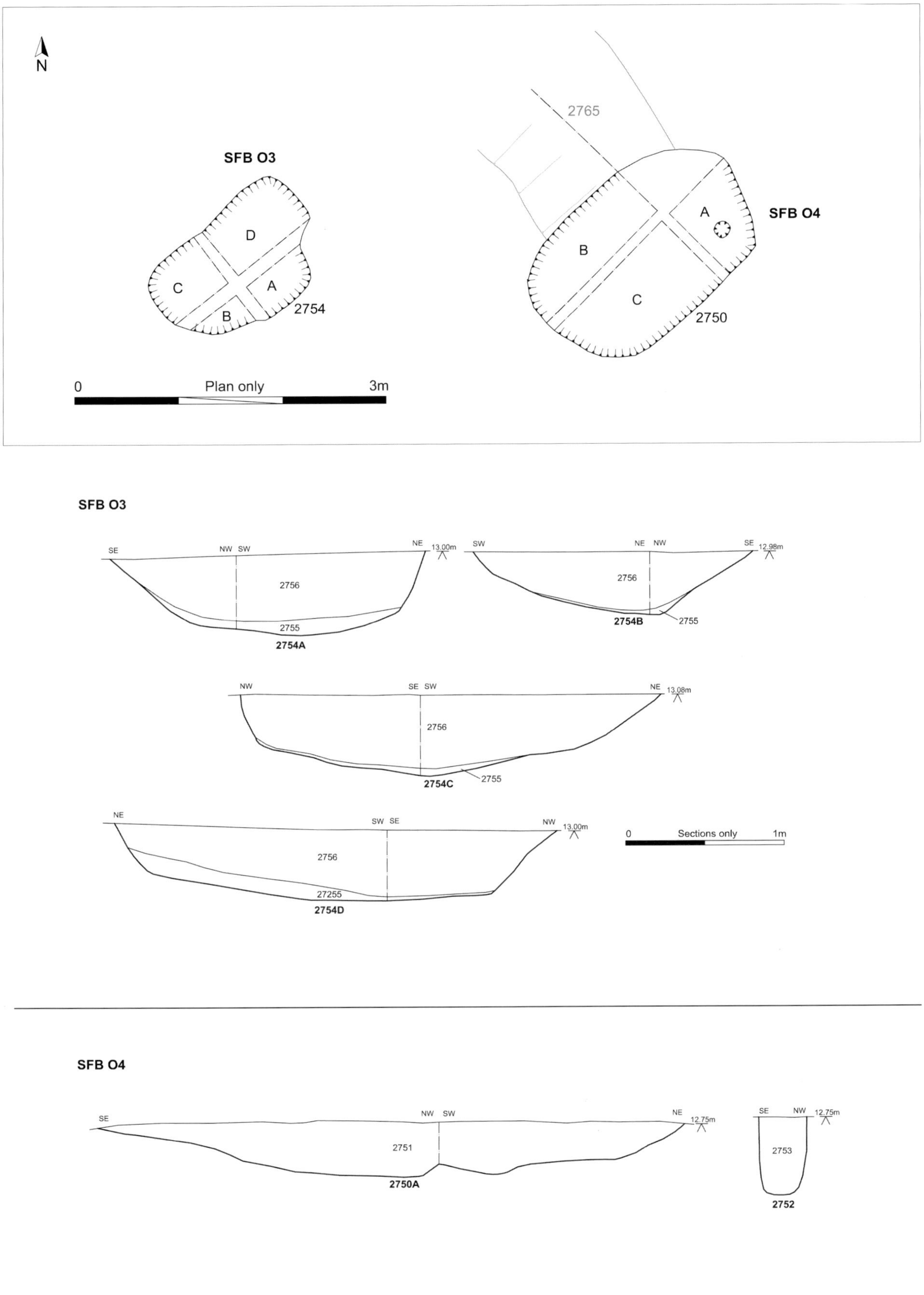

Fig. 9 Plans and sections of Sunken-Featured Buildings O3 and O4 at Lime Avenue, Oulton

of regional sites, including Hertismere High School in Suffolk, Mucking in Essex and Spong Hill in Norfolk.[58] The ledge within SFB 3161 at Spong Hill was lined with an internal wattle revetment on three sides of the sunken feature, and was thought to represent either a step or lined 'cellar'. Other interpretations of sills within SFBs include remnant floor surfaces[59] and sitting platforms.[60] While the original presence of upright stakes in the base of SFB S3 at Snape may have provided additional sub-floor support, it must be acknowledged that direct evidence for the original presence or absence of a suspended wooden floor was absent.

A discrete layer of ?colluvium (L2457) had formed around the *in situ* stakes within SFB S3 and was sealed in turn by a post-abandonment fill (L2407; Fig. 7). It is generally accepted that the fills of SFBs – which classically display a bi-partite or tri-partite pattern of infilling[61] – are the result of secondary or even tertiary deposition of material from other locations, post-abandonment (e.g. surface middens[62]). As such, although largely resulting from broadly contemporary activity, the finds from these fills have no provable relationship with the buildings themselves.

At both sites, the orientation of SFBs was predominantly east to west or north-east to south-west (where discernible; Tables 4 and 5), running across slope. This layout and orientation are mirrored at other settlements, including the Norfolk sites of Brandon Road, Thetford and Redcastle Furze,[63] while a uniformity of building alignment was also noted at Spong Hill, Norfolk and Duxford in Cambridgeshire.[64] At Pennyland, Milton Keynes the east-to-west orientation of SFBs was thought to reflect the deliberate placement of entrances away from prevailing winds,[65] a traditional interpretation attached to these structures.[66] A predominantly south-westerly wind is recorded for the East of England,[67] and may have influenced the placement of SFBs at the current sites. Possible entrances were identified at the south-eastern corners of SFBs S2 and S3 (Figs. 6 and 7); however, Tipper notes a considerable variation in the positioning of SFB entrances.[68]

Re-used Roman Pottery at Church Road, Snape

with Andrew Peachey

A series of fragments from samian ware vessels and an imported Roman storage vessel are of intrinsic interest in association with the Snape SFBs.

The samian ware comprises entirely material from east Gaul – Rheinzabern (RHZ SA) and Trier (TRI SA)[69] – which would originally have been imported to Britain in the late second to mid-third centuries AD. The penultimate stage in the 'life-cycle' of these sherds appears to have been as curated fragments in the fifth to seventh centuries AD. SFB S2 yielded the base of a RHZ SA Dr.31 bowl with the edge of a rosette stamp, and a rim sherd from a RHZ SA Curle 11 bowl with trailed decoration. SFB S3 contained a rim sherd from a TRI SA Dr.37 bowl with abraded moulded decoration including an ovolo (not identifiable). The fragments are sized between 70–100 × 70 mm with approximately triangular or rhomboid profiles and with edges, including the break, that had become rounded in antiquity (though had not been filed). The slip on all fragments is also worn but generally intact, except on rims or foot rings that form the edge of a fragment, where it has been removed. It is unclear where the Anglo-Saxon occupants of the SFBs sourced the samian ware, as it was distinct from the bulk of Roman pottery recovered from the Church Road site; the latter largely comprised locally manufactured mid- to late-first-century AD coarse wares.[70] The samian ware may have been sourced from an exposed or disturbed Roman midden or dump in the locality, or possibly arrived after being carried by occupants from a more distant source, but either way the distinct glossy, red-slipped sherds appear to have been deliberately selected.

Based on comparable evidence for the collection and re-use of Roman red-coloured pottery sherds (including samian ware) in southern and eastern Britain, Cool has identified a distinctive 'suite' of Anglo-Saxon material culture in the fifth and sixth centuries AD,[71] including counters and spindle whorls, and the samian ware from Snape may fall into the former category. It has also been speculated that such distinctly coloured fragments may have been imbued with some magical or symbolic significance.[72] The base of a similar samian ware bowl has previously been recorded in the hollow of an early Anglo-Saxon SFB at Harston Mill, Cambridgeshire,[73] while numerous re-used Roman objects, mainly brooches and metal implements, have been recorded from SFBs at sites including West Stow.[74] The deliberate selection of Roman fine wares by the post-Roman population was also apparent at Heybridge and Mucking (Essex), where they made up a significant proportion of the post-Roman assemblages.[75] The large amount of late Roman pottery in these assemblages, dominated by Lower Nene Valley colour-coated wares, Oxfordshire red-slipped wares and samian ware, was thought to suggest its continued use alongside post-Roman wares,[76] but the bias towards these fine wares may be more consistent with the selection of broken sherds based on aesthetic properties. At Mucking, more than 50% of the Roman sherds from Saxon SFBs 8 and 9 were of samian ware and were classified as 'significant';[77] however, it was considered uncertain whether this reflected deliberate selection of particular sherds by the site's Anglo-Saxon occupants.

A single rim sherd (138 g) of Mayen coarse ware[78] imported from the Rhineland was recovered from the subsoil, directly above the sunken feature of SFB S3. The vessel comprised a storage jar with an angular deep ledge/lid-seated rim that corresponds with Gose type 545,[79] and is comparable to vessels recorded in post-Roman deposits at Colchester.[80] These exceptionally hard storage jars were imported between the mid-fourth and mid-fifth centuries AD, and may have contained honey or corn.[81] Vessels have been recorded primarily at Canterbury, Richborough,

Colchester and London, but a sparse distribution has also been recovered on the eastern and southern coastlines, including at Burgh Castle and Caistor-by-Sea, while a further vessel has also been recorded at Gestingthorpe, close to the River Stour.[82] Although a direct association between the Snape sherd and the use/backfilling of SFB S3 cannot be proved, its contemporaneity with Anglo-Saxon activity at this site may suggest extensive trade links with mainland Europe.

The Burnt Flint Pits at Snape and Oulton

Notable among the remaining settlement evidence were a number of burnt flint pits, numbering two at Snape and five at Oulton (Table 6; Figs. 4, 5 and 12). This feature type is well documented on Anglo-Saxon sites across East Anglia, although under various names, e.g. 'hearth/pits' and 'flint-burning pits'.[83] They tend to be sub-rectangular in plan and of generally uniform size, although they range considerably in depth: seventeen pits excavated at Eye in Suffolk varied between 0.12 m and 0.54 m depth,[84] with a mean depth of 0.27 m, while the mean depth of seven pits at Kilverstone, Norfolk was 0.50 m.[85] The Snape and Oulton examples displayed similar variance, with the Snape pits ranging between 0.29 m and 0.58 m depth (mean = 0.44 m), while those at Oulton were between 0.19 m and 0.80 m (mean = 0.40 m).

Like most previously documented examples, the burnt flint pits at Snape and Oulton contained clearly laminated fills, including notable concentrations of charcoal and burnt flint. These layers were most clearly defined in Pit F2365 at Snape. As well as abundant charcoal inclusions, the primary fill of Pit F2058 at Snape yielded two sherds (99 g) of residual mid- to late first century AD pottery and two fragments of burnt Roman brick. Fill L2732 of Pit F2731 at Oulton contained 83 g of residual late Bronze Age/early Iron Age pottery. Similar instances of residual material within Anglo-Saxon burnt flint pits have been recorded at a number of sites, including Flixton Quarry and Kilverstone.[86] Despite the presence of Iron Age/ Romano-British pottery in its fills, two samples of charcoal from the Flixton pit produced radiocarbon date ranges of 420–545 cal AD and 430–555 cal AD (at 95% confidence).[87] Similarly, samples of charcoal from the Snape pits produced calibrated radiocarbon date ranges of 241–554 cal AD and 406–538 cal AD (at 95.4% confidence; Fig. 3).

The function of Anglo-Saxon burnt flint pits remains a topic of much debate. At Kilverstone, these features were interpreted as fulfilling a periodic industrial function of uncertain character,[88] while a domestic cooking function is favoured elsewhere (e.g. Redcastle Furze[89]). The Flixton pit was thought to be associated with ritual feasting, given its location with respect to neighbouring cemeteries of the same date, and a similar function was tentatively suggested for seven pits at Snape Anglo-Saxon cemetery.[90] At Hartismere High School, Eye it was suggested that the function of these features most probably required the slow release of latent heat within the flint, with the fires themselves being quickly smothered following the introduction of the latter.[91] The highly volatile nature of heated flint was also noted,[92] possibly undermining any domestic function(s).

Table 6 Summary of the burnt flint pits

Site	Pit No.	Length (m)	Width (m)	Depth (m)	No. of Fills
Snape	2058	2.00	1.15	0.58	2
	2065	1.61	1.28	0.29	4
Oulton	2331	1.54	1.10	0.47	6
	2683	1.26	1.25	0.22	3
	2707	1.18	1.08	0.30	3
	2717	3.60	2.60	0.80	5
	2731	1.48	1.30	0.19	4

Middle to Late Anglo-Saxon activity at Oulton

The middle to late Anglo-Saxon period at Oulton was characterized by a large, rectilinear enclosure, delineated to the north and west by a system of trackways (Fig. 4). While most of the constituent ditches had been backfilled at some point between the ninth and mid-twelfth centuries, those forming the enclosure's south-eastern corner had been backfilled no later than the ninth century. While probably implying an earlier date for the enclosure as a whole, this chronologically stratified sequence of backfilling and abandonment may be linked to a shifting focus of activity (and associated discard) over time. Certainly, the easternmost area of the site was largely devoid of later Anglo-Saxon features (Fig. 4).

Ditched enclosures are a common new feature during the middle Anglo-Saxon period in the East of England, and are sometimes linked to a concurrent shift towards more intensive husbandry practices.[93] In contrast, pre-seventh century AD enclosures tend only to occur on a small number of high-status sites,[94] although possible livestock pens or paddocks are sometimes found.[95] Unenclosed early settlements include Melford Meadows, Brettenham (Thetford), which dates from the fifth century AD,[96] while examples of later enclosures include Harston Mill, Cambridgeshire[97] and Pennyland, Milton Keynes.[98] The main enclosure ditches at Harston Mill, dating to *c.* AD 850–925, were the culmination of a developmental sequence of lesser ditches and gullies.[99] At Warmington, near Peterborough, a *c.* eighth-century system of enclosures was established in conjunction with timber structures, represented by clusters of postholes.[100] Possible structural features were also encountered at Oulton, close to the southern edge of the middle to late Anglo-Saxon enclosure (Fig. 4), although their precise nature/function could not be determined. It is suggested that the principal focus of domestic or other activity had shifted away from the excavated area by this time. Nonetheless, this period did produce a highly significant assemblage of Late Saxon or Viking (late ninth to early tenth century) weights from Pit F2162 (L2163) (see below).

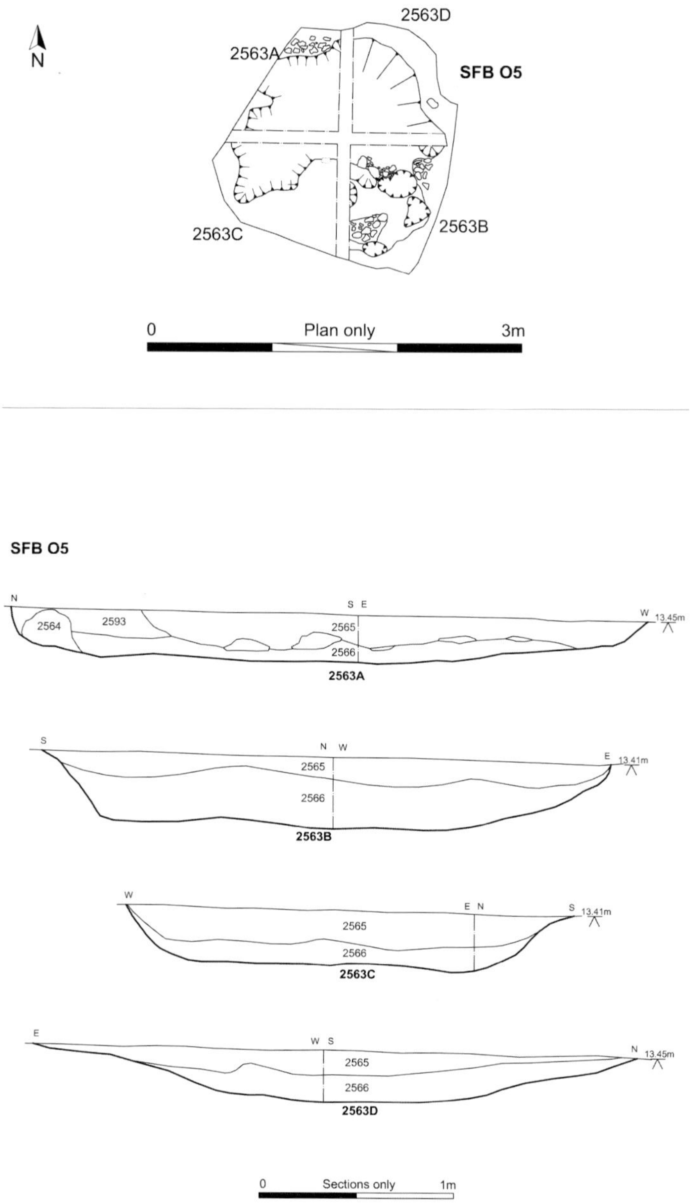

Fig. 10 Plan and sections of Sunken-Featured Building O5 at Lime Avenue, Oulton

The Economic Evidence

The animal bone
by Julia E.M. Cussans

Lime Avenue, Oulton

Bone preservation was poor. The small assemblage from Oulton was largely made up of unidentifiable fragments (mostly only recordable as large or medium-sized mammal). Cattle dominated the identifiable assemblage from the early to middle Anglo-Saxon phase of occupation – teeth and tooth fragments were most abundant – but sheep/goat, pig and horse were also represented. The single pig element, an upper deciduous fourth premolar, displayed very slight wear on the tips of the cusps, indicating a fairly young animal. It is very likely that pigs are under-represented, however, as they are noted as a key element of the Anglo-Saxon economy.[101] Bones/teeth were found in SFBs O1, O2, O3 and O4 but not SFB O5. Bone was also present in contemporary, dispersed pits. SFB O2 yielded the largest bone assemblage but no additional patterning could be detected. Individual fragments of cattle, sheep/goat and horse were present from the middle to late Anglo-Saxon period at Oulton.

Church Road, Snape

Following assessment of the Snape bone assemblage, a small sample of the two best preserved Anglo-Saxon contexts was selected for detailed analysis. These were the basal fill of SFB S3 and the fill of Pit F2238 (a feature of uncertain primary function which yielded a small quantity of domestic rubbish). Accepting possible biases introduced by poor preservation, some comparisons can be drawn between the bone assemblage from Snape and other Anglo-Saxon sites in the region. However, it must be borne in mind that the Snape assemblage is from feature fills, whereas at sites such as West Stow only occupation deposits were examined.[102] The different formation processes responsible for these distinct deposit types will have considerably affected their content in terms of animal bone (and other materials).

Elements of the head, particularly loose teeth, were the dominant body parts present, most probably relating to the better preservation of tooth enamel. Due to the fragmentary and friable state of the assemblage the vast majority of bones could not be identified to species. Approximately half of the bone fragments were recorded as unidentified, while a large number of fragments were only recordable as large or medium mammal. Identified mammal taxa, in order of abundance, were cattle, pig, sheep/goat and red deer; the red deer bone was a left distal tibia. A single indeterminate bird long bone fragment, thought to be from a chicken-sized bird, was also present.

The dominance of domestic mammals is not unusual for sites of this date.[103] The relative proportions of the three main taxa (cattle, sheep/goat and pig) do, however, seem to vary from site to site. At Spong Hill, cattle were dominant, followed by sheep, with only a small incidence of pig bones;[104] goats were not thought to be present. The low incidence of pigs was considered to be unusual for an Anglo-Saxon site as substantial quantities of pig remains are a 'hallmark of Anglo-Saxon sites in Britain'.[105] It was postulated that poor bone preservation at Spong Hill was likely to have affected pig bones more than those of sheep or cattle, due to their greater porosity. The same bias may have resulted in a lower-than-expected incidence of pig remains at Snape.

At West Stow, sheep/goat was the dominant taxon, followed by cattle and then pig, with pigs making up between 14 and 21% of the domestic mammal assemblage.[106] The difference in species dominance between

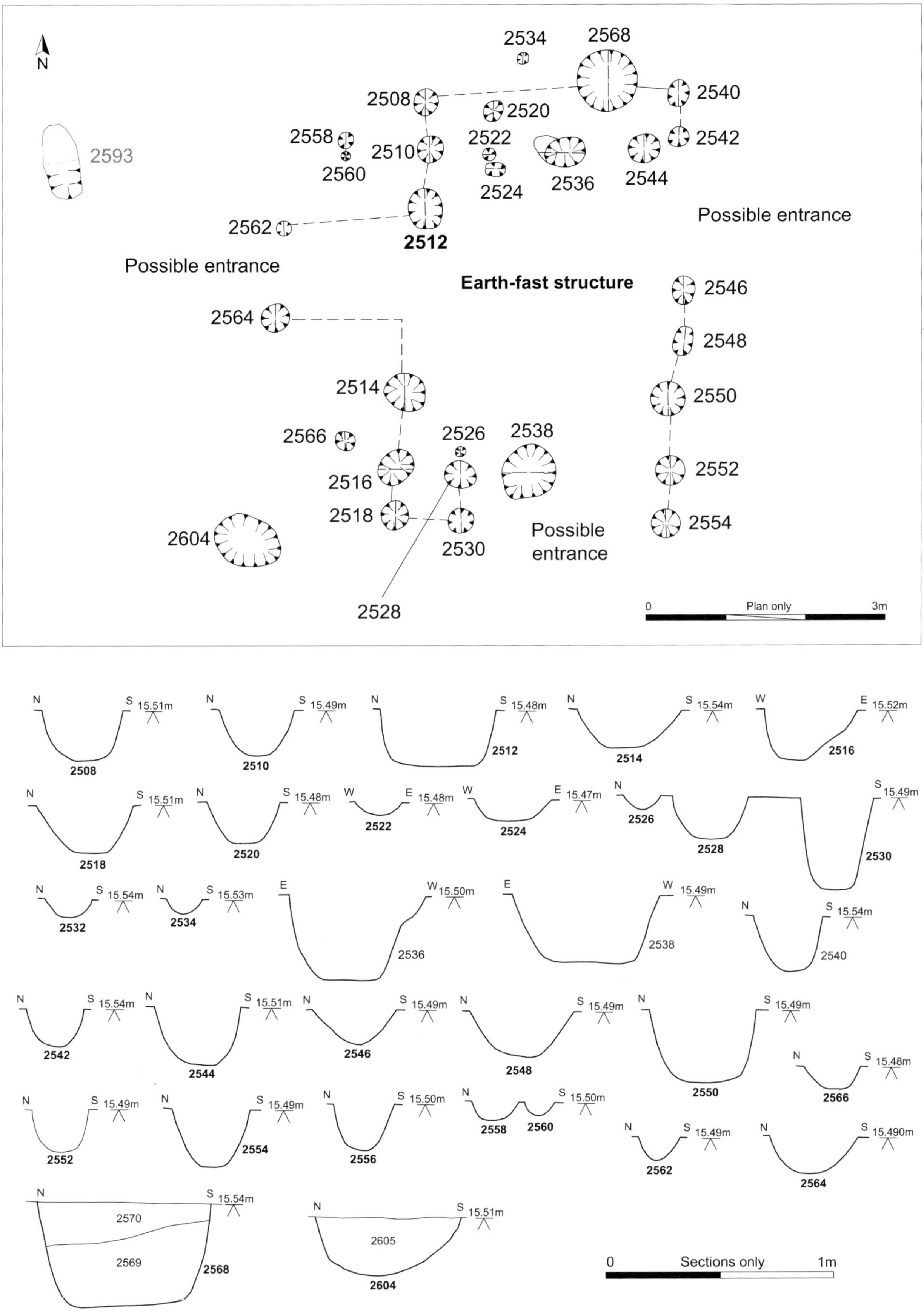

Fig. 11 Plan and sections of Earth-fast structure at Church Road, Snape

West Stow and Snape may well be accounted for by the difference in deposit types (feature fills versus occupation deposits), formation processes and methods of recovery, for example larger cattle bones being more likely to be cleared away from occupation surfaces during the life of a site and smaller ones having a greater chance of being left. Additionally, bones from West Stow were noted to be in an excellent state of preservation.

The anatomical distribution of bones of the three main domesticates was calculated in a similar way for West Stow and Snape, thus allowing for direct comparison between the two sites. While the West Stow cattle assemblage, like Snape, was dominated by head and foot elements, this dominance was not so substantial and West Stow had a considerably better representation of limb bones. This probably relates to the better state of preservation noted at West Stow. Similarly, for the pig remains, although head elements were dominant, other body areas are better represented at West Stow than at Snape.

A small number of cattle and pig teeth at Snape were available for ageing. These were assigned to age categories following Halstead for cattle and Hambleton for pig.[107] Of the six ageable teeth and mandibles available for cattle, three were assigned as age stage E, with an indicated age of 30–36 months, two were at age stage F (young adult) and one at stage I (senile). This would indicate that in the main animals were killed for meat, with a few older animals used as breeding stock and possibly for milk production. Age data from Spong Hill are very similar in nature to those from Snape. Given the poor preservation at both sites, the data are sparse and show a lack of unfused or juvenile bones and teeth of young animals. As has been noted for Snape, Bond was wary of over-interpreting the lack of young animals at Spong Hill, as this may well be a product of poor preservation rather than a specific economic strategy.[108]

A small number of butchery marks were observed at Snape. Large blade chop marks were only found on cattle, large mammal and medium mammal bones; knife marks were found on all of the main taxa. The majority of butchery marks were found on cattle and large mammal bones, with a single mark each being noted for pig and sheep/goat and only two marks on medium mammal bones.

Very few pathologies or abnormalities were observed at Snape and all of these occurred on cattle bones and teeth. Exostosis was found on an articulating proximal metatarsal and naviculocuboid. This is symptomatic of a number of different conditions, but as no other symptoms were present a diagnosis cannot be made.[109] Of the six cattle lower third molars (M3s) present, two had a missing or reduced hypoconulid (third cusp). The cause of this malformation is unknown, but has been thought to possibly indicate a narrow gene pool.[110] At Anglo-Saxon Flixbrough this condition was noted on 3.9% of mandibles.[111] In comparison, the 33% incidence seen here seems very high, although the small sample size may be a biasing factor. The final abnormality to be observed was a lower M3 which had partly sheared off on the lingual side during life and had continued to be worn; it would seem likely that this would have caused the animal some considerable pain.

Overall, despite the poor preservation and various taphonomic issues hindering the interpretation of the Snape animal bone assemblage, some useful information has been recovered. Cattle dominated the assemblage, with pig and sheep/goat possibly under-represented. It also seems likely that young animals are under-represented and that a considerably greater quantity of bone will have been deposited within SFB S3 and Pit F2238 than was recovered. Overall, the Snape assemblage appears to fit within the broader pattern seen for Anglo-Saxon sites in the East of England.

The archaeobotanical evidence
by John R. Summers

A total of seventy bulk environmental samples (879 litres) were taken and processed from Anglo-Saxon features at Snape, while fifty-one samples (670 litres) and thirteen samples (130 litres) were taken from early to middle Anglo-Saxon and middle to late Anglo-Saxon contexts at Oulton, respectively. The fully quantified samples from Snape derived from SFBs S1 and S3, while those for Oulton were taken from a range of feature types.

General Results

At Snape, cereals were present in 45.71% of samples. Wheat (*Triticum* sp.) was slightly more common than barley, occurring in 27.14% of samples compared to 22.86% for barley (*Hordeum* sp.). Within the wheat assemblage, free-threshing -type wheat (*T. aestivum/compactum* type) was the dominant variety (24.29% ubiquity compared to 1.43% glume wheat). The percentage presence of oat (*Avena* sp.) appeared to imply local cultivation, with 18.57% of samples containing oat remains, predominantly in the form of carbonized grains. Rye was present in a relatively small number of samples (2.86%), being concentrated in the SFBs. In addition, evidence for pulses, in the form of both horse bean (*Vicia faba* var. *minor*) and pea (*Pisum sativum*), was also common, with such remains present in 8.57% of samples. As with rye, these were most common from SFBs. Flax (*Linum* sp.) was present in a single sample from Posthole F2219 (SFB S3). SFB S1 yielded a fragment of plum/cherry (*Prunus* sp.) stone, which may represent wild foods gathered from surrounding hedgerow or woodland habitats. However, such material may have entered hearths with fuel wood, since charcoal from fill L2576 (Segment D) contained a small quantity of *Prunus* sp. fragments.

The early to middle Anglo-Saxon period at Oulton produced only low concentrations of carbonized material. Cereal remains were present in 43.14% of samples, which suggests fairly common usage of cereals but, coupled with low concentrations, indicates that there was no bulk processing or storage carried out at the site. Most of the cereal remains could not be identified. Wheat, including free-threshing-type wheat (*T. aestivum/turgidum* type), was present in 5.88% of samples; barley (*Horderum* sp.), including hulled grains, was present in 7.84% of samples; and oat (*Avena* sp.) and rye (*Secale cereale*) were each present in 1.96% of samples. Pulses (*Fabaceae*) were also recorded, although only in two samples (3.92%).

In the thirteen samples from the middle to late Anglo-Saxon period at Oulton, carbonized macrofossils were again rather sparse. Cereals were recorded in 30.77% of the samples, which included a small number of wheat (*Triticum* sp.) and oat (*Avena* sp.) remains. A single knotweed (*Persicaria* sp.) seed was recorded in L2730. Charcoal, including oak (*Quercus* sp.) and probable gorse (cf. *Ulex* sp.), was quite common. This indicates the deposition of fuel debris with few associated remains from the use and processing of cereals.

The Sunken-Featured Buildings

The fills of the Oulton SFBs produced only sparse carbonized plant macrofossils. Such low densities are most likely to represent scattered background debris which became incorporated into the feature fills. It seems unlikely that the use or processing of cereals was strongly associated with any of the five SFBs at this site.

The results from the SFBs S1 and S3 at Snape have the appearance of material derived from the day-to-day processing and use of cereals and other plant foods (i.e. pulses). The sampled fills are thought to represent post-abandonment fills of the sunken features rather than debris directly related to occupation. However, the remains do reflect contemporary occupation around these buildings and the site's economy at this time. The mixed nature of the crop remains from these buildings, along with the presence of charcoal remains, lead to an interpretation of domestic refuse in the form of hearth rake-out. The presence of both crops and weed seeds indicates that the hearths were receiving a mixture of remains from the daily processing and use of cereals and other crops.

The predominance of barley in both SFB fills indicates that it is likely to have made a significant dietary contribution. Whether this means that it was the primary crop is difficult to determine, although it appears to have been in roughly equal use to wheat during the early to middle Anglo-Saxon period. The dominant wheat variety was of a free-threshing type, which is quite typical for the period;[112] this also appears to have made a significant contribution to the diet and economy of the Church Road site.

The significant proportion of oat, particularly in SFB S3 at Snape, would appear to be an indication that it was also important for human consumption. Oat has also been reported in significant quantities from Anglo-Saxon contexts at Stansted and Springfield Lyons in Essex.[113] The status of rye is much less certain, although it is a drought-tolerant crop that would be well suited to Snape's free-draining, sandy soils.

The presence of pulses in a set of samples with a domestic appearance suggests that these crops were also making a significant contribution to the dietary economy at Snape. However, in other contexts, such crops have also been considered to have a potential role as fodder.[114]

Although there are several crop taxa (oat, rye and barley) which indicate the exploitation of local sandy soils for arable production, there is good evidence from the non-cereal taxa that a more extensive territory was exploited. In particular, the presence of stinking chamomile (*Anthemis cotula*) within the fills of SFB S3 is an indication of the use of heavier clay or loam soils, most probably for the cultivation of free-threshing-type wheat. Whether this was the direct result of cultivation by the site's inhabitants or present as imported grain is difficult to determine based on the present evidence. However, the number of weed seeds, particularly stinking chamomile seeds in SFB S3, which are likely to be associated with the free-threshing-type wheat remains, may indicate some on-site processing of the wheat crop.

Summary

Cereal production and processing at Oulton appears to have been of little significance during the Anglo-Saxon period. Remains of cereals were present in less than half of deposits and only in low densities. This is consistent with background debris, most likely originating from low level cereal use on the site.

At Snape, although there appears to have been extensive use of the local sandy soils for crops such as oat, rye and potentially barley during the early to middle Anglo-Saxon period, it appears that the area's heavier soils were also exploited for the cultivation of free-threshing-type wheat. It is also possible, however, that the presence of wheat within the environmental assemblage reflects trade and/or co-operation with neighbouring settlements situated closer to heavier soils.

The charcoal
by John R. Summers

Introduction

At Snape, rich deposits of charcoal were present in the burnt flint pits, along with a small amount of material from SFBs S1 and S3. Charcoal was also abundant within the fills of the Oulton burnt flint pits; particularly rich was L2748 (F2717), which contained 1,358 g of charcoal >2 mm in just 10 litres of sediment.

The Burnt Flint Pits

Church Road, Snape

The material from Burnt Flint Pit F2365 (L2366) at Snape (see Fig. 5) was composed predominantly of oak (*Quercus* sp.) charcoal (96% by weight), with a much smaller amount of hazel (*Corylus* sp.). Tyloses were present in 39% of oak fragments and ring curvature was judged weak or moderate for most fragments, with no small-diameter roundwood present. The largest ring count was twenty-two from a fragment of oak, although this is a minimum age, based on the absence of either pith or bark. The assemblage appears to indicate the burning of wood from mature oak trees, supplemented by a small amount of hazel. A small number of insect holes were also noted, indicating the presence of dead wood.

Remains from the other Snape pit (F2058 (L2060); see Fig. 5) were more varied, with oak (*Quercus* sp.), hazel (*Corylus* sp.), plum/cherry (*Prunus* sp.) and *Sorbus/Malus/Pirus/Crataegus* sp. group (*Maloideae*) all present. *Maloideae* was dominant by weight (54%) and fragment count, followed by oak (35%), hazel (11%) and a trace amount of plum/cherry. Most fragments from L2060 displayed some curvature in the growth rings and no evidence of heartwood was encountered. This indicates that large, mature trees were not felled to fuel the activities associated with Burnt Flint Pit F2058 at Snape. Where fragments were suitable for an assessment of age through ring counting, a maximum age of thirty-one years was obtained from a piece of hazel wood. A fragment of oak showing a complete sequence gave an age at death of twenty-two years and another fragment provided an age in excess of twenty-four years. Fragments of *Maloideae* provided ages from around fourteen years up to twenty-eight years and over.

Hazel and numerous *Maloideae* genera commonly occur in oak woodland and it seems likely from the ring counts and the taxa present that the fuel wood was gathered from young, mixed woodland communities. The felling of 20–30 year old trees in such a habitat could have been part of a thinning out process in managed woodland.

Two fragments provided evidence of seasonality, one oak and one hazel. Both had complete outer rings, indicating that they were cut at the end of the growing season (autumn/winter).

Lime Avenue, Oulton

The fills of the five burnt flint pits at Oulton were generally rich in charcoal. Charcoal remains were predominantly identified from primary fills unless the assessment found these to contain low concentrations. Oak (*Quercus* sp.) was the most abundant taxon in all five pits. In most instances, weak ring curvature and the presence of tyloses in the vessels indicated heartwood and the burning of mature oak timber. Occasional pieces of round wood probably represent smaller branches from the felled trees. Hazel (*Corylus* sp.) was recorded in four of the samples, while hazel was more prominent in one, although oak still predominated. It is likely that in this instance, a mixed fuel source of oak and hazel was burned.

The Sunken-Featured Buildings

A single sample from SFB S1 (Fill L2576) contained just fourteen charcoal fragments. However, a wide range of taxa was present, including elm (*Ulmus* sp.), oak (*Quercus* sp.), plum/cherry (*Prunus* sp.), *Sorbus/Malus/Pirus/Crataegus* sp. group (*Maloideae*) and holly (*Ilex* sp.). A small number of fragments allowed identification of moderate to strong ring curvature, demonstrating the presence of small-diameter wood. The diverse taxa, despite the low density of material, indicate exploitation of a wide range of sources of fuel wood.

Three samples were analyzed from fills L2407 and L2408 of SFB S3. Once again the density of charcoal fragments was quite low. The range of taxa included elm (*Ulmus* sp.), oak (*Quercus* sp.), hazel (*Corylus* sp.) and *Sorbus/Malus/Pirus/Crataegus* sp. group (*Maloideae*). Oak was the dominant taxon by both fragment count and weight. The range of taxa implies some flexibility in fuel wood choice but the dominance of oak may imply a greater degree of selection than indicated by the material from SFB S1.

Discussion

Oak was the overwhelmingly dominant species of charcoal within the Oulton burnt flint pits and Pit F2365 at Snape. In contrast, Pit F2058 at Snape yielded a much more varied assemblage; a similarly diverse assemblage was noted in a burnt flint pit at Flixton, Suffolk.[115] This is of interest since it indicates that very careful selection of timber may not have been considered necessary in relation to the activities associated with these features. The difference in this fuel to that from F2058 could indicate that either a different area of woodland was exploited or that it was imported from elsewhere. This said, however, the dominant taxa within F2058 (Maloideae and oak) are both high- quality hard wood fuels which would burn slowly and evenly. The universal dominance of oak charcoal at Oulton may reflect local woodland availability, especially as assemblages from other sites, including Snape, indicate a less rigid selection of fuel resources.

The material from SFBs S1 and S3 is likely to represent hearth ash and debris deposited in the sunken features following abandonment. The diverse assemblage of fuel wood shows limited concern with wood selection. This indicates that the wood is likely to have been gathered from a range of suitable habitats, including hedgerows and woodland. This is what might be expected for general domestic purposes, where specific temperature control is less significant.

The Late Anglo-Saxon or Viking weights

by Nicholas J. Cooper, with Carolingian coin identifications by Simon Coupland, and conservation and photography by Graham Morgan.

Introduction

A group of eleven late Saxon or Viking-period (late ninth to early tenth century) weights was recovered from Pit F2162 (L2163) at Lime Avenue, Oulton (see Fig. 4), shown as excavated below, prior to conservation (Fig. 12).

The weights comprise eight short cylindrical lead pan weights (nos. i–viii in the catalogue below) and three

Fig. 12 Group of weights from Pit F2162, comprising eight cylindrical lead pan weights arranged in two rows of four (left and central) and three oblate-spheroid iron weights with copper alloy sheaths (right). Lead weights: top row (i), (iii), (v), (ii), bottom row (vii), (iv), (vi), and (viii). Iron weights: top (xi), middle (ix) and bottom (x)

oblate-spheroid pan weights of diagnostically Viking type, with iron cores and copper alloy sheaths (nos. ix–xi in the catalogue). Of particular significance is the fact that four of the eight lead pan weights have coins embedded into their upper surfaces, two of Roman date and two Carolingian, dating to the later ninth or early tenth century (Fig. 13). The following catalogue describes each weight from the smallest to the largest by type.

Catalogue

Cylindrical pan weights

i) Short lead cylinder with straight sides. Diameter 15 mm, thickness 8 mm, weight 15.9 g.

ii) Short lead cylinder with convex sides. Diameter 17 mm, thickness 8 mm, weight 16.2 g.

iii) A slightly tapering or conical lead cylinder with a core of black vitreous material with a crazed surface. Diameter 25 mm, thickness 16 mm, weight 78.2 g.

iv) Short cylindrical lead weight with a Roman copper alloy coin, possibly a *sestertius*, or more likely a *dupondius*, inset into the top (Fig. 13 left); 31 mm in diameter, 11 mm thick, weighing 94.5. The coin is heavily worn and only the reverse is visible. The legend is worn except for the exergue, below the seated figure, TRP (tribunician power). The representation of the seated female figure holding a cornucopia in the cruck of the left arm, and possibly scales in the outstretched right arm, is similar to late-second-century issues.

v) Short cylinder lead weight; diameter 27 mm, thickness 17 mm, weight 98.2 g.

vi) Cylindrical lead weight with a silver coin, in an extremely fine condition, inserted into the upper surface, with only the reverse visible (Fig. 13 centre). Simon Coupland identifies this as a denier of the Gratia D-i rex type, minted from 864 onwards, of the Palace mint: +PALATINAMONE: MG 629, Depeyrot 750, cf. MEC 1.884 (MONET). The mint's precise location is uncertain. Diameter 30 mm, thickness 19 mm, weight 135.1 g.

vii) Short cylindrical lead weight with an inset copper alloy coin; diameter 38 mm, thickness 12 mm, weight 141.5 g. The coin is illegible but likely to be a later-second-century *sestertius* or *dupondius*.

viii) Large cylindrical lead weight with a coin, in an extremely fine condition, inserted into the upper surface, with only the reverse visible (Fig. 13 right). Simon Coupland identifies this as a *denier* of the same Gratia D-i rex type, of the Laon mint, LVGDVNICLAVATI, MG 794, Depeyrot 482, MEC 1.869. Diameter 35 mm, thickness 24 mm, weight 292.5 g.

Oblate-spheroid weights of iron and copper alloy

ix) Oblate spheroid weight with iron core and copper alloy sheath open at both poles. Diameter 13 mm, height 12 mm, weight 7.7 g.

x) Oblate spheroid weight with iron core and copper alloy sheath, open at the top. The bottom is flat and decorated with a ring of punch marks around the circumference and a central 'triskele' motif (Fig.14 left). Diameter 18 mm, height 17 mm, weight 23.8 g.

xi) Oblate spheroid weight with an iron core and copper alloy sheath (open at both poles). The surface of the copper sheath is decorated with triangles of punch marks with groups of three 'grapes' at each corner (Fig.14 right). Diameter 18 mm, height 18 mm, weight 24.1g.

The Dating of the Weights

The occurrence of a group of eleven weights from the single fill of a small pit strongly suggests that they originally comprised a coherent set, deposited in the ground at the same time and therefore presumably manufactured in accordance with the prevailing weight standard. The only

Fig. 13 Cylindrical lead pan weights with embedded coins. Roman (iv) and Carolingian (vi) and (viii).

dating is provided by the two Carolingian coins embedded in weights (vi) and (viii), both in extremely fine condition, suggesting that they had been set into the lead without previously circulating for long as currency. Simon Coupland states that both coin types are often attributed to Charles the Bald (AD 840–77) and are found in numbers in several hoards of the 880s. They remained in circulation until the tenth century, when an identical type was minted between 898 and 923 by Charles the Simple. It is thus impossible, without other evidence, to date the removal of these two specimens from circulation more precisely than to the late ninth or early tenth century. Once embedded in the weights, the coins would have avoided further wear and so it is not possible to demonstrate how long the weights remained in use before their deposition in the pit. However, as argued below, the typology of the weights and their metrology suggest that they were in use during the late ninth or early tenth century, either within a Viking-period cultural context or within a Late Saxon cultural context influenced by Viking-period activity.

The Typology of the Weights

Disc-shaped or cylindrical pan weights in lead are widely paralleled at medieval urban centres such as Winchester and London,[116] whilst elsewhere, smaller numbers are securely identified as pre-Conquest, but associated primarily with Viking activity.[117] Amongst those identified as pre-Conquest is a distinctive group with coins or other decorative items embedded in their tops, which are consistently associated with Viking activity; the small examples at least, are considered to have been used specifically for the weighing of bullion.[118] Whilst the Oulton weights vary in diameter and height, they all appear to have been cast by pouring molten lead into circular, straight-sided moulds. This method of manufacture suggests an attempt at standardization which is investigated below in terms of the metrology of the weights. Alongside the lead weights were three iron weights with copper alloy sheaths of the kind found across Scandinavia and in areas of Viking settlement in Britain, such as the winter camp at Torksey in Lincolnshire.[119]

The Metrology of the Weights

The weights vary between 7.7 g and 292.5 g and any attempt to equate them with their original weights and, indeed, any theoretical weight standard, would first need to take into account losses caused by oxidation. Deposits of white lead oxide are clearly visible on the upper surfaces of the unconserved cylindrical weights (Fig. 12) and the oxidation of the iron in the oblate-spheroid weights is quite extensive and probably enough to noticeably reduce their weight, although the copper alloy is unaffected. The second difficulty is knowing how closely weight standards were adhered to, and what degree of variation was recognized or tolerated. If the smaller weights were being used to weigh bullion, then a high degree of regulation might have been expected and, given the potential error that might occur in the larger weights, they may have been used to weigh lower-value items where perceived variation was tolerable.

The weights do not conform closely to the systems in use during the medieval period, usefully summarized by Egan,[120] and this supports the contention that they should potentially conform to a pre-Conquest system of weight standards within a late Saxon or Scandinavian context. Therefore, any assumption that this collection of weights relates to Viking-period activity would need to be tested against the currently understood standards of the period. This has most recently been reviewed in the study of the collection of fifteen lead weights from the Viking Age site at Cottam on the Yorkshire Wolds,[121] as well as during the study of eighteen Viking coin weights by Williams.[122] The Cottam weights compared favourably with the Scandinavian standard proposed by Brogger, based on his 1921 study of the weights found in Norwegian Viking-Age graves.[123] Brogger proposed the existence of a 'light' ounce or *ore* of 24.59 g, divided into three units, or *ertogs*, of 8.19 g, which had superseded the heavier 'old Norwegian' ounce of 26.5 g. When compared to these units, and multiples

Fig. 14 Fig. 14 Oblate-spheroid weights of iron with decorated copper alloy sheaths. Left to right: (x) and (xi).

thereof, the similarities between the Oulton weights and the Cottam collection are notable (Table 7).

The tabulation of the Oulton weights in ascending order by weight, within each type, highlights the clustering of single or paired weights around recognized multiples of the *ore* or *ertog*. The deviation from the theoretical weight is, with one exception (iii), consistently negative and might be explained by oxidation, as they are not otherwise damaged. Whilst the raw weight deviation ranges from 0.2 g to 12.5 g, the % deviation this represents ranges from 0.2% to 8.4%, with an average of 3.5%. The % error is not markedly greater amongst the heavier weights and, indeed, the largest weight (viii), at nearly 300 g, is only 0.9% less than its theoretical equivalent.

Despite some clear loss of weight through oxidation (up to 4.9%), the iron weights appear to cater for the lower multiples not covered by the lead weights and, perhaps,

Table 7 A comparison of the Oulton weights with a unit of 24.59 g (rounded to 24.6 g)

Lead and iron weights from Oulton (Suffolk) compared to unit of 24.6 g				
No.	**Actual wght (g)**	**Theoretical wght (g)**	**Deviation (g)**	**% Deviation**
Cylindrical lead weights				
i)	15.9	16.4 = two *ertogs*	−0.5	3.0
ii)	16.2	16.4 = two *ertogs*	−0.2	1.2
iii)	78.2	73.8 = three *ore*	+4.4	6.0
iv)	94.5	98.4 = halfmark (4 *ore*)	−3.9	4.0
v)	98.2	98.4 = halfmark (4 *ore*)	−0.2	0.2
vi)	135.1	147.6 = six *ore*	−12.5	8.4
vii)	141.5	147.6 = six *ore*	−6.1	4.1
viii)	292.5	295.1 = three halfmarks	−2.6	0.9
Iron & copper alloy oblate-spheroid weights				
ix)	7.7	8.1 = one *ertog*	0.4	4.9
x)	23.8	24.6 = one *ore*	−0.8	3.2
xi)	24.1	24.6 = one *ore*	−0.5	2.0

confirm that they were added to the proposed 'set' due to this complementarity. The smallest (ix) is close to one *ertog*, whilst the larger pair, (x) and (xi), are close to one *ore*. Between these, the smallest of the lead weights (i) and (ii) are close to two *ertogs*. The multiple then jumps to three *ore* (iii), with two examples, (iv) and (v), at four *ore*, equivalent to the Viking half-mark. The next pair, (vi) and (vii), are equivalent to six *ore*, and the largest of all (viii) represents three Viking half-marks or twelve *ore*.

The collection from Cottam shows a remarkably similar pattern of deviation from the theoretical standards seen at Oulton, although eight of the fifteen are positive values.[124] Calculating the % deviation within these data demonstrates a similar range to Oulton, from 0.5% to 8.4%, with an average value of 3%. The range of weight represented is, however, narrower, from 8.42 g (one *ertog*) to 94.89 g (four *ore* or one Viking half-mark). In terms of the multiples between these, four of the weights recognized at Cottam are not represented at Oulton; namely the half *ore* of 12.29 g, the one-third plus one-half *ore* at 20.49 g, the one-and-a-third *ore* at 32.78 g, and the two *ore* at 49.18 g. Although the Cottam collection represents unconnected examples from across the settlement, rather than a coherent set, it still reflects the need for greater precision (using narrower weight intervals) when weighing lighter items of high value which might include bullion. In contrast, the Oulton set is perhaps geared to heavier items, at the half-mark or above, with the smaller weights allowing some flexibility and precision between these higher intervals. This brings the discussion towards the significance of the weights with coins inserted, since these are absent from the Cottam collection and appear only to be used in weights at the half-mark, or above, at Oulton, the largest here being equivalent to three half-marks. Smaller weights bearing coins are, however, found elsewhere.

The Occurrence of Viking Coin Weights

The occurrence of coins set into the top of lead weights, referred to as 'Viking coin weights' by Williams,[125] has been reviewed by a number of authors,[126] and seems to be part of a wider phenomenon linked to Viking activity, that also included the insertion of other fragments of decorated metalwork and glass into weights, either for decorative effect or to provide a way of identifying the weights during transactions.[127] Since those reviews, many more weights of early medieval date have been discovered through metal detection and have been recorded under the Portable Antiquities Scheme (PAS).[128] A search of the PAS database (dated 30/11/2017) reveals a total of 408 weights in all base metals (293 of lead or lead alloy, 103 in copper alloy, and four in iron) attributed to the early medieval period, with most being referred to as of 'Viking-type'. Those with inserted items are all in lead or lead alloy, whilst the copper alloy and iron weights include examples of the oblate-spheroid weights (often referred to in the database as barrel-shaped) of the kind found at Oulton, which will be discussed in more detail below.

Amongst nearly 300 lead weights are twenty that include fragments of decorated metalwork and three that include glass, the latter paralleling the insertion of dark vitreous material into the core of weight (iii). In addition, there are twelve weights with coins embedded, ten of the early medieval period and two of probable Roman date. Although the weights are Viking products and, with a few explainable exceptions (see below), are found within the Danelaw or other Viking settlements, the coins inserted into them, up until recently at least, have invariably been Anglo-Saxon. The most common belong to the copper alloy *styca* coinage of the Northumbrian kings between the 830s and 850s,[129] as overviewed by Pirie and Kruse.[130] Twelve of the eighteen Viking coin weights studied by Williams incorporated *stycas* and he has argued that they were commonly used to decorate the weights precisely because the Vikings did not value them as coins and they rarely used them as such.[131] Four of the remaining Viking coin weights in the study incorporated ninth-century issues of Wessex and Mercia, three of which came from outside the Danelaw, two from the Isle of Purbeck and one from Cirencester, and may relate to Viking activity there in the 870s.[132] Occasionally, coins that were already old, such as 'porcupine' *sceattas* of the early eighth century, were used.[133]

In terms of their distribution within the Danelaw and other Viking settlements, Williams' study included a find local to Oulton – a weight containing a Northumbrian *styca* of the 840s from Lowestoft, found by metal detector in 1998 – as well as one from Colchester found in 1993, and another from Faversham in Kent, found in 1996.[134] Otherwise, the pre-millennial finds tend to have been to the north, in Lincolnshire, Yorkshire and from Viking graves on the Scottish Islands of Colonsay and Arran, and in Norway.[135] The picture painted by the Portable Antiquities data over the last two decades is very similar, with eight of the ten early medieval coin inserts being Northumbrian *stycas*, found in Lincolnshire, Yorkshire and Merseyside, with just one *styca* of Redwulf found in Norfolk.[136] One other bearing a coin of Wiglaf of Mercia (AD 830–40) came from North Lincolnshire.[137] The remaining early medieval coin find is discussed below as it is of particular relevance to the Oulton group.

The Oulton Viking coin weights stand out from previous discoveries because they incorporate complete silver coins of Carolingian origin as well as worn examples of Roman coins. Although Carolingian coins have not until recently been recognized on such weights, it is not surprising that they were used in this way, since they commonly occur in Viking coin hoards in Britain, and they join the example of a weight bearing a fragment of Carolingian metalwork found at the Benedictine nunnery at Clementhorpe in York.[138] Most significantly, shortly before the discovery of the Oulton weights, an example bearing a fragment of another Carolingian coin was found near Walsingham, in Norfolk, in 2013.[139] The fragment belongs to an example of a CHRISTIANA RELIGIO *denier* of the Carolingian king Loius the Pious (AD 814–40).

The use of Roman coins in these weights is also unusual but a small number of examples are now known. One of the first recognized was an example in the Rogers collection employing a late Roman coin of Constantine,[140] and since then two have been recorded under the PAS: the first, a radiate of AD 260–75, from Norton Disney in North Lincolnshire,[141] and the second a very worn fourth-century coin found on Canvey Island in Essex.[142] Given the poor condition of these two coins and the two from Oulton, it seems doubtful that their antiquity or design had any bearing on their selection for insertion. The possible exception to this conclusion is that the reverse of the coin in weight (iv), bearing a cornucopia and possibly scales, in the arms of the seated female figure (Fig. 12), may have been recognized as symbolic of trade.

The Occurrence of Oblate-spheroid Weights

In addition to the three examples from Oulton, seven examples of iron oblate-spheroid weights with copper alloy sheaths have been recorded by the PAS, three of which come from Suffolk, namely Saxmundham, Laxfield and St Edmundsbury, and another from Little Wilbraham in south Cambridgeshire. The remaining three come from Sevenoaks in Kent, North Cave near Hull, and 'near Stamford Bridge' in Yorkshire.[143] In four cases, the flat bases and tops (where preserved) are decorated with a central cross motif surrounded by a ring of punched dots. In style they are similar to the *triskele* on weight (x), but on the examples from Little Wilbraham and Stamford Bridge, the motif is clearly a swastika with curving arms, whilst on the example from Hull, it is a straight-armed cross with a trefoil of dots at each terminal and S-shaped curls extending at right-angles to these. The examples from Saxmundham and Sevenoaks bear a double crown motif, thought to be derived from Arabic symbols. In addition, there are three other weights listed on the PAS database (two from Lincolnshire and one from Buckinghamshire) which, though similar in shape, are cast entirely in copper alloy and not directly comparable to the Viking type.

Interestingly, two examples of this type of weight, one possibly bearing the worn remains of a 'triskele' motif, have been published from residual contexts in London.[144]

The seven diagnostic weights within the PAS record vary between 30.1 g (close to the one-and a-third *ore* weights from Cottam, with another closer at 32.39 g) and 137.95 g (close to the six *ore* weights from Oulton (v) and (vi)), with the intervals covered by two weights of around 40 g (39.21 g and 40.29 g), one of 56.6 g, and the last of 91 g, none of which are represented at Cottam or Oulton. They could, however, represent multiples of the half *ertog* of 4.1 g which Haldenby and Kershaw suspect is the base unit that correlates most closely with the Cottam weights, and appears frequently in Scandinavia.[145]

Discussion

Settlement form and function

Overall, settlement form at the Church Road and Lime Avenue sites is difficult to define as only a portion of the early to middle Anglo-Saxon landscape was excavated in each case. However, the location of these settlements and the nature of the features encountered display strong similarities. Both occupied elevated positions overlooking river valleys, on free-draining sandy soils, and both were also principally characterized by unenclosed groups of SFBs and burnt flint pits (Figs. 1, 4 and 5). The lack of settlement enclosures is typical of the early to middle Anglo-Saxon period in the region, where their widespread emergence is dated from the mid-seventh century AD.[146]

The sunken-featured buildings

At both sites SFBs were the dominant or only form of building present. The predominance of SFBs is usual for sandy/gravelly sites where posthole structures or 'halls' tend to be scarcer.[147] SFBs are also broadly indicative of an early settlement date as this structural form is seen to decline during the middle Anglo-Saxon period and is absent at most later-seventh- to ninth-century sites.[148] Where orientation could be ascertained, the SFBs at Snape and Oulton also appeared to be similarly aligned (approximately east to west), perpendicular to the slope of the ground. This 'across-slope' alignment of the SFBs is mirrored at numerous sites and reflects the deliberate placement of entrances away from prevailing winds.[149]

SFBs are the most commonly encountered form of Anglo-Saxon structure on archaeological sites and are ubiquitous throughout southern Britain.[150] Other East Anglian examples include those from Brandon Road, Thetford,[151] Harston Mill, Cambridgeshire,[152] Dernford Farm, Sawston,[153] the Old Bell, Marham,[154] and Hartismere High School, Eye.[155] Although the function of these structures is still widely debated, the surviving sunken features generally display similar overall dimensions (mean = 3 × 4 m in plan by 0.30–0.50 m deep).[156] Some later (seventh-century) examples can be considerably larger, however.[157]

Although broadly contemporary, the SFBs at each site may have represented a chronological succession of buildings (at least in part). It is possible that SFBs S1 and S2 at Snape and SFBs O3 and O4 at Oulton represented short 'sequences' of structures with one building replacing the other in each case. Both pairs were closely spaced, separated by just *c.* 2 to 6.5 m (Figs. 6 and 9). However, the stratigraphic evidence could not confirm any structural sequence and scientific dating was only possible in one instance (SFB S1; Table 3).

Structural typologies

Where evidence of superstructure survived, the Snape and Oulton SFBs appeared to conform to established two- or six-post typologies.[158] It is possible that local, sandy turf formed an important building material at both sites, although no evidence of such was found. Nonetheless, weight-bearing turf walls have been widely suggested elsewhere,[159] and it would be almost inconceivable to think that such a freely available material would not be utilized. A more complex structural form should not be discounted, however. Exceptional preservation of charred plank/wattle walls and thatch was recorded within Hut [SFB] 15 at West Stow,[160] one of two such structures at the site that had burnt down. Although similar building materials did not survive at Snape or Oulton, the poor preservation of all (un-charred) organic building remains can be postulated in each case based on the poor condition of recovered animal bone.

Only SFB S3 at Snape included structural evidence to suggest the presence of a suspended wooden floor overlying the sunken feature. It is acknowledged, however, that direct evidence for the presence or absence of floors was lacking in all instances. Corresponding beam slots (F2411 and F2470) were cut to the level of a well-defined 'sill', running around the edge of Sunken Feature F2406 (SFB S3), while a linear group of stakeholes truncated its base (Fig. 7). The beam slots are thought to have housed a substantial timber crossbeam, possibly mirrored by additional beams resting on the internal sill. Whether or not such beams constituted sub-floor supports remains open to debate. The purpose of a sub-floor void within SFB S3 may well have been ventilation,[161] especially considering the possible investment in timber thought to be represented by the surviving elements of this building.

The Early to Middle Anglo-Saxon economy
with Julia E.M. Cussans and John R. Summers

Plant and Animal Remains

It is difficult to infer much regarding the nature of the earlier Anglo-Saxon economy at Oulton. Plant remains from this period are only representative of low-level cereal use, while the animal bone assemblage is small. Despite this, the faunal remains include a reasonable diversity of identified taxa, dominated by cattle, with sheep/goat, pig and horse also present. However, no reliable conclusions can be drawn about the relative abundance or economic utility of different domestic species. The lack of fish and bird bones is notable given the location of the Lime Avenue site in respect to the River Waveney and associated wetlands, some 1.9 km to the west. Wildfowling was well attested at West Stow, for example, with seventeen individual species represented,[162] while the site at Dernford Farm yielded remains of woodcock, goose and wild boar.[163] Fish species from a variety of habitats were also recorded at Bloodmoor Hill,[164] just 4.2 km to the south of Oulton.

The animal bone assemblage from Snape was also dominated by domestic species, notably cattle, with sheep/goat and pig present in fewer numbers. This relative abundance of species may not reliably represent past economic strategy, however. Two fragments of red deer bone – a rare occurrence in such assemblages – were also recorded. Wild species typically represent less than 1% of bone assemblages dating between the fifth and seventh centuries AD, with red deer remains usually confined to shed antler.[165] This makes the occurrence of a left distal tibia at Snape all the more notable, possibly indicating the specific targeting of red deer by the local population for uses other than craft-level production.[166]

Age-at-death calculations at Snape indicated the raising of cattle for meat, with possible breeding and milking animals (of an older age) also represented. Although younger animals were not present, this most probably reflects poor bone preservation. The butchery evidence was principally representative of skinning and dismemberment/food procurement, with possible horn working and the splintering of bone for marrow extraction or the production of material for pin manufacture (or similar) also attested. A small number of bone pathologies and abnormalities were observed but no firm conclusions could be drawn.

Overall, the Snape bone assemblage represents an economy based on farming, supplemented by hunting, typical of the period in East Anglia and in keeping with evidence from other sites, e.g. Melford Meadows, West Stow and Bloodmoor Hill.[167] Although the remains of fish and fowl were once again absent, this was no doubt the result of poor preservation. The location of the Church Road site, overlooking the Alde estuary, *c.* 7.6 km from the coast, would have afforded easy access to such resources.

Plant remains from Snape, mostly recovered from SFBs S1 and S3, attest to a varied agrarian economy similar to that seen at other regional sites. The presence of barley, rye and oat is strongly suggestive of local cultivation on sandy, free-draining soils, while wheat grains suggest the exploitation of heavier clay soils (examples of which are present *c.* 2 km to the north). Barley (probably a hulled, six-row variety) and wheat (predominantly free-threshing type) appear to have been of equal economic utility, while material from SFB S3 attests to the potential dietary importance of oats. Pulses also appear to have played a notable economic role, while a single cherry or plum stone fragment from the basal fill of SFB S1 might also attest to the gathering of uncultivated foodstuffs. Overall, however, material from the Snape SFBs is typical of day-to-day processing and use of cereals and other cultivated foodstuffs.

The Finds Evidence

Artefacts from Oulton are few, but include an iron knife from the secondary fill of SFB O2 (L2634). Knives are a multi-functional tool, however, and no firm use can be assigned to this example, especially considering the secondary or even tertiary nature of L2634.

The two spindle whorl fragments from SFB S1 at Snape attest to the spinning of wool at this site. No contemporary evidence for the weaving of textiles was encountered, however. Limited craft activity is also indicated by a possible awl handle from SFB S3 at this site. Anglo-Saxon SFBs are often associated with textile manufacture,[168] and Crummy suggests that early settlements were self-sufficient in terms of this industry.[169] Regional examples of textile-related artefacts were also found within SFBs at Billingford,[170] Brandon Road, Thetford,[171] Hartismere High School, Eye,[172] Spong Hill,[173] West Stow,[174] and Bloodmoor Hill.[175] The latter included a very large assemblage of fired and unfired clay loom weight fragments.[176] Although the fills of the Snape SFBs may not directly relate to their use, it is clear that the spinning of wool played a part in the settlement's economy.

A single rim sherd from a Mayen coarse ware storage jar was found within the subsoil directly overlying SFB S3. Although a direct association between the Snape sherd and the use/backfilling of SFB S3 cannot be proved, the date of the jar – a mid-fourth- to mid-fifth-century import from the Rhineland – is possibly contemporary with Anglo-Saxon activity at the site. However, no firm conclusions can be drawn. Vessels of this type have primarily been recorded at Canterbury, Richborough, Colchester and London, but there is also a sparse distribution on the eastern and southern coastlines.

Although the limited finds evidence cannot be used to assign any particular function to the SFBs at either site, it is almost certain that spinning occurred at Snape. SFBs are generally viewed as multi-functional buildings, however,[177] and it is likely that none of the current examples had a specialized use.

The Burnt Flint Pits

The burnt flint pits at both sites were substantial features containing clearly defined fills yielding large quantities of burnt flint and charcoal. Despite the Romano-British spot date from Pit F2058, both pits at Snape were radiocarbon-dated to between the early fifth and sixth centuries AD. Comparable features have been widely encountered on Anglo-Saxon sites, both in domestic and funerary contexts.[178] However, the absence of any other diagnostic ecofactual or artefactual remains makes it impossible to narrow down the interpretation of these features from previously presented hypotheses.[179] In addition to heat treatment of flint and pit cooking, a further interpretation is that they could have been used for charcoal production.

The excellent preservation of the charcoal from Snape and Oulton indicates that the fires provided suitable reducing conditions and some traditional charcoal burners take the form of similarly sized rectangular pits. However, it is difficult to rationalize the presence of large quantities of flint, which has no obvious role in charcoal production.

Middle to Late Anglo-Saxon activity at Lime Avenue, Oulton

A large rectangular enclosure was dated to the middle to late Anglo-Saxon period at Oulton, but appeared to have origins in the earlier settlement period at this site (Fig. 4). The enclosure was bounded to the north and west by contemporary sections of ditched trackway, the westernmost section of which narrowed towards the south and may have been designed to control the movement of livestock. Although small, the middle to late Anglo-Saxon faunal assemblage from Oulton includes a good spread of taxa with cattle, sheep/goat and horse all represented. However, the few fragments recovered cannot be used to infer the relative economic importance of these species. Plant remains were also sparse from this period of activity. As a result, it is difficult to determine the function(s) of the Anglo-Saxon enclosure, although an agricultural use seems most likely. Enclosures of this date are often viewed as reflecting changing crop and animal husbandry regimes in the mid-Saxon period.[180]

The Weights

by Nicholas J Cooper

The set of weights from Oulton represents a significant find, not only in terms of its coherent metrology, but also in what it adds to our knowledge of the characteristically Viking-period phenomenon of inserting decorative objects into the tops of these otherwise rather unprepossessing and functional objects. Metrologically, the set adheres to Scandinavian weight standards based on units of 24.59 g, representing the *ore* or ounce, and its subdivision, the *ertog*, of 8.19 g, or one-third of an *ore*. It therefore chimes with the results of another recent study of weights from Cottam on the Yorkshire Wolds,[181] as well as demonstrating Scandinavian practice in the south of the Danelaw area on the East Anglian coast. Haldenby and Kershaw's overview of current knowledge on Viking-period lead weights places the known assemblages firmly within a Scandinavian rather than a late Anglo-Saxon cultural context. The paucity of lead weights in southern English urban centres such as Winchester and London at this time, compared with the large numbers at Viking urban settlements such as York and Dublin, the Viking winter camp at Torksey, and sites such as Llanbedrgoch and Flixborough,[182] demonstrate a specific need for these simple, functional objects at a particular time when the new settlers were in transition from a bullion, or metal weight, economy to a coin-based economy.[183] However, the set from Oulton appears to cater for heavier commodities than silver, unless the amounts were very large; and so its exact function within the economy is unclear, with no other artefactual evidence from the site to offer any clues.

Regarding the insertion of coins and other objects into the tops of weights, the combined distribution of PAS data and the earlier finds gathered by Williams coincides with the Danelaw or other areas of Viking settlement, and confirms that it is a phenomenon related to Viking activity. Why the Vikings did this for certain weights and not others is a matter of debate. Williams originally considered that the Vikings, before they themselves used coinage, may have been influenced by the early use of coin dies on late-Saxon coin weights, of which at least four are known; the earliest in one of Alfred dated 871–99.[184] The early settlers were illiterate and as they became familiar with the use of coinage, the visual symbols they contained could have been an important way of imparting authority or denoting a weight standard during transactions.[185] However, this did not translate into a coherent pattern of use in regard to coin types or the display of obverse or reverse images, and it is perhaps more likely that inserted objects including coins were personal identifiers that allowed owners to identify specific weights within their sets, making it impossible for them to be switched mid-transaction.[186]

Landscape and infrastructure

The sites at Lime Avenue, Oulton and Church Road, Snape occupy similar topographical and geological locations on locally elevated ground overlooking river valleys and close to the Suffolk coast. The gently sloping site at Oulton overlooks the historical course of the River Waveney – now Oulton Broad – and would have been well placed to monitor passing river traffic. The location of the Snape settlement is similarly advantageous, commanding a panoramic view of the local landscape, approximately 1 km north of Snape Bridge.[187] First depicted on Saxton's map of 1575, the bridge's location at the head of the Alde estuary is likely to have been used as a crossing and/or mooring point for much longer. The deliberate positioning of Anglo-Saxon structures on high ground is mirrored at other regional sites including Brandon Road in Thetford, Duxford in Cambridgeshire and Bloodmoor Hill in Carlton Colville.[188] The Duxford site also occupies a position of potential importance, overlooking the point at which a branch of the Icknield Way, a major communications route in the middle Anglo-Saxon period,[189] crosses the River Granta.[190] The Brandon Road settlement overlooks the course of the Little Ouse,[191] while the Bloodmoor Hill settlement and cemetery overlook the floodplain of the River Waveney.[192] This deliberate placement of settlements above navigable rivers and other routes would have provided essential trade and communications links to the wider region and beyond.

As a key to better understanding local navigation, it is important to consider once again the juxtaposition of the Church Road site and Snape Anglo-Saxon cemetery (Fig. 1). While the choice of cemetery location was no doubt influenced by the existence of Bronze Age earthworks at this location, the placement of Mound I (housing the sixth-century ship burial) may have been more specifically intended to provide an aid to navigation.[193] At the time of construction, Mound I would have occupied a largely treeless heathland, and would have been clearly visible as a silhouette from both the sea and the River Alde.[194] Furthermore, a direct line of sight between the cemetery and Snape Bridge, an obvious landing point at the head of the Alde estuary (see above), passes just *c.* 200 m to the east of the Church Road site. It is not unreasonable to suggest, therefore, that anyone landing at Snape Bridge and travelling towards the cemetery would have passed close to or possibly through the early to middle Anglo-Saxon settlement; the local topography strongly suggests that any additional part of the Church Road site – very probably including habitations – would have been located to the east, beneath the modern village. However, extensive test pitting of the area in 2016 revealed no further Anglo-Saxon remains.[195] Since the completion of fieldwork in 2015, investigations by Archaeology South-East have revealed an additional SFB to the immediate north of the Church Road site;[196] however, at the time of writing this had not yet been reported on.

As well as contemporary infrastructure, it is probable that early Anglo-Saxon settlements made use of Romano-British roads and trackways. Although no major roads are known close to Oulton or Snape, both sites contained evidence of Romano-British activity which would have relied on good communication and transportation links. The Roman pottery production site at Snape, especially, would probably have had close ties to local market centres such as the large Romano-British settlement at Hacheston,[197] *c.* 9.2 km to the west, for the trading of surpluses;[198] coastal trade may have also been conducted via the Alde estuary.

Wider trade and communications

The early Anglo-Saxon period at Snape produced possible evidence for long-distance trade with mainland Europe. A single sherd of Mayen coarse ware jar – possibly associated with the importing of corn or honey between the mid-fourth and mid-fifth centuries AD[199] – was present in the subsoil above SFB S3. Comparable vessels are known from post-Roman deposits at Colchester.[200] Examples from East Anglia are known from Burgh Castle and Caistor-by-Sea, and a vessel has also been recorded at Gestingthorpe, close to the River Stour.[201] Despite the tentative link between the Snape sherd and the use/backfilling of SFB S3, its date suggests a possible – although not provable – link with the Anglo-Saxon settlement, perhaps being imported from the coast via the River Alde.

The significance of the Oulton weights to this site's wider social and economic context has been discussed by Cooper (above).

Conclusions

The current sites add usefully to our understanding of early Anglo-Saxon settlement in Suffolk and the wider region. Both settlements were defined by sunken-featured buildings (SFBs), while an earth-fast structure was also identified at Snape. Where definable, the SFBs conformed to established typologies. The sunken features themselves displayed no signs of trampling, and the sub-floor spaces did not appear to have been utilized for storage.

Activity within the SFBs was difficult to define in most cases, as the bulk of finds from these buildings were thought to derive from secondary or even tertiary sources. However, at Snape the presence of spindle whorl fragments from SFB S1 suggests that spinning of wool formed part of the site's economy. This is in keeping with existing interpretations of SFBs as having strong ties to textile manufacture,[202] with early settlements being thought self-sufficient in terms of this industry.[203] A possible awl handle from SFB S3 might also be linked to craft activities. Mixed farming appeared to form the economic mainstay of both Anglo-Saxon settlements, although interpretations were hampered to some extent by poor bone preservation. An under-representation of pigs and wild species, including fish and fowl, was thought likely in both cases. The sites' locations in respect to nearby rivers and wetland habitats would strongly suggest that both fishing and wildfowling were carried out by the early to middle Anglo-Saxon populations, as has been evidenced elsewhere.[204] Cereal cultivation was apparent at Snape and Oulton, with assemblages being dominated by species tolerant to the local free-draining, sandy soils.

Possible trade links were demonstrated at Snape by the presence of imported Mayen coarse ware in the subsoil above SFB S3. Although an absolute relationship with the early to middle Anglo-Saxon settlement cannot be proven, the date of the pottery strongly suggests that the local population had access to imported goods from the Continent. Similarly, later Anglo-Saxon trade links were demonstrated at Oulton by a collection of eleven Anglo-Saxon or Viking weights, four of which have Carolingian coins (×2) and Roman coins (×2) embedded in their upper surfaces; the system of measurement appears to be Viking. The Carolingian coins are particularly notable as they may suggest a European origin for the weights. Alternatively, the coins may have been imported independently, only being set within the weights at a later date.

The local river networks represent obvious trade and communication links. Both the Alde and Waveney would have provided navigable access to the coast, while the Waveney also passes close to the Anglo-Saxon complex at Bloodmoor Hill. Although no major Roman roads are known to pass near Snape or Oulton, both sites produced plentiful evidence of Romano-British activity,[205] and it is suggested that local systems of Roman trackways would have endured into the earlier Anglo-Saxon period.

Acknowledgements

Archaeological Solutions Ltd (AS) would like to thank Hopkins Homes Ltd, Persimmon Homes Ltd and Oldman Homes Ltd for funding the projects at Oulton and Snape, and for their cooperation and assistance. AS is also pleased to acknowledge the input and advice of Dr Matthew Brudenell and Dr Jess Tipper (formerly of Suffolk County Council Archaeological Service Conservation Team).

The author would like to thank Dr Zoe Outram (Science Advisor (East of England), Historic England) for her advice regarding radiocarbon dating. Nicholas J. Cooper would like to thank Simon Coupland for identifying the Carolingian coins, as well as Martin Allen, Yolanda Courtney, Jo Story and Paul Withers for their help in researching the weights.

Notes

1 Medlycott 2011, 58.
2 SHER SNP 103 and SHER OUL 037 respectively in the Suffolk Historical Environment Record (hereafter 'SHER').
3 Newport 4 and Wick 3 Associations, respectively; Soil Survey of England and Wales 1983, 9–10.
4 *Ibid.*
5 Lucy, Tipper and Dickens 2009.
6 Wade 1997, 46, fig. 8.
7 SHER LWT Misc.
8 Wade 1997, 46, fig. 8.
9 SHER SNP 007; NGR TM 4014 5932.
10 West 1999, 44–5.
11 Filmer-Sankey and Pestell 2001, 5 and 11.
12 Müller-Wille 1970, 9; after Filmer-Sankey and Pestell 2001, 193.
13 Filmer-Sankey and Pestell 2001, 194.
14 *Ibid.*, 198.
15 Evison 1982.
16 Filmer-Sankey and Pestell 2001, 195–6.
17 *Ibid.*, 195–8.
18 Filmer-Sankey and Pestell 2001.
19 *Ibid.*, 199.
20 *Ibid.*, 204ff.
21 Cf. Hamerow 2010, 72.
22 Mustchin 2014; Mustchin and Peachey 2018.
23 Mustchin 2014; Mustchin and Walker 2016.
24 Tipper 2009, 208.
25 See Thompson in Mustchin 2016.
26 McCarthy and Brooks 1988, 162 and 168.
27 West 1985, fig. 165.4.
28 See Blinkhorn in Mustchin 2014.
29 See Mustchin 2014, appendix 2.
30 See Summers in Mustchin 2014). Recommendations for radiocarbon dating were made by Dr Jess Tipper (formerly of Suffolk County Council Archaeological Service Conservation Team), while the availability and suitability of material for dating was determined by Dr John Summers (Archaeological Solutions Ltd).
31 Grocock 2010, 25.
32 West 1999, 44.
33 Mudd 2002, 3; Williamson 2010, 146, 152.
34 Wade 1999, 46; West 1999, 44.
35 Hamerow 2012, 94.
36 See West 1971; 1985 for West Stow; Boulter and Walton Rogers 2012, 269 for Flixton Quarry.
37 Tipper 2004 183.
38 *Ibid.*, 162.
39 West 1985.
40 R. J. Williams 1993.
41 *Ibid.*
42 Newton forthcoming.
43 Tipper 2004, 64–5.
44 E.g. Mackreth 1996.
45 Hamerow 2011, 146; 2012; 54.
46 Von Guyan 1952; Ahrens 1966.
47 After Tipper 2004, 68.
48 See reconstruction drawing in Hamerow 2012, 56, fig. 2.13; after Heidinga and Offenberg 1992.
49 Defined by von Guyan (1952).
50 Tipper 2004, 69; after West 1985, 121.
51 Rickett 1995; West 1971; 1985.
52 Cf. Tipper 2004, 71.
53 *Ibid.*, 84.
54 Rickett 1995, 54; West 1985, 120.
55 Cf. Tipper 2004, 84.
56 Newton 2013, 335–6.
57 Hope-Taylor 1977, 103–5 and fig. 48; after Tipper 2004, 84.
58 For Hertismere High School, Suffolk see Caruth and Goffin 2012, 38; for Mucking, Essex see Hamerow 1993, 11; for Spong Hill, Norfolk see Rickett 1995, 54.
59 Hamerow 1993, 11.
60 Berisford 1973, 122–3.
61 Cf. Tipper 2004, 99ff.
62 After Hamerow 2012, 60–1.
63 Andrews 1995, 13ff; Atkins and Connor 2010, 112.
64 Rickett 1995, 47; Roberts, Spoerry and Lyons 2011, 123.
65 R. J. Williams 1993, 79.
66 Tipper 2004, 81.
67 http://www.metoffice.gov.uk/climate/uk/regional-climates/ee.
68 Tipper 2004, 81, table 26.
69 Tomber and Dore 1998, 41–3.
70 Mustchin and Peachey 2018, 25.
71 Cool 2000, 52–3.
72 Eckardt and Williams 2003, 155–7.
73 O'Brien 2016.
74 West 1985, 122.
75 Going 1993, 71–2.
76 Drury and Wickenden 1982, 20-5; Going 1993, 71–2.
77 *Ibid.*
78 Tomber and Dore 1998, 70.
79 Gose 1950.
80 Symonds and Wade 1999, 466: fig. 6.115.64.
81 Fulford and Bird 1975, 181; Pollard 1988, 149.
82 Fulford and Bird 1975, 180.
83 Boulter and Walton Rogers 2012, 94, and Garrow, Lucy and Gibson 2006, 184 respectively.
84 Caruth and Goffin 2012, 45, table 8.
85 Garrow *et al.* 2006, 184.
86 Boulter and Walton Rogers 2012, 94–5, fig. 6.3), and Garrow *et al.* 2006, 184–6, fig. 5.16, plate XXI respectively.
87 Boulter and Walton Rogers 2012, 94.
88 Garrow *et al.* 2006.
89 Andrews 1995.
90 Filmer-Sankey and Pestell 2001; H. Williams 2008, 248.
91 Carruth and Goffin 2012, 45–6.
92 *Ibid.*
93 Hamerow 2012, 88–9 and 163.
94 *Ibid.*, 72ff.
95 *Ibid.*, 71.
96 Mudd 2002.
97 O'Brien 2016.
98 R. J. Williams 1993, 48–9, fig. 25 and 93.
99 O'Brien 2016, 94–5, fig. 6.1.
100 After Hamerow 2012, 78.
101 Crabtree 1985.
102 *Ibid.*

103 E.g. Ashwin 2011; Baxter 2011; Bond 1995; Crabtree 1985; Newton, Morris and Leach 2012.
104 Bond 1995.
105 Crabtree 1985, 89.
106 Crabtree 1985.
107 Halstead 1985; Hambleton 1999.
108 Bond 1995.
109 Baker and Brothwell 1980, 114.
110 O'Connor 2000.
111 Dobney, Jacques, Barret and Johnstone 2007, 182.
112 E.g. Ballantyne 2005; Carruthers 2008; Murphy 2005.
113 Carruthers 2008, 13.15–13.16; Murphy 2005.
114 E.g. Murphy 2005.
115 Boulter and Walton Rogers 2012, 94.
116 See Biddle 1990, 918, fig. 280 and Egan 1998, 301–22, fig. 235 respectively.
117 G. Williams 1999.
118 Biggs and Withers 2000, 18; G. Williams 1999, 32.
119 Blackburn 2011.
120 Egan 1998, table 14.
121 Haldenby and Kershaw 2014, 106–23.
122 G. Williams 1999, 32.
123 Haldenby and Kershaw 2014, 112–13, table 1.
124 *Ibid.*, table 1.
125 G. Williams 1999.
126 Archibald 1991; G. Williams 1999; Biggs and Withers 2000, 18–20; Pirie 2000.
127 G. Williams 1999, 34.
128 See www.finds.org.uk.
129 Biggs and Withers 2000, 18.
130 Pirie 2000, 25–9; Kruse 1992, 67–95.
131 G. Williams 1999, 35.
132 *Ibid.*, 28–32, nos. 18–21.
133 Biggs and Withers 2000, 19, no. 11; also included in G. Williams 1999, no. 5.
134 G. Williams 1999, 25, nos. 10, 9 and 8 respectively.
135 Biggs and Withers 2000, 19, no. 12; G. Williams 1999, 23–6, nos. 12, 14–16, 17, 6 and 7 respectively.
136 NMS-0D47D0.
137 NLM-5766.
138 J. Kershaw *pers. comm.*
139 NMS-16C428.
140 Biggs and Withers 2000, 18, fig. 1.
141 NLM-8F9E07.
142 SF-6536.
143 Saxmundham: SF-4B1547; Laxfield: SF-334CE5; St Edmundsbury: SF-042327; Little Wilbraham, Cambridgeshire: SF-B137C2; Sevenoaks, Kent: KENT-2080; North Cave, Hull: SWYOR-E16C55; 'near Stamford Bridge', Yorkshire: YORYM-01C134.
144 Egan 1998, 309, fig. 230.974–975; dated to Ceramic Phase 6, *c.* 1150–1200.
145 Haldenby and Kershaw 2014, 113–15.
146 Hamerow 2012.
147 Tipper 2004, 24.
148 *Ibid.*, 11–12.
149 R. J. Williams 1993, 79.
150 Hamerow 2011, 146; West 1971, 4.
151 Atkins and Connor 2010.
152 O'Brien 2016.
153 Newton forthcoming.
154 Newton 2013.
155 Caruth and Goffin 2012.
156 Tipper 2004, 64–5.
157 Cf. Hamerow 2011, 146.
158 Cf. Tipper 2004, 68–9.
159 *Ibid.*, 80.
160 West 1971, 5.
161 Rickett 1995, 54; West 1985, 120.
162 Crabtree 1990, after Sykes 2011, 330.
163 Newton forthcoming.
164 Parks and Barrett 2009, 305.
165 Sykes 2011, 328–9.
166 *Ibid.*, 328.
167 Melford Meadows: Powell and Clark 2002, 101ff: West Stow: Crabtree 1985, 85ff; Bloodmoor Hill: Higbee 2009.
168 Arnold 2005, 38; Hamerow 2002, 33.
169 Crummy 2002.
170 Wallis 2011, 32.
171 Atkins and Connor 2010, 24.
172 Caruth and Goffin 2012.
173 Rickett 1995, 50–3.
174 West 1985, 138–9.
175 Lucy *et al.* 2009. 44.
176 *Ibid.*, 45.
177 Cf. Lucy *et al.* 2009, 45 and Tipper 2004, 185.
178 E.g. Garrow *et al.* 2006, 184–6; Andrews 1995, 22; Caruth and Goffin 2012, 45–6; Boulter and Walton Rogers 2012, 94.
179 E.g. Andrews 1995, 22; Caruth and Goffin 2012, 45–6; Boulter and Walton Rogers 2012, 94.
180 Hamerow 2012, 88–9 and 163.
181 Haldenby and Kershaw 2014.
182 *Ibid.*, 119–20.
183 G. Williams 1999, 32.
184 *Ibid.*, 20.
185 *Ibid.*, 35–6.
186 G. Williams *pers. comm.*
187 SHER SNP 036.
188 Atkins and Connor 2010, 21; Lucy *et al.* 2009; Lyons 2011, 91ff.
189 Baker and Brookes 2013, 280.
190 Roberts *et al.* 2011, 124.
191 Atkins and Connor 2010, 2, fig. 1.
192 Lucy *et al.* 2009.
193 Cf. Filmer-Sankey and Pestell 2001, 233–4.
194 *Ibid.*, 1, 234 and fig. 3.
195 Ranson 2016.
196 Hoggett *pers. comm.*
197 Blagg, Plouviez and Tester 2004.
198 Mustchin and Peachey 2018, 30.
199 Fulford and Bird 1975, 181; Pollard 1988, 149.
200 Symonds and Wade 1999, 466: fig. 6.115.64.
201 Fulford and Bird 1975, 180.
202 Arnold 2005, 38; Hamerow 2002, 33.
203 Crummy 2002.
204 E.g. Crabtree 1990; Parks and Barrett 2009.
205 Mustchin and Peachey 2018; Mustchin and Walker 2016.

Bibliography

Ahrens, C. 1966. 'Vorgeschichte des Kriesen Pinneberg und der Insel Helgoland – Die Vor- und frühgeschichtliche Denkmäler und Funde in Schleswig-Holstein, VII', in K. Kersten (ed.), *Veröffentlichungen des Landesamtes für Vor- und Frühgeschichte in Schleswig*, 205, Neumunster: Wachholtz, GFR.

Andrews, P. 1995. *Excavations at Redcastle Furze, Thetford 1988–9*, East Anglian Archaeology Report, No. 72, Dereham: Field Archaeology Division, Norfolk Museums Service.

Archibald, M. M. 1991. 'Anglo-Saxon and Norman lead objects with official coin types', in A. G. Vince, (ed.), *Aspects of Saxon and Norman London II: Finds and Environmental Evidence*, 326–46, London: London and Middlesex Archaeological Society.

Arnold, C. J. 2005. *An Archaeology of the Early Anglo-Saxon Kingdoms* (New Edition, Taylor and Francis e-Library).

Ashwin, T. 2011. 'Animal bone', in H. Wallis, *Romano British and Saxon Occupation at Billingford, Central Norfolk*, East Anglian Archaeology Report, No. 135, 60, Norwich: NAU Archaeology/ Norfolk Historic Environment.

Atkins, R. and Connor, A. 2010. *Farmers and Ironsmiths: Prehistoric, Roman and Anglo-Saxon Settlement Beside Brandon Road, Thetford, Norfolk*, East Anglian Archaeology Report, No. 134, Cambridge: Oxford Archaeology East.

Baker, J. and Brookes, S. 2013. *Beyond the Burghal Hidage: Anglo-Saxon Civil Defence in the Viking Age*, Leiden: Koninklijke Brill NV.

Baker, J. and Brothwell, D. 1980. *Animal Diseases in Archaeology*, London: Academic Press.

Ballantyne, R. 2005. 'Plants and seeds', in R. Mortimer, R. Regan and S. Lucy, *The Saxon and Medieval Settlement at West Fen Road, Ely: The Ashwell Site*, East Anglian Archaeology Report, No. 110, 100–12, Cambridge: Cambridge Archaeological Unit.

Baxter, I. 2011. 'Animal and bird bone', in A. Lyons, *Life and Afterlife at Duxford, Cambridgeshire: Archaeology and History in a Chalkland Community*, East Anglian Archaeology Report, No. 141, 99, Cambridge: Oxford Archaeology East.

Berisford, F. 1973. *The Early Anglo-Saxon Settlement Sites in the Upper Thames Basin, with special reference to the area around Cassington and Eynsham*, unpublished BLitt thesis, University of Oxford.

Biddle, M. 1990. *Object and Economy in Medieval Winchester*, Winchester Studies 7(ii), Oxford: Oxford University Press.

Biggs, N. and Withers, P. 2000. *Lead Weights: The David Rogers Collection*, Llanfyllin: Galata Publications.

Blackburn, M. 2011. The Viking winter camp at Torksey, 872–3', in M. Blackburn (ed.), *Viking Coinage and Currency in the British Isles*, 221–64, London: Spink.

Blagg, T., Plouviez, J. and Tester, A. 2004. *Excavations at a Large Romano-British Settlement at Hacheston, Suffolk, 1973–74*, East Anglian Archaeology Report, No. 106, Bury St Edmunds: Suffolk County Council Archaeological Service.

Bond, J. M. 1995. 'Animal bone from Early Saxon sunken-featured buildings and pits', in R. Rickett, *The Anglo-Saxon Cemetery at Spong Hill, North Elmham, Part VII: The Iron Age, Roman and Early Saxon Settlement*, East Anglian Archaeology Report, No. 73, 142–6, Dereham: Field Archaeology Division, Norfolk Museums Service.

Boulter, S. and Walton Rogers, P. 2012. *Circles and Cemeteries: Excavations at Flixton. Volume 1*, East Anglian Archaeology Report, No. 147, Bury St Edmunds: Suffolk County Council.

Carruthers, W. J. 2008. 'Charred, mineralized and waterlogged plant remains', in N. Cooke, F. Brown and C. Phillpotts, *From Hunter-Gatherers to Huntsmen: A History of the Stansted Landscape*, Framework Archaeology Monograph, No. 2, Chapter 34 on CD.

Caruth, J. and Goffin, R. 2012. *Land South of Hartismere High School, Eye, Suffolk, EYE 083: Post-Excavation Assessment Report*, Suffolk County Council Archaeological Service Unpublished Report, No. 2012/067.

Cool, H. 2000. 'The parts left over: material culture into the fifth century', in T. Wilmott and P. Wilson (eds.), *The Late Roman Transition in the North*, British Archaeological Reports (British Series) 299, 47–65, Oxford: Archaeopress.

Crabtree, P. 1985. 'The faunal remains', in S. West (ed.), *West Stow: The Anglo-Anglo-Saxon Village, Volume 1: Text*, East Anglian Archaeology Report, No. 24, 85–96, Ipswich: Suffolk County Planning Department.

Crabtree, P. 1990. *West Stow, Suffolk: Early Anglo-Saxon Animal Husbandry*, East Anglian Archaeology Report No. 47, Ipswich: Suffolk County Planning Department.

Crummy, N. 2002. 'From self-sufficiency to commerce: structural and artefactual evidence for textile manufacture in Eastern England in the pre-Conquest period', in D. G. Koslin and J. E. Snyder (eds.), *Encountering Medieval Textiles and Dress: Objects, Texts, Images*, 25–43, London: Palgrave Macmillan.

Dobney, K., Jaques, D., Barret, J. and Johnstone, C. 2007. *Farmers, Monks and Aristocrats: the Environmental Archaeology of Anglo-Saxon Flixbrough*, Oxford: Oxbow Books.

Drury, P. J. and Wickenden, N. P. 1982. 'An Early Saxon settlement within the Romano-British small town at Heybridge, Essex', *Medieval Arch.*, **26**, 1–40.

Eckardt, H. and Williams, H. 2003. 'Objects without a past? The use of Roman objects in early Anglo-Saxon graves', in H. Williams (ed.), *Archaeologies of Remembrance, Death and Memory in Past Societies*, 141–70, New York: Springer.

Egan, G. 1998. *The Medieval Household: Daily Living c.1150–c.1450*, London: Museum of London.

Evison, V. 1982. 'Anglo-Saxon glass claw beakers', *Archaeologia*, **107**, 43–76.

Filmer-Sankey, W. and Pestell, T. 2001. *Snape Anglo-Saxon Cemetery: Excavations and Surveys 1824–1992*, East Anglian Archaeology Report, No. 95, Ipswich: Suffolk County Council.

Fulford, M. and Bird, J. 1975. 'Imported pottery from Germany in Late Roman Britain', *Britannia*, **6**, 171–81.

Garrow, D., Lucy, S. and Gibson, D. 2006. *Excavations at Kilverstone, Norfolk: An Episodic Landscape History*, East Anglian Archaeology Report, No. 113, Cambridge: Cambridge Archaeological Unit.

Going, C. J. 1993. 'Roman pottery from the Grubenhäuser', in H. Hamerow (ed.), *Excavations at Mucking, Vol. 2: The Anglo-Saxon Settlement*, English Heritage Archaeological Report, 21, 71–2, London.

Gose, E. 1950. *Gefäßtypen der römische Kermalik im Rheinland*, Beihefte der Bonner Jahrbücher, 1, Kevelaer: Butzon und Bercker.

Grocock, C. 2010. 'Barriers to knowledge: coppicing and landscape usage in the Anglo-Saxon economy', in N. J. Higham and M. J. Ryan (eds.), *Landscape Archaeology of Anglo-Saxon England*, 23–38, Woodbridge: The Boydell Press.

Haldenby, D. and Kershaw, J. 2014. 'Viking-Age lead weights from Cottam', *Yorkshire Archaeological Journal*, **86**, 106–23.

Halstead, P. 1985. 'A study of mandibular teeth from Romano-British contexts at Maxey', in F. Pryor, C. French, D. Crowther, D. Gurney, G. Simpson and M. Taylor (eds.), *The Fenland Project: Archaeology and Environment in the Lower Welland Valley, Volume 1*, East Anglian Archaeology Report, No. 27, 219–24, Cambridge: Cambridgeshire Archaeological Committee).

Hambleton, E. 1999. *Animal Husbandry Regimes in Iron Age Britain: A Comparative Study of Faunal Assemblages from British Iron Age Sites*, British Archaeological Reports (British Series) 282, Oxford: Archaeopress.

Hamerow, H. 1993. *Excavations at Mucking, Volume 2: The Anglo-Saxon Settlement*, London: English Heritage.

Hamerow, H. 2002. *Early Medieval Settlements: The Archaeology of Rural Communities in North-western Europe 400–900*, Oxford: Oxford University Press.

Hamerow, H. 2010. 'Communities of the living and the dead: the relationship between Anglo-Saxon settlements and cemeteries, c. AD 450–850', in M. Henig and N. Ramsey (eds.), *Intersections: The Archaeology and History of Christianity in England, 400–1200*, British Archaeological Reports (British Series), 505, 71–6, Oxford: Archaeopress.

Hamerow, H. 2011. 'Anglo-Saxon timber buildings and their social context', in H. Hamerow, D. A. Hinton and S. Crawford (eds.), *The Oxford Handbook of Anglo-Saxon Archaeology*, 128–55, Oxford: Oxford University Press.

Hamerow, H. 2012. *Rural Settlements and Society in Anglo-Saxon England*, Oxford: Oxford University Press.

Heidinga, H. A. and Offenberg, G. A. M. 1992. *Op zoek naar de vijfde eeuw: de Franken tussen Rijn en Maas*, Amsterdam: Der Bataafsche Leeuw.

Higbee, L. 2009. 'Mammal and bird bone', in S. Lucy, J. Tipper and A. Dickens, *The Anglo-Saxon Settlement and Cemetery at Bloodmoor Hill, Carlton Colville, Suffolk*, East Anglian Archaeology Report, No. 131, 279–304, Cambridge: Cambridge Archaeological Unit.

Hope-Taylor, B. 1977. *Yeavering. An Anglo-British Centre of Early Northumbria*, DoE Archaeological Report, 7, London: HMSO.

Kruse, S.E. 1992. 'Late Saxon balances and weights from England', *Medieval Arch.*, **36**, 67–95.

Lucy, S., Tipper, J. and Dickens, A. 2009. *The Anglo-Saxon Settlement and Cemetery at Bloodmoor Hill, Carlton Colville, Suffolk*, East Anglian Archaeology Report, No. 131, Cambridge: Cambridge Archaeological Unit.

Lyons, A. 2011. *Life and Afterlife at Duxford, Cambridgeshire: Archaeology and History in a Chalkland Community*, East Anglian Archaeology Report, No. 141, Cambridge: Oxford Archaeology East.

Mackreth, D. F. 1996. *Orton Hall Farm: A Roman and Early Anglo-Saxon Farmstead*, East Anglian Archaeology Report, No. 76, Peterborough: Nene Valley Archaeological Trust.

McCarthy, R. and Brooks, C. 1988. *Medieval Pottery in Britain AD 800 to 1600*, Leicester: Leicester University Press.

Medlycott, M. (ed.) 2011. *Research and Archaeology Revisited: A Revised Framework for the East of England*, East Anglian Archaeology Occasional Paper, No. 24, ALGAO East of England Region.

Mudd, A. 2002. *Excavations at Melford Meadows, Brettenham, 1994: the Romano-British and Early Saxon Occupations*, East Anglian Archaeology Report, No. 99, Oxford: Oxford Archaeology.

Müller-Wille, M. 1970. 'Bestattung im Boot. Studien zu einer nordeuropäischen Grabsitte', *Offa*, **25/26 (1968/69)**, 7–203.

Murphy, P. 2005. 'Environmental evidence', in S. Tyler and H. Major, *The Early Anglo-Saxon Cemetery and Later Saxon Settlement at Springfield Lyons, Essex*, East Anglian Archaeology Report, No. 111, 149–63, Chelmsford: Essex County Council.

Mustchin, A. R. R. 2014. *An Archaeological Excavation on Land North of Blyth Houses, Church Road, Snape, Suffolk. Research Archive Report*, Archaeological Solutions Ltd Unpublished Report, No. 4471, Bury St Edmunds.

Mustchin, A. R. R. and Peachey, A. 2018. 'An early Romano-British double flue pottery kiln at Church Road, Snape, Suffolk', *Journal of Roman Pottery Studies*, **17**, 22–31.

Mustchin, A. R. R. and Walker, J. 2016. *Land off Lime Avenue, Oulton, SUFFOLK (Phase 1). An Archaeological Excavation: Research Archive Report*, Archaeological Solutions Ltd Unpublished Report, No. 5069, Bury St Edmunds.

Newton, A. A. S. 2013. 'Saxon and Medieval Settlement at The Old Bell, Marham', *Norfolk Archaeology*, **46**, 331–56.

Newton, A. A. S. forthcoming. 'Prehistoric and Anglo-Saxon activity at Dernford Farm, Sawston, Cambridgeshire', East Anglian Archaeology Report, Bury St Edmunds: Archaeological Solutions Ltd.

Newton, A. A. S., Morris, J. and Leach, S. 2012. 'Animal bone present in the sunken-featured building', in A. A. S. Newton, 'Saxon and medieval settlement at the Old Bell, Marham', *Norfolk Archaeology*, **46**, 331–56.

O'Brien, L. 2016. *Bronze Age Barrow, Early to Middle Iron Age Settlement and Burials, and Early Anglo-Saxon Settlement at Harston Mill, Cambridgeshire*, East Anglian Archaeology Report, No. 157, Bury St Edmunds: Archaeological Solutions Ltd.

O'Connor, T. P. 2000. *The Archaeology of Animal Bones*, Stroud: Sutton Publishing.

Parks, R. and Barrett, J. 2009. 'Fish bone', in S. Lucy, J. Tipper and A. Dickens, *The Anglo-Saxon Settlement and Cemetery at Bloodmoor Hill, Carlton Colville,* Suffolk, East Anglian Archaeology Report, No. 131, 304–5, Cambridge: Cambridge Archaeological Unit.

Pirie, E. J. E. 2000. *Thrymsas, Sceattas and Stycas of Northumbria: An Inventory of Finds Recorded to 1997*, Llanfyllin: Galata Publications.

Pollard, R. 1988. *The Roman Pottery of Kent*, Kent Archaeological Society (available online at: http://www.kentarchaeology.org.uk/Research/Pub/RPofK/Contents.htm).

Powell, A. and Clark, K. M. 2002. 'Animal bones', in A. Mudd, *Excavations at Melford Meadows, Brettenham, 1994: the Romano-British and Early Saxon Occupations,* East Anglian Archaeology Report, No. 99, 101–8, Oxford: Oxford Archaeology.

Ranson, C. 2016. *Archaeological Test Pitting in Snape, Suffolk, 2016*, Access Cambridge Archaeology: University of Cambridge.

Rickett, R. 1995. *The Anglo-Saxon Cemetery at Spong Hill, North Elmham, Part VII: The Iron Age, Roman and Early Saxon Settlement*, East Anglian Archaeology Report, No. 73, Dereham: Field Archaeology Division, Norfolk Museums Service.

Roberts, J., Spoerry, P. and Lyons, A. 2011. 'Anglo-Saxon', in A. Lyons, *Life and Afterlife at Duxford, Cambridgeshire: Archaeology and History in a Chalkland Community*, East Anglian Archaeology Report, No. 141, 123–6, Cambridge: Oxford Archaeology East.

Soil Survey of England and Wales 1983. *Legend for the 1:250,000 Soil Map of England and Wales*, Harpenden: Soil Survey of England and Wales.

Sykes, N. 2011. 'Woods and the wild', in H. Hamerow, D. A. Hinton and S. Crawford (eds.), *The Oxford Handbook of Anglo-Saxon Archaeology*, 327–45, Oxford: Oxford University Press.

Symonds, R. and Wade, S. (eds.) 1999. *Roman Pottery from Excavations in Colchester, 1971–86*, Colchester Archaeological Report, No. 10.

Thompson, P. 2016. 'The Post-Roman pottery', in A. R. R. Mustchin, *Land off Lime Avenue, Oulton, Suffolk (Phase 1). An Archaeological Excavation: Research Archive Report*, Archaeological Solutions Ltd Unpublished Report, No. 5069, Bury St Edmunds.

Tipper, J. 2004. *The Grubenhaus in Anglo-Saxon England: An Analysis and Interpretation of the Evidence from a Most Distinctive Building Type*, Yedingham: English Heritage/The Landscape Research Centre.

Tipper, J. 2009. 'Pottery', in S. Lucy, J. Tipper and A. Dickens (eds.), *The Anglo-Saxon Settlement and Cemetery at Bloodmoor Hill, Carlton Coalville, Suffolk*, East Anglian Archaeology Report, No. 131, 202–43, Cambridge: Cambridge Archaeological Unit.

Tomber, R. and Dore, J. 1998. *The National Roman Fabric Reference Collection*, London: Museum of London.

von Guyan, W. U. 1952. 'Einige Karten zur Verbreitung des Grubenhases in Mitteleuropa im ersten nachchristlichen Jahrtausend und einige Hinweise auf des archäologische Problem der völkerwanderungszeitlichen Hausformen der Schweiz', *Jahrbuch der Schweizerischen Gesellschaft für Urgeschichte*, **42**, 174–97.

Wade, K. 1997. 'Anglo-Saxon and medieval (rural)', in J. Glazebrook (ed.), *Research and Archaeology: A Framework for the Eastern Counties, 1. Resource Assessment*, East Anglian Archaeology Occasional Paper, No. 3, 46–58, Norwich: Scole Archaeological Committee for East Anglia.

Wade, K. 1999. 'The Later Anglo-Saxon Period', in D. Dymond and E. Martin (eds.), *An Historical Atlas of Suffolk* (revised and enlarged edition, 46–7, Ipswich: Suffolk County Council/Suffolk Institute of Archaeology and History.

Wallis, H. 2011. *Romano British and Saxon Occupation at Billingford, Central Norfolk*, East Anglian Archaeology Report, No. 135, Norwich: NAU Archaeology/ Norfolk Historic Environment.

West, S. 1971. 'The Anglo-Saxon village of West Stow: an interim report of the excavations 1965-8', *Medieval Arch.*, **13**, 1–20.

West, S. 1985. *West Stow: The Anglo-Anglo-Saxon Village, Volume 2: Figures and Plates*, East Anglian Archaeology Report, No. 24, Ipswich: Suffolk County Planning Department.

West, S. 1999. 'The Early Anglo-Saxon Period', in D. Dymond and E. Martin (eds.), *An Historical Atlas of Suffolk* (revised and enlarged edition, 44–5, Bury St Edmunds: Suffolk County Council/ Suffolk Institute of Archaeology and History.

Williams, G. 1999. 'Anglo-Saxon and Viking coin weights', *British Numismatics Journal*, **69.4**, 19–36.

Williams, H. 2008. 'Towards an archaeology of cremation', in C. W. Schmidt and S. A. Symes (eds.), *The Analysis of Burned Human Remains*, 239–70, London: Academic Press.

Williams, R. J. 1993. *Pennyland and Hartigans: Two Iron Age and Saxon Sites in Milton Keynes*, Buckinghamshire Archaeological Society Monograph Series, No. 4.

Williamson, T. 2010. 'The environmental contexts of Anglo-Saxon settlement', in N. J. Higham and M. J. Ryan (eds.), *The Landscape Archaeology of Anglo-Saxon England*, 133–56, Woodbridge: The Boydell Press.

Websites

https://finds.org.uk/database/search/results/q/weight/objectType/WEIGHT/broadperiod/EARLY+MEDIEVAL (consulted 30/11/2017).

http://www.metoffice.gov.uk/climate/uk/regional-climates/ee (consulted 24/03/2016).

www.ingramcontent.com/pod-product-compliance
Lightning Source LLC
LaVergne TN
LVHW081337300926
849161LV00008B/1998
* 9 7 8 1 5 2 2 5 7 5 1 3 9 *